Corruption in the Americas

Corruption in the Americas

Edited by
Jonathan D. Rosen and Hanna S. Kassab

LEXINGTON BOOKS
Lanham • Boulder • New York • London

Published by Lexington Books
An imprint of The Rowman & Littlefield Publishing Group, Inc.
4501 Forbes Boulevard, Suite 200, Lanham, Maryland 20706
www.rowman.com

6 Tinworth Street, London SE11 5AL, United Kingdom

British Library Cataloguing in Publication Information Available

Library of Congress Cataloging-in-Publication Data

Names: Rosen, Jonathan D., editor. | Kassab, Hanna Samir, editor.
Title: Corruption in the Americas / edited by Jonathan D. Rosen and Hanna S. Kassab.
Description: Lanham, Maryland : Lexington Books, 2020. | Includes bibliographical
    references. | Summary: "This edited collection analyzes trends of corruption in
    countries throughout the Americas. The contributors examine the main actors
    involved in corruption as well as the linkages between organized crime and state
    institutions" — Provided by publisher.
Identifiers: LCCN 2020031559 (print) | LCCN 2020031560 (ebook) |
    ISBN 9781793627216 (cloth) | ISBN 9781793627230 (pbk)
    ISBN 9781793627223 (epub)
Subjects: LCSH: Political corruption—Latin America. | Corruption—Latin America. |
    Organized crime—Latin America. | Political stability—Latin America. | Legitimacy
    of governments—Latin America.
Classification: LCC JF1525.C66 C677 2020 (print) | LCC JF1525.C66 (ebook) |
    DDC 364.1/323098—dc23
LC record available at https://lccn.loc.gov/2020031559
LC ebook record available at https://lccn.loc.gov/2020031560

To my loving wife:
Karina Castillo Vargas

Contents

Acknowledgments

We would like to thank the contributors for their hard work and dedication.

Thank you to the wonderful staff at Lexington Books for this excellent opportunity.

Both Hanna and Jonathan would like to thank their respective families for their love and support. Jonathan would like to give a special thanks to his loving wife, Karina Esmeralda Castillo Vargas.

Introduction

Jonathan D. Rosen and Hanna S. Kassab

Latin American countries have witnessed seemingly endless corruption scandals. In 2018, for example, Elías Antonio "Tony" Saca, the former president of El Salvador, received a ten-year prison sentence.[1] Saca and his coconspirators stole more than $300 million from El Salvador. Saca used the power of the presidency to enrich himself. Parker Asmann, an organized crime expert, maintains: "Former President Saca's corruption network penetrated all aspects of Salvadoran society, from government institutions to prominent business elites and the country's media. But Saca, who headed the network, didn't receive the harshest sentence."[2] Corruption did not end with Saca and future presidents did not heed the lesson from his case. In fact, Mauricio Funes, the successor of Saca, stole more than $300 million. Funes left El Salvador and moved to Nicaragua to escape extradition.[3]

Not surprisingly, the high levels of corruption have resulted in general distrust among the El Salvadoran population. According to Vanderbilt's Latin American Public Opinion Project (LAPOP) 2016/2017 survey in El Salvador, 27.98 percent of the survey respondents contended that all politicians are corrupt, while 27.44 percent maintained that more than half of them are corrupt. Only 3.98 percent of respondents contended that none of the politicians are corrupt (see figure 0.1). Meanwhile, 33.29 percent of the El Salvadoran population answered "not at all" when asked their level of trust in the executive, compared to only 7.96 percent of the population that responded that they have "a lot" of trust in the executive.

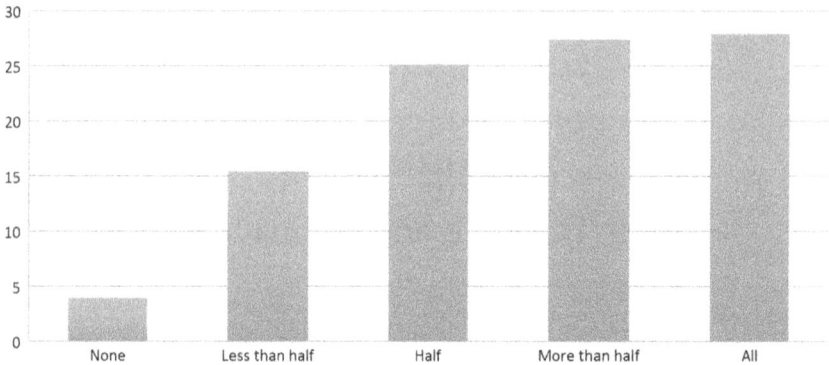

Figure 0.1 The Perception of the Amount of Corrupt Politicians in El Salvador (2016/2017). Created by authors with data from the Latin American Public Opinion Project (LAPOP) 2016/2017.

THE CASE OF ODEBRECHT: THE TENTACLES OF CORRUPTION

The Odebrecht scandal reveals the systemic corruption present in Latin America.[4] Odebrecht, a construction company, paid millions in bribes to secure public works contracts throughout the region. Between 2001 and 2016, bribes totaling approximately $788 million were paid out to at least ten governments in Latin America.[5] The return on investment was approximately a $1 bribe for $8 in profit. In the end, the company must pay $3.5 billion in bribes. The company's chief executive, along with many other executives, is now behind bars.[6] However, the damage had already been done. For fifteen years, the company won contract after contract, beating out other firms without the financial fire power to pay those bribes. This type of behavior results in an uneven economic playing field and creates few (corrupt) winners. The state also pays too much for the project putting pressure on governmental expenditures. Social programs also suffer as a result of such activities.

The Odebrecht scandal was brought to light during the Brazilian Petrobras corruption investigation. For some states in Latin America, corruption is not simply an industry, but rather it is part of the political system. Success can be determined whether one greases the wheels of the government. The state may punish the perpetrators and remove corrupt officials, but the fact is that corruption remains part of the way states conduct business and business people behave.

The problem of corruption goes beyond economic realms and impacts political stability.[7] Corruption eats away at the legitimacy of the government. If a government is seen as corrupt, working only for a select few, then people are going to start questioning its source of authority. This may begin to explain the proliferation of violent non-state actors (e.g., organized criminal actors) residing within the state. The state and its authority become further undermined because of several non-state groups competing for authority within a geographical space.[8]

CORRUPTION AND IMPUNITY IN LATIN AMERICA

According to the 2018 Corruption Perceptions Index (CPI), Venezuela scored an 18 out of 100, with zero being the most corrupt and 100 being the cleanest. Countries throughout the region did not fare much better. Mexico, for instance, scored a 28 out of 100, while Guatemala scored a 27. Meanwhile Honduras received a score of 29, and El Salvador received a 35 out of 100. In South America, Colombia received a 36, while Peru scored a 35 out of 100. Meanwhile, Brazil had a score of 35, while Bolivia received a 29 out of 100 (see figure 0.2).[9]

Corruption is a debilitating factor for many states and inhibits the implementation of the rule of law and the strengthening of institutions.[10] High levels of corruption can help weaken the state and functions as a corrosive factor for democratic consolidation.[11] Weak institutions foster corruption and help strengthen ties between organized crime groups and government officials. Kyra Gurney explains the links between the state and organized crime, contending: "Ties between criminal groups and public officials play a crucial role in facilitating criminal activity and creating a culture of impunity. Corrupt security forces can keep criminal groups informed, shield them from law enforcement operations, and facilitate drug shipments, while ties to politicians and local elites lend criminals a facade of legitimacy."[12] In sum,

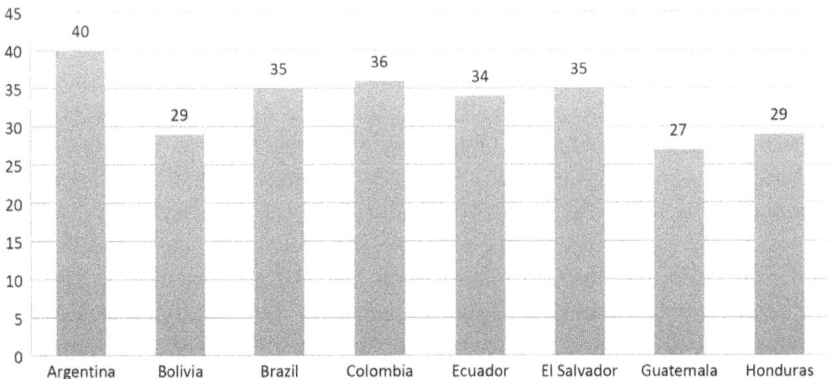

Figure 0.2 2018 Corruptions Perceptions Index. Created by authors with data from Transparency International's Corruptions Perceptions Index, 2018.

corruption is a key component that corrodes the state apparatus and helps weaken countries.

While there are differences between every country in Latin America and the nature and degree of fragility is quite distinct (i.e., Honduras and El Salvador are not Brazil and Mexico), one key factor is institutional weakness. Many countries in the Americas are plagued by extremely weak institutions that do not function efficiently. A key factor that contributes to the state fragility in the region is high levels of impunity. Human rights abuses and major crimes go unpunished as some countries have impunity rates of over 90 percent. In Mexico, for example, impunity rates are approximately 98 percent.[13] The rate of impunity is high in Mexico because the judicial system[14] does not function effectively, and corruption is rampant throughout governmental institutions.

Colombia, like Mexico, has faced major problems with extremely high levels of impunity. Despite being Latin America's oldest democracy, Colombia is plagued by weak institutions that are riddled with corruption and high levels of citizen insecurity.[15] The number of human rights abuses against journalist, community leaders, and trade unionists have been well documented and represent serious concerns for citizen security in Colombia.[16] Journalists play a fundamental role in any democracy as they hold politicians and public officials accountable through investigative reporting. Human Rights Watch notes some of the recent abuses against community activists, journalists, and trade union members:

- For years, Colombia has led the world in killings of trade unionists, with more than 2,600 reported killings since 1986, according to the National Labor School, Colombia's leading NGO monitoring labor rights. The bulk of the killings are attributed to paramilitary groups, which have deliberately targeted unionists.
- Though the number of killings annually has dropped from its peak in the 1990s, when the paramilitaries were in the midst of their violent expansion, more than 400 trade unionists have been killed during the Uribe government. In 2008, the number of killings went up again, to forty-one as of October, according to the National Labor School. Unionists working in the education sector comprise a high proportion of the victims.
- Impunity in the killing of trade unionists is widespread: in about 97 percent of cases there has been no conviction and the killers remain free. The rate of convictions for unionist killings under the Uribe administration was consistently low until 2007, when the number of convictions jumped to forty-three. As of October the Attorney General's Office reported there had been fifty-three convictions in 2008. This sudden increase is primarily due to pressure from the US Congress.[17]

Moreover, Amnesty International reveals that "a staggering 95 per cent of the roughly 3,000 cases of assassination of union members committed over the last 30 years remain unprosecuted."[18] Human Rights Watch contends, "The National Labor School (ENS), Colombia's leading labor rights NGO, continues to report killings of trade unionists. As of September 2014, the special prosecutorial unit dedicated to anti-union violence had opened investigations into more than 110 cases of trade unionist killings committed since 2009, but obtained convictions in just 9 of them."[19] The high impunity rates send a perverse message to criminal groups: it is extremely unlikely that you will be prosecuted if you kill a union worker. Therefore, people "resolve" their problems with union workers by disappearing them. These cases demonstrate the alarming trends in Colombia (see figure 0.3).[20]

Moreover, the global impunity index indicates that Latin American countries score as some of the countries with the highest levels of impunity in the world. In addition, the impunity problem in Latin America is not concentrated in only Central America or parts of South America. Instead, countries throughout the region face alarming levels of impunity. According to the 2017 Global Impunity Index, Mexico scored a 69.21 in 2017, with zero being the least amount of impunity and 100 being the highest level. In addition, Peru received a score of 69.04, while Venezuela received a score of 67.24. Brazil, Colombia, and Nicaragua each scored more than 66 on the impunity scale. Furthermore, Honduras and El Salvador scored a 65.04 and 65.03, respectively. In summary, Latin American countries have been plagued by high levels of impunity, which has contributed to the corruption problem impacting the region (see figure 0.4).[21]

Some states in Latin America have such high levels of corruption, impunity, violence, and human rights abuses that experts have debated whether some countries in the region can be classified as failed states. While various states in the Americas have been labeled as failed states, calling a country a failed state

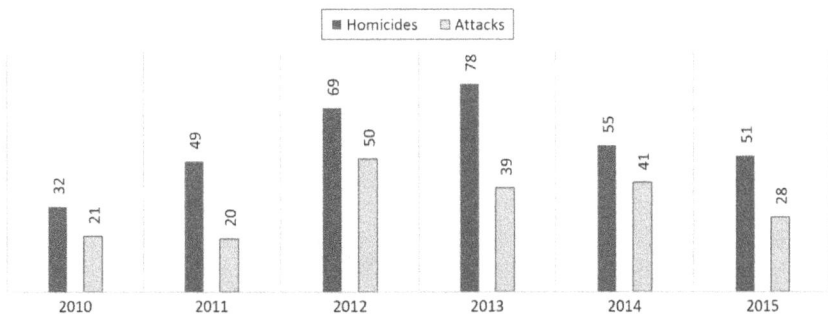

Figure 0.3 Attacks and Killings of Defenders of Human Rights. Created by authors with data from "15th Anniversary of Plan Colombia: Learning from Its Successes and Failures," Washington Office on Latin America, February 1, 2016; Somos Defensores.

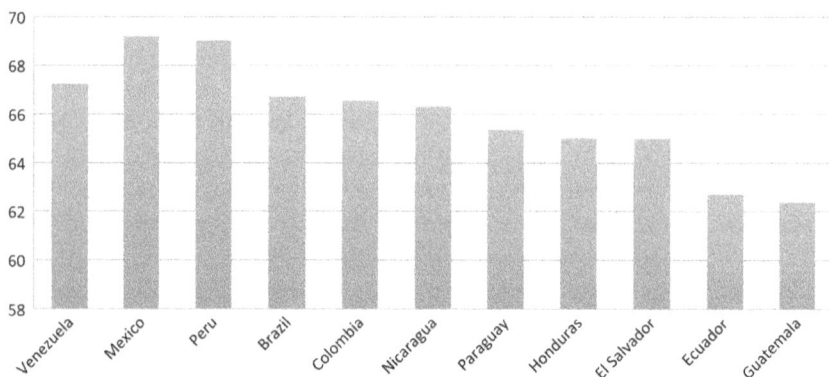

Figure 0.4   2017 Global Impunity Index (0-100 score). Created by authors with data from Juan Antonio Le Clercq Ortega and Gerardo Rodríguez Sánchez Lara, *Global Impunity Dimensions: GG-2017 Global Impunity Index* (Pubela, Mexico: University of the Americas Puebla, 2017).

is quite controversial and requires a precise definition of what constitutes a failed state.[22] Some experts, for example, have argued that Mexico was a failed state. While Mexico has high levels of drug trafficking and organized crime, it should not be classified as a failed state as Mexico is not Afghanistan. Ted Galen Carpenter, an expert on security and organized crime, discusses Mexico and the failed state argument, stating: "Concerns that Mexico might become a 'failed state'—which had gained traction during the most turbulent years of Calderón's presidency—are again on the rise. . . . Mexico is not Somalia, Bosnia, Yemen, Sudan or other failed states, where such stabilizing features are largely absent; nor is it fractured by bitter ideological or religious conflicts, as those countries have been."[23] Thus, the concept of what is and what is not a failed state is problematic. What constitutes a failed state is in the eye of the beholder. Noam Chomsky,[24] for instance, argues that the United States is a failed state. This volume uses the term "fragile states"[25] as opposed to failed states in part because the term "failed states" is a loaded term and is quite controversial in nature.[26] Fragile states are weak states[27] that are fertile grounds for organized crime groups and illegal actors as such groups can infiltrate the state apparatus through corruption and other mechanisms such as extortion.

FACTORS INFLUENCING TRUST AND PERCEPTIONS OF CORRUPTION

What factors influence perceptions about corruption? This is a question that will be explored in the following chapters. The LAPOP 2016/2017 Colombia data,[28] for example, reveals that 31.30 percent of respondents believed that all politicians are corrupt. The regression model controls for age, sex, political ideology, whether someone has been asked to pay a bribe to the municipal government, which is coded no and yes, and trust in political parties, coded one for "Not at All" and seven for "A Lot" (see table 0.1). The age variable is from eighteen to eighty-eight, but it has been recoded into six categories.[29] The dependent variable is coded "None," "Less than half of them," "Half of them," "More than half of them," and "All."[30]

The model reveals that being asked to pay a bribe and trust in political parties is statistically significant at the 95 percent confidence level. A one-unit increase in being asked to pay a bribe (i.e., moving from no to yes) leads to a .447 shift in the dependent variable. This means that people who have been asked to pay a bribe, on average, are more likely to believe that politicians are corrupt. Moreover, a one-unit shift in trust in political parties leads to a -.180 shift in the dependent variable. In other words, people who have more trust in political parties, on average, are less likely to perceive them as corrupt.

The high amounts of corruption have created large levels of distrust in other Latin American countries, such as Honduras, which is facing a political and institutional crisis. In fact, the 2016/2017 LAPOP data reveal that 34.64 percent of respondents contended "Not at All," when asked their levels of trust in the Honduran executive. Regression helps determine the different factors that influence trust in the executive, which is coded one for "Not at All" and seven for "A Lot." The independent variables are age, which is recoded as mentioned earlier, sex, urban, monthly household income, education, skin color, ideology, and whether a government employee asked for a bribe.

Table 0.1   Factors Influencing Perceptions of Corruption among Politicians

	Coeff	
Variable	*(SE)*	*t-test*
Age	0.047	0.77
	(0.061)	
Sex	0.004	0.03
	(0.144)	
Ideology	−0.016	−0.50
	(0.031)	
Asked for Bribe Mun. Gov.	0.447***	3.27
	(0.137)	
Trust in Political Parties	−0.180***	−3.18
	(0.057)	
Constant	4.252***	12.31
	(0.345)	
Observations	145	
R-squared	0.140	

Robust standard errors in parentheses.
*** $p < 0.01$, ** $p < 0.05$, * $p < 0.1$.
Source: Created by authors with data from LAPOP.

Ideology is coded one for left and ten for right, while government employees asked for a bribe is coded no and yes. The coding of the rest of the variables has been defined in the previous sections (see table 0.2).[31]

The regression results indicate that age, monthly household income, ideology, and whether a government employee asked for a bribe are statistically significant at the 95 percent confidence level. The regression reveals that a one-unit shift in age leads to a .206 change in the dependent variable, which means that people who are older, on average, have more trust in the executive. Moreover, a one-unit change in monthly household income leads to a -.033 shift in the dependent variable. This means that people who have higher monthly household incomes, on average, have less trust in the executive. Meanwhile, a one-unit shift in the ideology variable (i.e., moving from left to right) leads to a .176 change in the dependent variable. This means that people who have a more conservative ideology, on average, have higher levels of trust in the executive. Finally, a one-unit shift in the bribe variable (i.e., moving from no to yes) leads to a -.960 shift in the dependent variable. Therefore, people who have been asked for a bribe by a government employee, on average, are less likely to trust the executive.

Table 0.2 Factors Influencing Trust in the Executive

Variable	Coeff. (SE)	t-test
Age	0.206***	4.11
	(0.050)	
Sex	0.032	0.24
	(0.130)	
Urban	0.151	1.14
	(0.133)	
Monthly Household Income	−0.033**	−2.36
	(0.014)	
Education	−0.028*	−1.66
	(0.017)	
Skin Color	−0.070*	−1.71
	(0.041)	
Ideology	0.176***	8.29
	(0.021)	
Gov Employee Asked Bribe	−0.960***	−4.60
	(0.209)	
Constant	2.640***	6.08
	(0.434)	
Observations	1,117	
R-squared	0.133	

Robust standard errors in parentheses.
*** $p < 0.01$, ** $p < 0.05$, * $p < 0.1$.
Source: Created by authors with data from LAPOP.

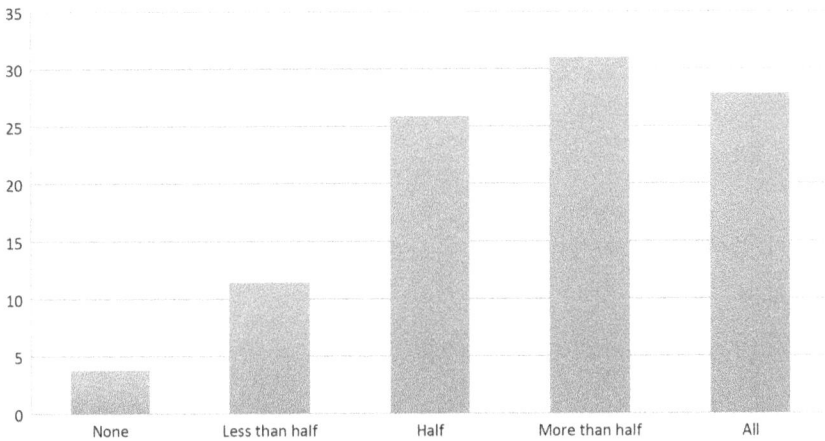

Figure 0.5   Perception about the amount of Corruption among Politicians (2016/2017).
Created by authors with data from LAPOP 2016/2017.

The high levels of corruption also have generated high levels of distrust of Honduran politicians, which is similar to the context of some other Central American countries examined in this volume. In fact, the LAPOP Honduran survey data reveal that 27.88 percent of participants responded that all politicians are corrupt (see figure 0.5). A regression model helps determine what factors influence perceptions of corruption among politicians, which is coded "None," "Less than half of them," "Half of them," "More than half of them," and "All." The independent variables are age, urban, monthly household income, education, and ideology (see table 0.3).[32]

The model reveals that age, monthly household income, and ideology are statistically significant at the 95 percent confidence interval. A one-unit change in age leads to a -.076 shift in the dependent variable. This means that people who are older, on average, are more likely to believe that politicians are less corrupt. Moreover, a one-unit shift in monthly household income leads to a .014 change in the dependent variable. Therefore, people who have larger monthly household incomes are more likely to believe that politicians are corrupt. Finally, a one-unit change in ideology (i.e., left to right) results in a -.040 shift in the dependent variable. Thus, people who are more conservative, on average, are more likely to believe that there is less corruption among politicians.

SATISFACTION WITH DEMOCRACY

The seemingly endless corruption scandals, the collusion between transnational organized crime and the state, and violence have contributed to the

Table 0.3   Factors Influencing Perceptions of Corruption among Politicians

Variable	Coeff (SE)	t-test
Age	−0.076***	−2.98
	(0.026)	
Urban	0.004	0.06
	(0.068)	
Monthly Household Income	0.014**	2.00
	(0.007)	
Education	−0.003	−0.31
	(0.009)	
Ideology	−0.040***	−3.66
	(0.011)	
Constant	3.977***	22.87
	(0.174)	
Observations	1,082	
R-squared	0.031	

Robust standard errors in parentheses.
*** p < 0.01, ** p < 0.05, * p < 0.1.
Source: Created by authors with data from LAPOP.

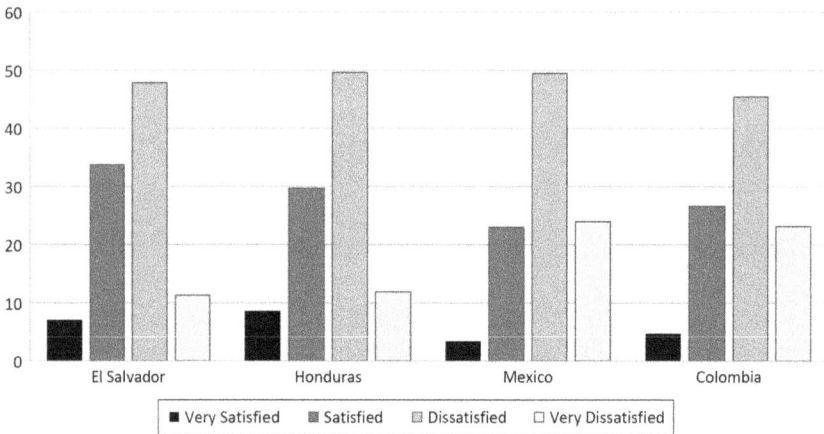

Figure 0.6   Satisfaction with Democracy. Created by authors with data from LAPOP. The data is from the most recent year of the individual country surveys.

high levels of distrust that citizens of the countries examined in this study have in the political system. For instance, the most recent individual country survey data conducted by LAPOP reveals that 3.46 percent of Mexicans are very satisfied with democracy compared to 4.77 for Colombians, 7.08 for El Salvadorans, and 8.67 percent of Hondurans. Most people living in El Salvador, Honduras, Mexico, and Colombia, therefore, are dissatisfied with the state of democracy in their respective countries (see figure 0.6).

Low levels of trust in democracy can create a variety of challenges. Citizens who are jaded by the high levels of impunity and corruption will likely believe that democracy is not working for them. This could lead to people feeling that it is a futile effort to participate in the political system. People also may be less likely to report crimes due to general levels of distrust in institutions, such as the police. Therefore, there is a need for all the countries examined in this book to strengthen institutions and consolidate democracy.[33]

ORGANIZATION OF THE VOLUME

There are countless books that discuss drug trafficking, organized crime, and violence in Latin America. Many of these works analyze state fragility and corruption, but they often focus on several cases, or even one country.[34] We believe that the scholarly literature is missing a comprehensive volume on corruption in Latin America. This book, therefore, is an effort to fill this void in the literature and provide both theoretical and policy insights into this important topic.

This volume consists of works of experts from around the region who are country specialists. The authors in this work have diverse scholarly backgrounds and theoretical and methodological orientations. The volume is divided into case studies of countries throughout the Americas. The authors in the case studies have been asked to think about the following questions:

- What is the nature of corruption?
- What are the recent trends in corruption?
- Who are the main actors involved in corruption (e.g., state, non-state actors, and companies)?
- What is the linkage between corruption and organized crime?
- How has corruption impacted governance and state fragility?
- How has the government responded to corruption?

In chapter 1, Bradford R. McGuinn provides a conceptual review of the corruption literature. In the chapter, McGuinn analyzes the concept of intention, focusing on how it has evolved over time. McGuinn highlights the different theoretical constructs, looking specifically at realism, liberalism, and a structuralist-institutional perspective. In summary, this work provides an excellent overview of the different paradigms designed to explain the nature of corruption.

In chapter 2, Roberto Zepeda and Jonathan D. Rosen explore corruption and state fragility. The chapter starts by analyzing the democratization process in Mexico. It utilizes survey data to determine different factors that influence trust in institutions and perceptions about democracy. The chapter then examines the linkages between Mexico's war on drugs, corruption, and violence in Mexico. The authors highlight the different trends in violence and corruption, particularly during the Felipe Calderón and Enrique Peña Nieto administrations. The chapter then turns to the election of Andrés Manuel López Obrador (AMLO) and the different policy approaches of the new president, who campaigned on a platform of the need to reduce corruption.

In chapter 3, Adriana Beltrán examines corruption in Guatemala. She focuses on the evolution of the International Commission against Impunity in Guatemala, known as CICIG. She examines the nature of corruption in this country and how CICIG sought to reduce corruption and reform institutions. She provides countless examples of corruption and argues that the Guatemalan state can be described as a captured state. Beltrán then analyzes how various actors led to the demise of CICIG. In this chapter, she also explores the role of the United States and the current political landscape in Guatemala and how this will impact efforts to combat corruption.

In chapter 4, Fernando Cepeda Ulloa analyzes corruption in Colombia. He starts by focusing on what he refers to as the "crisis of the traditional value system" as well as structural changes in the political system, particularly the weakening of political parties. Cepeda Ulloa then analyzes the role of the judicial system, a system characterized by what he refers to as "legal fetishism" and efficiencies. In this chapter, Cepeda Ulloa also highlights the impact that drug trafficking and organized crimes have had on corruption as well as the centralization of power after the 1991 Constitution. The chapter then explores the different mechanisms that are available to combat corruption and the impact of recent events on the various instruments designed to diminish corruption.

In chapter 5, Cynthia McClintock examines the case of corruption in Peru. The chapter begins with a historical analysis of corruption in Peru and how it has evolved over time. She then turns to the Odebrecht case and examines how five former presidents have received bribes from this Brazilian construction company. The chapter also examines what McClintock refers to as the "battle against corruption" between 2016 and 2019 as well as the importance of the economic, political, and judicial contexts that help explain the nature of corruption in this country. The chapter focuses on the role of investigative journalism and changes in the country's judiciary. Finally, McClintock highlights the various initiatives designed to reform the system and combat the pervasive levels of corruption plaguing Peru.

In chapter 6, Marten Brienen analyzes corruption in Bolivia. He begins the chapter with an analysis of some of the recent trends in corruption, citing a litany of cases as well as survey data on corruption. He explores the role of institutions and state fragility in Bolivia. Brienen uses the police to demonstrate the high levels of state weakness that is present throughout the state apparatus. He concludes by arguing that institutions, despite their names and appearances, do not carry out their intended duties and responsibilities, but rather serve as mechanisms for extracting resources, often through bribes. The high levels of distrust in institutions and lack of the rule of law have led some marginalized communities to take the law into their own hands.

In chapter 7, Michael Jerome Wolff examines the nature of organized crime and corruption in Brazil and highlights the intricate linkages between the state and organized crime. He analyzes the different organized crime groups operating in Brazil. Moreover, Wolff examines the various government strategies designed to combat drug trafficking, organized crime, and violence and the consequences of these policies. The chapter then turns to the role of the police and their involvement in death squads. It also examines the role of the penitentiary system, an institution that has been plagued by corruption scandals, overcrowding, and human rights abuses.

NOTES

1. Hilary Goodfriend, "Prosecuting Presidents in El Salvador: Corruption prosecutions against former presidents in El Salvador did little to punish thieving public officials, but they did help tip the balance of power back toward the Right—revealing the limits and biases of anti-corruption discourse today," *NACLA Report on the Americas* 51, no. 2 (2019): pp. 141–145.

2. Parker Asmann, "Despite confession, Former El Salvador President's sentencing is bittersweet," *InSight Crime*, September 13, 2018, https://www.insightcrime.org /news/brief/despite-confession-former-el-salvador-presidents-sentencing-bitterswee t/, accessed September 11, 2019, p. 2.

3. Héctor Silva Ávalos and César Castro Fagoaga, "The Funes and Saca Tapes in El Salvador: A plot revealed," *InSight Crime*, December 21, 2018, https://www .insightcrime.org/news/analysis/funes-saca-tapes-el-salvador/, accessed September 11, 2019.

4. For more, see: Francisco Durand, "The Odebrecht Tsunami: The Odebrecht scandal highlights the phenomenon of corporate capture of the state in Brazil and Peru. Yet new investigative tools show promise in detecting and responding to multinational graft," *NACLA Report on the Americas* 51, no. 2 (2019): pp. 146–152; Ben Marques, "From The Panama Papers To Odebrecht: Illicit financial flows From Brazil," *Business and Public Administration Studies* 13, no. 1 (2019): pp. 22–31.

5. Charles Orta, "How Odebrecht profited from corrupting LatAm political elites," *InSight Crime*, https://www.insightcrime.org/news/analysis/how-odebrecht -profited-from-corrupting-latam-political-elites/, accessed September 12, 2019.

6. Daniel Gallas, "Brazil's Odebrecht corruption scandal explained," *BBC News*, April 17, 2019.

7. For more, see: Per G. Fredriksson and Jakob Svensson, "Political instability, corruption and policy formation: The case of environmental policy," *Journal of Public Economics* 87, no. 7–8 (2003): pp. 1383–1405; Damarys Canache and Michael E. Allison, "Perceptions of political corruption in Latin American democracies," *Latin American Politics and Society* 47, no. 3 (2005): pp. 91–111.

8. For more, see: Tim Hall, "Where the money is: The geographies of organised crime," *Geography* 95 (2010): p. 4; Tim Hall, "Economic geography and organized crime: A critical review," *Geoforum* 41, no. 6 (2010): pp. 841–845.

9. For more, see: Transparency International's "Corruption Perceptions Index 2018," https://www.transparency.org/cpi2018, accessed September 12, 2019.

10. For more, see: Susan Rose–Ackerman, "Corruption and government," *International Peacekeeping* 15, no. 3 (2008): pp. 328–343.

11. A few sections of this chapter are from Jonathan D. Rosen and Hanna S. Kassab, eds., *Fragile States in the Americas* (Lanham, MD: Lexington Books, 2016), introduction.

12. Kyra Gurney, "Why are the World's Most Violent Cities in Latin America?" *InSight Crime*, p. 6.

13. Laura Carlsen, "Obama should not prop up Mexico's president," *Huffington Post*, January 6, 2015, 1; Juan Antonio Zúñiga M., "Impunes, 93.8% de los delitos perpetrados en 2013: Inegi," *La Jornada*, 16 de octubre de 2015.

14. See: Silvia Inclán Oseguera, "Judicial reform in Mexico: Political insurance or the search for political legitimacy?" *Political Research Quarterly* 62, no. 4 (2009): pp. 753–766; Juan D. Lindau, "The drug war's impact on executive power, judicial reform, and federalism in Mexico," *Political Science Quarterly* 126, no. 2 (2011): pp. 177–200.

15. See: Bruce M. Bagley and Jonathan D. Rosen, eds., *Colombia's Political Economy at the Outset of the Twenty-First Century: From Uribe to Santos and Beyond* (Lanham, MD: Lexington Books, 2015).

16. Adam Isacson, "Optimism, pessimism, and terrorism: The United States and Colombia in 2003." *The Brown Journal of World Affairs* 10, no. 2 (2004): pp. 245–255

17. Quoted from Human Rights Watch (HRW), "Colombia: Events of 2009," *HRW*, https://www.hrw.org/world-report/2010/country-chapters/colombia, accessed May 15, 2019, p. 6.

18. "Impunity," Amnesty International, http://www.amnestyusa.org/our-work/countries/americas/colombia/impunity, accessed October 2015.

19. "World Report 2015: Colombia," https://www.hrw.org/world-report/2015/country-chapters/colombia, accessed October 2015, p. 6.

20. Adam Isacson, "Optimism, pessimism, and terrorism: The United States and Colombia in 2003"; Washington Office on Latin America (WOLA), "The Human Rights Landscape in Colombia: Adam Isacson's testimony before the Tom Lantos Human Rights Commission."

21. Juan Antonio Le Clercq Ortega and Gerardo Rodríguez Sánchez Lara, *Global Impunity Dimensions: GG-2017 Global Impunity Index* (Pubela, Mexico: University of the Americas Puebla, 2017).

22. A few sections of this chapter are from Rosen and Kassab, eds., *Fragile States in the Americas*, introduction.

23. Ted Galen Carpenter, "Watch out, America: Mexico may be the next failed state," *CATO Institute*, January 29, 2015, http://www.cato.org/publications/comment ary/watch-out-america-mexico-may-be-next-failed-state, accessed October 2015, 2; see also: Adam David Morton, "The war on drugs in Mexico: A failed state?" *Third World Quarterly* 33, no. 9 (2012): pp. 1631–1645.

24. Noam Chomsky, *Failed States: The Abuse of Power and the Assault on Democracy* (New York, NY: Owl Books, 2006).

25. For more on this debate, see: Robert I. Rotberg, "Failed states in a world of terror," *Foreign Affairs* (2002): pp. 127–140; Volker Boege, M. Anne Brown, and Kevin P. Clements, "Hybrid political orders, not fragile states," *Peace Review* 21, no. 1 (2009): pp. 13–21; Seth Kaplan, "Identifying truly fragile states," *The Washington Quarterly* 37, no. 1 (2014): pp. 49–63; Eka Ikpe, "Challenging the discourse on fragile states," *Conflict, Security & Development* 7, no. 1 (2007): pp. 85–124.

26. For more on fragile states, see David Carment, Stewart Prest, and Yiagadeesen Samy, *Security, Development and the Fragile State: Bridging the Gap between Theory and Policy* (New York, NY: Routledge, 2009); Wim Naude, Amelia U. Santos-Paulino, and Mark McGillivray, eds., *Fragile States: Causes, Costs, and Responses* (New York, NY: Oxford University Press, 2011).

27. Hanna Samir Kassab, *Weak States in International Relations Theory: The Cases of Armenia, St. Kitts and Nevis, Lebanon, and Cambodia* (New York, NY: Palgrave Macmillan, 2015).

28. LAPOP indicates that the following command should be used to weight the data: svyset upm [pw=wt], strata (estratopri).

29. The recode is as follows: recode q2 (18/28=1) (29/39=2) (40/50=3) (51/61=4) (62/72=5) (73/88=6), gen (age).

30. The linktest produces as hatsq of 0.43, which reveals that the model does not have issues with specification. The model has a Mean VIF of 1.04, meaning that the model does not have issues with multicollinearity. Finally, the Breusch-Pagan/Cook-Weisberg test for heteroskedasticity produces a Prob > chi2 of 0.003, indicating that the model must be readjusted using the vce (robust) command in Stata 15.1.

31. The model is tested for specification, multicollinearity, and heteroscedasticity. The linktest produces a hatsq of 0.418, indicating that the model does not have issues with specification. The model has a Mean Vif of 1.14. Thus, there are not issues of multicollinearity. The Breusch-Pagan / Cook-Weisberg test for heteroscedasticity had a Prob > chi2 of 0.001, which is statically significant at the 95 percent confidence level. The model is adjusted using the vce (robust) command).

32. The model does not have issues with specification as the linktest produces a hatsq of 0.96. Moreover, the model has a Mean VIF of 1.18, which means that the model does not have issues with multicollinearity. Finally, Breusch-Pagan/Cook-Weisberg test for heteroscedasticity produces a Prob > chi2 of 0.02, indicating that the model needs to be corrected using the vce (robust) command in Stata 15.1.

33. For more on consolidating democracy, see: Jenny Pearce, "Civil society, the market and democracy in Latin America," *Democratization* 4, no. 2 (1997): pp. 57–58; Larry Diamond, "Consolidating democracy in the Americas," *The Annals of the American Academy of Political and Social Science* 550, no. 1 (1997): pp. 12–41.

34. Benjamin Lessing, *Making Peace in Drug Wars: Crackdowns and Cartels in Latin America* (New York, NY: Cambridge University Press, 2018); Enrique Desmond Arias, *Criminal Enterprises and Governance in Latin America and the Caribbean* (New York, NY: Cambridge University Press, 2017); Bruce M. Bagley and Jonathan D. Rosen, eds., *Drug Trafficking, Organized Crime, and Violence in the Americas Today* (Gainesville, FL: University Press of Florida, 2015); Jennifer S. Holmes, Kevin M. Curtin, and Sheila Amin Gutiérrez de Piñeres, *Guns, Drugs, and Development in Colombia* (Austin, TX: University of Texas Press, 2008).

Chapter 1

A Little Lower than the Angels

*Problems of Corruption and
Obligation: A Conceptual Review*

Bradford R. McGuinn

As widely condemned as it is practiced, inveighed against by some in the name of public integrity, weaponized by others for political advantage, the term "corruption" is associated with Latin America in indiscriminate ways. Linked etymologically with "debasement" or "decay," joined in the popular imagination with "misconduct," and more generally still with the "misuse of public office for private gain," corruption is as much a condition as it is a specific criminal act. It is suggested here that considerations of corruption are animated by normative as well as legal judgments regarding ideal balance between public and private responsibilities, socially constructed notions of right conduct from which corrupt practice would constitute deviation.[1] Informing practice is a concept of *obligation*, what Margaret Gilbert called a "forceful species of reason for action."[2]

This chapter examines forms of reasoning that privilege private, rather than public, conceptualizations of obligation, theoretical insights that help us understand the manner by which corruption challenges the processes of institutionalization that are the basis of impersonal public rule. The chapter begins with an overview of Latin America's current encounter with corrupt practices, then considers definitional and theoretical treatments of corruption and obligation, before examining the manner by which the trajectories of political theory might offer insight into the directing of obligation toward private rather than public ends, concluding with a consideration of the trials associated with corruption's remedy.

PLUNDERGROUND

"It is a cancer which destroys all healthy tissues," the Italian journalist Luigi Barzini said of the corruption that menaced his native realm during the years after the defeat of fascism,[3] a time when much of Latin America was drifting toward military rule. The region's subsequent democratic revolution brought about pluralistic politics, and also a condition today of corruption, misrule and mistrust between state and society. Brazil's experience with the *Operacao Lava Jato* investigation, or "Operation Carwash,"[4] brought to grief the careers of former president Luiz Inácio Lula de Silva and his successor, Dilma Rousseff. So too the impact of the Odebrecht scandal has registered across the region,[5] taking an extraordinary toll on Peru's leadership, where one president was forced to resign, a previous president committed suicide as police were moving to apprehend him, and a third was arrested in California.[6] Argentina's "Notebook Scandal" and a host of other extravagant cases throughout Latin America speak to a crisis of governance that threatens the region's democratic promise,[7] risking the "criminalization" of its politics.[8]

The trial of Joaquín Guzmán Loera, or "El Chapo,"[9] leader of what has been described as "the largest drug-trafficking organization in the world,"[10] made vivid the capacity of drugs cartels to institutionalize corrupt practice amid a "swamp of bribery"[11] and extreme violence,[12] the regime of *plata o plomo*, silver or lead.[13] From "border and customs officials,"[14] to law enforcement officers, and some of the region's the top most political leaders, illicit enterprises have penetrated the mechanisms of governance. In some countries, where efforts have been undertaken to combat corruption, such as with the International Commission against Impunity in Guatemala (Comisión Internacional contra la Impunidad en Guatemala—CICIG), a body that brought charges "against some 700 people involved in more than 60 criminal networks,"[15] the exertions of convicted "[f]ormer presidents and ministers, legislators, judges and business owners," was sufficient to "crush the anti-corruption drive that put them in jail."[16]

The corruption cases associated with corporate leaders and national presidents, cartel chieftains and disgraced civil servants, are associated too with the pathologies of narcotics trafficking, gang violence, and the migration crisis in Central America.[17] "At the root of all the problems in Honduras is corruption and impunity," a Honduran businessman noted.[18] It is, he suggested, a force "provoking massive migration."[19] Where governments have failed to create "opportunities for the people," another observer noted, "the corruption is tremendous."[20] From bus owners forced to pay extortion to gangs,[21] to the "nonprofits" obtaining government contracts for work not performed,[22] or for teachers that do not exist,[23] is a "system,"[24] one in which traffickers prey upon the vulnerable across Central America, sending migrants[25] upon their danger-ous journeys toward the United States to a fate of increased uncertainty.[26] Meantime, populations across the region, long liberated from the fear of mili-tary regimes, are consigned to the highest rates of homicide in the world.[27] The only region of the world to experience a growth in lethal violence since 2000, with only eight percent of the world's population, "Latin America accounts for roughly a third of global murders,"[28] a distressing number of which will go without prosecution.[29]

That Latin America risks becoming a "plunderground," as a Senate Crime Committee said of Miami in 1950,[30] that "the core of government" is vul-nerable to corruption's poison,[31] speaks to a disturbance of obligation, an imbalance in fealty between public and private responsibilities. To the many historical factors that inform this unhappy condition—legacies of colonial-ism, polarization between wealth and poverty, the shadow of the *caudillo*, the nexus between oligarchs and commodities of unstable valuation, rapid urbanization, homes broken by war and migration, the proliferation of guns and overcrowded prisons, impunity and the temptation of personalized vengeance, the geographies of violence within the narcotics ecosystem, the impact of populist politics and frequent electoral swings from right to left—can be added larger patterns of international deinstitutionalization which have redirected once settled patterns of obligation in chaotic trajectories. [32]

INTENTION

Once removed from a legal context, where corruption might be seen as a spe-cific "form of crime,"[33] the term becomes a concept descriptive of a condition. The "intentional misperformance or neglect of a recognized duty," as Robert C. Brooks had it over a century ago, "or the unwarranted exercise of power, with the motive of gaining some advantage more or less directly personal,"[34] serves to highlight the concept of intentionality, which is featured in the well-known description of corruption as "a crime of calculation, not passion."[35]

An act of intention,[36] at odds with notions of "duty," suggesting "formal" obligations associated with a public role:[37] such an understanding pres-ages too Samuel Huntington's emphasis upon "behavior of public officials which deviates from accepted norms in order to serve private ends,"[38] what Joseph Nye would call deviation from "the formal duties of a public role" on behalf of "private-regarding" interests.[39] Central to this view is the concept of "office," with its role obligations, statutory authority, fiduciary duties and moral requirements, a concept of order from which corruption implies deviation: duties shirked, office abused, morality subverted, all in intentional fashion.

It is with some caution that the heuristic traditions associated with what Martin Wight called "international theory" are engaged in a discussion of corruption. Less preoccupied with what these theoretical approaches might emphasize on matters of international politics, and more with their utility in the realm of social theory, especially upon the narrower point of obligation, the reasoning of realism, liberalism, critical theory and constructivism do point us in different directions. Realism with its grounding in self-interest and power, associates obligation with survival, whereas liberalism, with its faith in cooperation, progress, and the efficacy of institutions, considers obligation in terms of a suspension of absolute self-interest in favor of mutuality. Critical theory, with its Marxian genealogy, its emphasis on the struggle between socioeconomic or cultural aggregates, and its emancipatory urgings, will view obligation in teleological terms, as fealty to a trajectory of liberation, while constructivist theory, by virtue of its granting to language primary ontological status as the means by which our "reality" is fashioned, is likely to guide us toward a contingent view of obligation. Corruption is, then, for the realist political struggle by other means, for the liberal a failure of the moral imagination and institutions, for the critical theorist the very emblem of oppressive power and for the constructivist, corruption will be "what people make of it."

CONSTRUCTS

That humankind exists "a little lower than the angels" is a theme central to classical and scriptural understandings of corruption, and a view foundational to political realism. "Man has always been his most vexing problem,"[40] Reinhold Niebuhr wrote, reminding us of "tragic heroes," whose hubris causes them to disregard the "prudent advice of moderation,"[41] and violate the "principle of order and measure.[42] From the classical world we are also provided an association between corruption and decay.[43] Where evil is only dormant and "prudence,"[44] what Aristotle called the "crown of values,"[45] gives way to avarice, the "voluntary partnership that people form for their common good,"[46] or polis, is placed in jeopardy.

"Man is like to vanity," the Psalmist tells us.[47] His sin, his corruption, Niebuhr suggests further, is "defined as rebellion against God,"[48] through the assertion of his will.[49] Between the realms of the terrestrial and the celestial,[50] as much of Christian doctrine would have it, is the view of earthy life as inherently corrupt,[51] conjoined with a longing for release from the "diseased body politic into the purifying body of Christ."[52] The roads from Athens and Jerusalem would shape the normative categories by which corruption would be viewed throughout the western experience. From the Puritan ethos,[53] to the modern concepts of "moral disengagement,"[54] systems of reasoning have been cultivated in order that the virtuous would have to "strain to do wrong,"[55] where "justice" might "well up like water," and "righteousness" flow "in an ever-flowing stream,"[56] where with the shields of honor and covenants, as "accountings for moral obligation,[57] we might be held safe from ourselves.

The early republican speculations of Niccolo Machiavelli would also associate corruption with the "pursuit of private interests" above the "common good,"[58] warning of "private loyalties" that imperil a polity.[59] "Corruption," S. M. Shumer said of Machiavelli's writings, "must be understood in relationship to its mirror-image concept, the healthy republic," measured by the vitality of "civic virtu."[60] "The concept of 'corruption'," he continues, "measures the failure to reach the norms expected of healthy politics."[61] For Thomas Hobbes too, corruption, with its origins in the realm of "faulty reasoning or emotions," constitute a danger to "civic peace,"[62] causing "citizens [to] think they benefit from sedition," "leading to disorder,"[63] toward civil war."[64]

From the republican to the liberal tradition of political theory would emerge a "conception of impersonal rule,"[65] an emphasis upon the "impersonal state."[66] Edmund Burke recognized the risks to the integrity of such an enterprise posed by the exercise of "public will,"[67] and expressed a wariness too regarding the exercise of public virtue, of which the anticorruption exertions seen in the French Revolution were emblematic, encouraging, instead, an understanding of the "middle tints and shades between the two extremes."[68] In the doctrines of Adam Smith would emerge a more direct assertion of "standard liberal values," those of "impartiality, universalism, neutrality," the idea of "formal equality of opportunity and rule of law,"[69] and the association of corruption with inefficiency.[70] The logic of a "hidden hand," the unseen force said to suppress corruption and maintain order, found application in the American constitution,[71] with its "distribution of its powers" meant to serve as a break upon avarice.[72]

Liberal doctrines were integral to the processes of Latin America's independence in the nineteenth century, and flourished into the first decades of the next,[73] associated as these ideas were with "positivism," reason and science, "a European concept of progress,"[74] challenging the authority of the Church.[75] Everywhere liberal politics implies a diffusion of power and competition toward its acquisition, a tension between the "subjective construction of psychological desires" and "objective social conditions."[76] Actors, "driven by interests"[77] within a culture of competition organic to "social systems based on industrial capitalism,"[78] risk competitive democracy being associated with "bribery of the electorate by politicians."[79] Safeguard from the implications of such a "security dilemma" would be provided by "independent, public-interest standards," in which "reciprocity of service"[80] is subject to the ideational and institutional restraints "potent enough to prevent different pockets of power from destroying one another (and the state) through uninhibited self-assertiveness."[81]

Directing concepts of obligation between citizen and state,[82] the private and public,[83] is the functional imperative of competitiveness, balanced by what Ronald Dworkin called "a certain conception of equality,"[84] reconciled with the "ideational imperative" of administrative integrity. To the need to accommodate competition while discouraging corruption, Max Weber would provide a point of reconciliation in a concept of public administration,[85] joining the "depersonalized state" with a "rationalized society."[86] In this view, "passion, avarice, and greed" were to be managed through institutions, with "bureaucracy as the legal-rational form of executing power, the *stahlhartes Gehause*, or iron cage,"[87] repressing "irrational behavior" and supplanting "patrimonial" forms of governance.[88] With the ascendency of "Western, impersonal, and universalistic norms of bureaucracy,"[89] public office, then, becomes "a public trust, not a personal domain,"[90] as considerations of "status" give way to those of "contract."[91]

But the association of modern liberalism and the concept of "western individualism,"[92] Weber's emphasis on the "Protestant Ethic," have stimulated questions regarding the universal application of normative constructs of corruption that begin with liberal assumptions regarding the "impersonal state."[93] While liberalism does not have difficulty dealing with concepts of corruption informed by moral failings, it might be inclined to the view, unlike realists, that "injustice is not a permanent aspect of community life."[94] Liberalism struggles also to explain why "strong kinship bonds," "personalistic and familialistic outlooks,"[95] should continue to "carry the weight of social compulsion."[96]

Primordial attachments, "traditional deference," charisma, the "locality orientation" or "ethnic concentration" of "family, or small group orientation," have long been central to our understanding of political corruption.[97] The old North American political machines were so animated, shaped in the popular imagination by figures sometimes "Hogarthian,"[98] other times derived from Damen Runyon or Mario Puzo.[99] Bribes, corrupt bidding processes, generating what Sergio Fernandez Moro has called "systemic corruption,"[100] of his native Brazil, operating, as another observer said of Mexico, upon a dialectic of *mordida*, or the "bite" of "lower-level bribes" and the *amparo*, or injunction from judges,[101] constitute a system not unknown to the political corruption of old Chicago, where the leap from the picaresque Michael "Hinky Dink" Kenna to the menace of Alfonse Capone was the distance of only a few decades and degrees of audacity.[102]

More mannered theoretical treatments might emphasize the influence of social change and mobility, ruptured "personal ties," and "value conflicts," stimulated by the force of "individualism and materialism"[103] weighing upon the new "marginal men," liminal in their status dilemmas. C. Wright Mills would direct readers to breakdown of "older values and codes of uprightness" that had not found sturdy sequel, while others would stress the problems of poverty and dependence as central to the corrupt political machine.[104] The attenuation of ethnic identities and the assimilation of their economic activities into the modern liberal state, Daniel Bell argued, would mark the passing of the "system of political bosses."[105] Such a view would prefigure much of the western developmental literature, with its emphasis on the problem of "political integration," the construction of "a single coherent political society" with increased "cultural homogeneity and value consensus," asking of the individual "deference and devotion to the claims of the state."[106]

In the liberal imagination the force of "personal loyalty," the ability of power-holders to draw their "clients" into "an intricate web of reciprocities,"[107] "reward networks,"[108] or "old-boy"[109] systems of moral obligation and "micro morality,"[110] often associated with "a populist ideological aura," and supported by violence, was meant to attenuate upon contact with modernity. But of a political culture, a "system of empirical beliefs, expressive symbols, and values which defines the situation in which political action takes place,"[111] informed by considerations of "cultural traditions" and "social norms,"[112] realist theory might provide a more direct accounting of the continuity in value orientations defined in terms of power. In the system of moral reasoning, as has been said of the Brazilian case, where tension exists between the *rua*, or street, and that of the *casa*, or house,[113] a struggle between "traditional morality, well-established friendships and the opportunity at hand," an environment in which crimes are "practiced with impunity," with the "intolerable arrogance" of entitlement, the "exclusive club with strict entrance requirements,"[114] challenges the efficacy of the depersonalized liberal construct while affirming the tenacity of tradition.

The matter is complex: discerning the relationship between what has been said of "subcultural" factors within Italian bureaucracy, between "*parentela* (kinship)" and those of a "*clientela* relationship,"[115] to the most nuanced of affective ties within post-Soviet space or Iraq after its de-Baathification, to say nothing of the diverse landscapes of Latin America, might require still finer theoretical instruments. Insights from psychology, sociology, or anthropology regarding the "basic personality structure" of a social system,[116] dimensions of ontological insecurity that might attend environments of systemic corruption, vulnerability, "powerlessness and rejection,"[117] or "shame and humiliation"[118] allow for consideration of corruption within "territories of the self."[119] The quartet of "mistrust, shame, inferiority, role confusion" meant to yield to "trust, autonomy, industry, identity"[120] has its counterpoint in theories of modernization juxtaposing "traditional, religious, familial, and ethnic political authorities" with "the rationalization of authority," the "single, secular, national political authority."[121]

Often, however, such authorities "expropriate" their states, allowing for the indulgence of elites.[122] The "bureaucratic polity," as was once said of Indonesia, represents one variation upon this theme: a fusion of "the military and the bureaucracy" creating "complex molecule"[123] of power obtained through "interpersonal competition within the elite orbiting the president, the atoms of which are held together through an elaborate system of personal ties and mutual obligations."[124] The example of the Philippines reminds us that a "politico-economic elite," constructed around personalities, rather process,[125] fashions not only a flamboyant style of politics, but through, "the use of traditional patron-client ties," presents a politics of "outright corruption, fraud, coercion, and violence."[126] Has not much the same been said of Latin America, with its irregular "exchange and transfer system of wealth and power"?[127] Realist theory would provide an accounting for the self-interested politics of personalism, its "system of exchange,"[128] and the manner by which an oligarchic elite enacts its predations upon state and society.[129] It might suggest too that the integration of politicians into family-centered criminal organizations, as has been said of Honduras, and throughout Central America's Northern Triangle, fashions a molecule of density, protected by a coating of democratic and international legitimacy, that that denies to the system the balancing mechanisms that might limit corruption.[130]

As committed to the "passing of traditional society," as is liberal theory, and resistant also to culturalist understandings of corruption, are the range of insights emanating from the Marxian tradition. In its dialectical reasoning, between "nature and freedom," desire and duty, contingency and progress,[131] Marxism enjoins teleological energy to the vision of alienation's abolition and the realization of the harmony of the classless society. Corruption in this telling is a structural property, the weight of repressive socioeconomic systems and the "false consciousness" they produce.[132] The traditions of critical theory, emanating from the Frankfurt School, with its emphasis upon the acquisition and production of knowledge in the service of dominating systems,[133] provides an understanding of Latin America's problem of corruption in terms of neocolonialism and the predations of the neoliberal state. It might direct us also to an understanding of corruption quite apart from government and public officials. "Corporate actors," in this view, are equally of account "when they exercise public power in a way that serves selfish ends at the expense of public ends."[134] Such an understanding of corporate culpability is structural in that it does not depend for its standard of corruption on either the illegality of action or the presence of public officials.[135]

The "mechanisms which allow the internal regulations of social interactions,"[136] what Frances Lieber long ago called "a group of laws, usages and

operations standing in close relation to one another, and forming an independent whole with a united and distinguishing character of its own,"[137] provides
us an emphasis on institutions. Older traditions of speculation on institutional
corruption and misdirected obligation might stress a "moralist" perspective,[138]
the presence within such aggregations of "bad apples."[139] Modernist accountings tend to begin with the assumption that "an institution can be better than
the individuals who constitute it,"[140] where "role obligations," as Michael
O. Hardimon argued in this fashion, "are defined in terms of institutions."[141]
A "structuralist-institutionalist" perspective might emphasize a culture of
corruption as an established interaction between the "supply side (private
bribers) and a demand side (public officials),"[142] whether of "corporate or
state provenance,"[143] associated with people of "respectability or high social
status,"[144] in which the "unethical practices by professionals,"[145] routes obligation toward "private gain."[146] The compromised "administrative system,"[147]
might then be captured in terms made well known by Robert Klitgaard, in
which "Corruption = Monopoly + Discretion – Accountability,"[148] an equa-
tion that must diminish "interpersonal trust, civil involvement and regime
legitimacy."[149]

Regarding the manner of accountability, Alberto Vannucci directs us
toward the "principal-agent model"[150] within the domain of neo-institution-
alist theory. With the burden of obligation is a fiduciary dimension, in which
an actor responsible for a "critical resource" bears obligations "in both law
and morality."[151] "Not honesty alone," Justice Cardozo once argued of this
matter, "but the punctilio of an honor the most sensitive, is then the standard
of behavior,"[152] to which the "morals of the marketplace" place especial pressure. The actor, "morally disengaging," might, it has been suggested, seeks to
normalize corruption and "advance more quickly" within their institution.[153]
A monitoring theory is provided in Peter Feaver's "principle-agent" theory
of civil-military relations, stipulating that without the direct supervision
of principles, agents will either "work" or "shirk" their responsibilities.[154]
"Working," and a positive sense of obligation, rests upon concepts of honor
embedded in the type of military professionalism that would inform codes
known to other professions,[155] but also by the willingness of the military, in
Feaver's case, to "be punished" for their "shirking" by civilian authorities.
After the tradition of Samuel Huntington's warning, that with "modernization in the absence of political institutionalization,"[156] there could emerge an
institutional "decay," with regimes dedicated to systemic "shirking."

Whereas our general understanding of institutional corruption turns on
an action that "must be some advantage more or less directly personal,"[157]
some theorists have sought to "weakened the insistence on individual gain,"
emphasizing instead a construct that would rely not upon "illegal or currently
unethical conduct" but a "system of influence," that "taints"[158] "the working

of institutions and process."[159] Such represents the approach of "normative institutionalism" associated with Dennis F. Thompson. Framed at a level distinct from individual corruption or the structural corruption identified by critical theorists,[160] distinguished also from the traditional notion of corruption as representing an imbalance between the personal and the public,[161] or even the utility of moral sanction needed to allow competition but limit corruption, the "normative institutionalist" understanding of corruption considers the ways in which modern competitive politics encourages institutional corruption through the influence of money. "Unlike bribes, which exemplify the personal gain found in individual corruption," Thompson asserted, "political gain involves goods that are usable primarily in the political process and are either necessary for doing the job or essential by-productions of doing it."[162] "Corruption is institutional," he argued further, "insofar as the gain a legislator receives is political rather than personal,"[163] a condition in which obligation has not been deflected from public to private, in which an actor's dutiful compliance with the demands of office create conditions of corruption.

Mark Warren has emphasized "the damage to democracy" through "duplicitous exclusion," violating "the norm of equal inclusion," by which, as he put it, "every individual potentially affected by a collective decision should have the opportunity to affect the decision proportional to his or her stake in the outcome."[164] But the "link between citizens and their representative is broken" when decisions result from "the whispered voices of those who have bought access through their campaign contributions,"[165] "the very link that defines democracy."[166] "Corruption," then, results in the reduction of "public agencies of collective action to instruments of private benefit."[167] Others would stress the utility of moving from a "formal" understanding of corruption as deviation from formal duties and public office, to a "functional" conceptualization that might focus upon the idea of "public power," the ability of corporations to cause and influence the direction of corruption.[168] The "functional" view focuses attention on "the actual power dynamics" of corruption, "not the form,"[169] emphasizing "the use of institutions, structures of authority and even collaboration to allocate resources and coordinate or control activity in a society or the economy."[170]

Popular treatments of political corruption in Latin America have pointed toward campaign costs enjoining politicians to "make a pact with the devil,"[171] in order to finance "the continent's largest political parties."[172] In the "polarized polity," as one analyst suggested, coalitions are fashioned not through "ideological coherence, but with money as the 'glue to keep them together.'"[173] It was said of Brazil that such a condition represented not "the failure of democracy," but "democracy at work,"[174] where "elections drive politicians to seek ever-more money and public attention."[175]

There is too the matter of "electoral corruption," the "electoral comedy," as Carlos Martinez Silva said of Colombia in 1898."[176] Reports of more recent elections in Honduras have spoken of "corrupt networks," "nonprofits," that profit political campaigns,[177] in ways that parallels, even replaces "formal legal and political practices."[178] For some theorists, the deregulatory emphasis inherent in the region's "neoliberal moment," contained the risk of "a regulatory and security vacuum," in which, during the period between 1980 and 2010, thirty-four former presidents in Latin America were subject to "criminal indictments."[179] For its part, much of the incumbent political class remains protected by regimes of legal immunity designed as a safeguard against political persecution, but serving also to shield politicians from criminal prosecution.[180]

A constructivist understanding of the institutional aspect of obligation and corruption might place emphasis upon what Aaron Wildavsky and Mary Douglas have called "culture theory," the view that the preexisting cultural preferences, especially attitudes regarding obligation to rules or group are likely to shape the interests of actors and the nature of their institutions.[181] An *individualist*, with a low sense of obligation to rules or group, an *egalitarian* with weak fealty to rules but strong attachment to the group, the *hierarchist* with strong commitment to both rules and group, and the *fatalist*, obedient to the rules but with weak ties to the group, present us differing routings of obligation: toward self, group, authority, and fate.

Concern regarding the ascendency of what Nicholas Lehmann has called "transaction man,"[182] with its individualist ethos of amoral self-interest, together with regimes of deregulation, have shaped coverage of industrial accidents in Latin America, such as Brazil's Vale Bridge Collapse in 2019,[183] while assertions of revolutionary egalitarianism have animated "new left" governments.[184] A culture theory might also offer a way for us to understand the deinstitutionalizing effects of Latin American populist politics,[185] in which ideology,[186] and the mobilization of various societal sectors,[187] "securitize" cultural anxiety.

REMEDY

To the problem of corruption can be added the trials of its corrective: the anticorruption campaign often central to populist assertions. Liberal theory has been vexed on this matter.[188] Tolerance for "some degree of corruption," seen as helpful for "groups which might otherwise be thoroughly alienated from society," or for the "maintenance of a political system" itself,[189] providing the "grease" "that gets the bureaucracy moving,"[190] has often been conjoined in liberalism with the scolding orientation of the Puritan inheritance. When Samuel Huntington argued that "the only thing worse than a society with a rigid, over centralized, dishonest bureaucracy"[191] would be a regime of "virtue," he may have, during the years of the Cold War, been stating a liberal-realist preference for a confusion of obligations over revolutionary clarity. But confusion has now brought in its revenges. As was pointed out in connection with Argentina's trials of politics, corruption and violence, for "countries with weak formal institutions, important sectors within the state broker informal deals with criminal actors, offering protection in exchange for material payoffs, information, or the promise of order."[192] A new form of "order" can be realized, as Hernan Flom argued, an environment of "police autonomy, decentralized drug trafficking,"[193] where violence spreads in horizontal fashion.[194]

Implicit also in the problem of corruption is the erosion of democracy. The weaponization of corruption by elites seeking to marginalize their rivals was apparent in Brazil's "Manifesto of the Colonels" generations ago, with its demand for order amid a "climate of shady business, peculation, and embezzlement."[195] Saving the country from "the brink of financial and economic ruin" owing to "the abuses of past governments," relief from "generalized corruption" can, it was argued, be best ensured by the "delivery of the government to a military dictatorship."[196] During their seasons of domination, the region's militaries would enjoy "opportunities to profit from their influence,"[197] while presenting themselves as "moral guardians of the nation."[198] Such was the premise behind the ideology of "guided democracy," with its privileging of national over individual freedom,[199] stressing "unity as against what is taken to be the dissipation of energies implied in liberal diversity."[200] Figures of the right and left might, in the face of their definition of a condition of corruption—threats from "above" for egalitarians, and from "below" for hierarchists—resort to "autocratic legalism,"[201] forcing new laws through parliament toward the "hyperpresidentialism" fashionable elsewhere.[202]

As corruption escalated during the time of democracy, heightened levels of crime have "spawned a growing security complex in most countries."[203] Home to "43 of the 50 most murderous cities" in the world,[204] with roughly 2.5 million people murdered in the years between 2000 and 2017, a figure that bears comparison with nearly 900,000 people "killed in the armed conflicts of Syria, Iraq and Afghanistan combined,"[205] Latin America's drift toward "stability maintenance," societal doubts regarding value of democracy,[206] could demand of its people increasingly illiberal patterns of political obligation,[207] amid slowing world economic growth, an attenuated commitment by the United States toward human rights and democratic consolidation, as well as the ascendency of the "new autocrats" elsewhere in the world.[208]

If a Colombian pamphlet in 1873 would declare the republic "a shameful market of vices and unpunished crimes,"[209] such judgment would need qualification today. Anticorruption campaigns in Colombia and throughout Latin

America have been vigorous, as *Operacao Lava Jato* reminds us. Officials in Brazil have evinced concern regarding the tradition of *foro privilegiado*, or "privileged forum."[210] Hegemonic parties have been voted out of power, only to return and be rejected again, as in Mexico.[211] So too, street protests against corruption and violence have been widespread.[212] Forces within Guatemala's civil society have vowed to press on with anticorruption efforts despite the end of the long-running effort of the international commission.[213] "As governments enhanced mechanisms of horizontal accountability," Catherine M. Conaghan argued along these lines, "civil society mobilized to advance 'social accountability.'"[214] Notable prosecutions have taken place in Honduras with the assistance of the Organization of American States.[215] Campaigns of "moral renewal," associated with "faith-based" actors within the region's "religious economy,"[216] as well as forces of secular civil society, have joined with a wealth of international and regional organizations, nongovernmental organizations and bilateral relationships across the world seeking to provide remedy to Latin America's problems with corruption.[217]

CONCLUSION

What New York City's famous mayor, Fiorello LaGuardia, called the "panorama of scheming and conniving"[218] is ubiquitous through time and space. About the complex processional of the mighty and meek, for whom obligation is directed toward private gain rather than public duty, an aggregating definition of their practice cannot issue. For their part, theories have been framed at individual, group, or structural levels, within the familiar idioms of political theory, some emphasizing our moral failings, others stressing factors of an economic social, political, or cultural nature.

Where realist theory reminds us that avarice remains our constant companion, that when confronted by the fear that often accompanies disorder, primordial obligations weaken *civitas*, where critical theory points us toward an obligation to solidarity in pursuit of emancipation and constructivism suggests that the world of corruption is one of our making, it is liberalism, as a theory and practical system of reason, that seems of greatest account here. With its plea to reason and cooperation, its association with a species of obligation freely given that rests as much upon trust as it does self-interest, liberalism asks that transactions be made in good faith, in transparent fashion, regulated by considerations of office and agreed upon procedure in the service of the institutions meant to manage the ambitions and anxieties of all those in the thrall of their vanities.

For all of this, perhaps a central question within the tangle of Latin America's problems with obligation and corruption, mistrust and misrule, would concern the matter of *purpose*. To what "larger social purposes" are the institutions of the region to be directed?[219] What is to be made of a condition in which fewer than half of people in Latin America "favor democracy," where fewer than a quarter are satisfied with its harvest,[220] and "one third of all Latin Americans would emigrate if given the choice"?[221] Theories may help us apprehend aspects of the problem afflicting Latin America, and perhaps even suggest to us remedy. But when? *One of These Days*, to take the title of the short story in which Gabriel Garcia Marquez presents us a Colombian Mayor who, when asked by his dentist whether the bill for services urgently needed should be sent, to "you or the town," the Mayor responded in most dismissive fashion, in a manner emblematic of a fusion of the personal and public, which cannot help create a confusion of institutional purpose, when he said: "It's the same damn thing."

NOTES

1. "Corruption," Susan Rose-Ackerman has written, "Is both a moral and a legal category," "Corruption and Purity," *Daedalus*, V. 147, N. 3 (Summer 2018): 99.

2. Margaret Gilbert, "Agreements, Coercion and Obligations," *Ethics*, V. 103, N. 4 (July 1993): 679.

3. Luigi Barzini, *The Italians* (New York: Atheneum, 1965): 275.

4. Uki Goni, "South America's Cultural of Graft," *The New York Times*, 30 December 2015.

5. Nicholas Casey and Andrea Zarate, "Former Peru President Arrested in U.S. as Part of Vast Bribery Scandal," *The New York Times*, 16 July 2019.

6. Casey and Zarate, "Former Peru President," 16 July 2019.

7. See Daniel Politi and Ernesto Londono, "Argentina's Top Spy Accused in Brazil Corruption Case," *The New York Times*, 1 March 2018 and Nicholas Casey and Andrea Zarate, "Corruption Scandals with Brazilian Roots Cascade across Latin America," *The New York Times*, 13 February 2017.

8. Sergio Fernando Moro, "Preventing Systemic Corruption in Brazil," *Daedalus*, V. 147, N. 3 (Summer 2018): 164.

9. Nicole Hong and Acacia Coronado, "El Chapo Sentenced to Life in U.S. Prison," *The Wall Street Journal*, 17 July 2019.

10. Alan Feuer, "El Chapo Trial Shows that Mexico's Corruption Is Even Worse Than You Think," *The New York Times*, 28 December 2018.

11. Feuer, "El Chapo Trial," 28 December 2018.

12. Hong and Coronado, "El Chapo Sentenced to Life in U.S. Prison," 17 July 2019.

13. Louise I. Shelly, "Corruption and Illicit Trade," *Daedalus*, V. 147, N. 3 (Summer 2018): 135.

14. Shelly, "Corruption and Illicit Trade," 135.

15. Elizabeth Malkin, "Guatemala's Anti-Corruption Fight Inspired Latin America, It May Be Shut Down," *The New York Times*, 18 May 2019.

16. Malkin, "Guatemala's Anti-Corruption Fight," 18 May 2019.

17. See Santiago Perez, "Violence Makes Mexico an Unwelcoming Refuge," *The Wall Street Journal*, 7 June 2019 and Jose de Cordoba, "Guatemalan City Fueling the Migrant Exodus to American," *The Wall Street Journal*, 21 July 2019.

18. Ryan Dube, "Honduras's Leader Struggles With Ills That Drive Migration," *The Wall Street Journal*, 24 June 2019.

19. Dube, "Honduras's Leader Struggles," 24 June 2019.

20. Dube, "Honduras's Leader Struggles," 24 June 2019.

21. Sonia Nazario, "Pay or Die," *The New York Times*, 26 July 2019.

22. Nazario, "Pay or Die," 26 July 2019.

23. Nazario, "Pay or Die," 26 July 2019.

24. Nazario, "Pay or Die," 26 July 2019.

25. See Dube, "Honduras's Leader Struggles," 24 June 2019 and Jonathan Hiskey, Abby Cordova, Mary Fran Malone, and Diana M. Orces, "Leaving the Devil They Know: Violence, Migration and U.S. Policy in Central America," *Panoramas: Scholarly Platform*, University of Pittsburgh, 9 June 2018.

26. Perez, "Violence Makes Mexico," 7 June 2019.

27. Perez, "Violence Makes Mexico," 7 June 2019.

28. David Luhnow, "Latin America is the Murder Capital of the World," *The Wall Street Journal*, 20 September 2018.

29. Anthony Harrup, "Mexico's Murder Rate Hit Record High," *The Wall Street Journal*, 25 July 2019.

30. Paul G. Ashdown, "WTVJ's Miami Crime War: A Television Crusade," *The Florida Historical Quarterly*, V. 58, N. 4 (April 1980): 427.

31. Uki Goni, "South America's Cultural of Graft," 30 December 2015.

32. Luhnow, "Murder Capital," 20 September 2018.

33. Wim Huisman and Gudrun Vande Walle, "The Criminology of Corruption," in Gjalt de Graff, Patrick von Maravic, and Pieter Wagenaar, *The Good Cause: Theoretical Perspectives on Corruption* (Verlag Barbara Budrich, 2010): 115.

34. Robert C. Brooks, "The Nature of Political Corruption," *Political Science Quarterly*, V. 24, N. 1 (March 1909): 4.

35. Omar Azfar, Young Lee, and Anand Swamy, "The Causes and Consequences of Corruption," *Annals of the American Academy of Political and Social Sciences*, V. 573 (January 2001): 51.

36. Brooks, "The Nature of Political Corruption," 6.

37. Azfar, Lee, and Swamy, "The Causes and Consequences of Corruption," 44.

38. Gjalt de Graaf, "Causes of Corruption: Towards a Contextual Theory of Corruption," *Public Administration Quarterly*, V. 31, N. 1/2 (Spring/Summer 2007): 43.

39. William D. Rubinstein and Patrick von Maravic, "Max Weber, Bureaucracy, and Corruption," in Gjalt de Graaf, Patrick von Maravic and Pieter Wagenaar, *Theoretical Perspectives on Corruption* (Verlag Barbara Budrich, 2010): 33. See. More specifically, J. S. Nye, "Corruption and Political Development: A Cost-Benefit Analysis," *The American Political Science Review*, V. 61, N. 2 (June 1967): 417–427.

40. Reinhold Niebuhr, *The Nature and Destiny of Man: A Christian Interpretation* (New York: Charles Scribner's Sons, 1964): 1.

41. Niebuhr, *The Nature and Destiny of Man*, 11.

42. Niebuhr, *The Nature and Destiny of Man*, 10.

43. Richard Mulgen, "Aristotle on Legality and Corruption in Manuchuia Barcham," in Barry Hindess and Peter Larmour, eds., *Corruption: Expanding the Focus* (ANU Press, 2012): 29.

44. Bruce Buchan, "Changing Contours of Corruption in Western Political Thought, c. 1200-1700," in Manuchuia Barcham, Barry Hindess and Peter Larmour, eds., *Corruption: Expanding the Focus* (ANU Press, 2012): 74.

45. Leo Strauss and Joseph Crospy, *History of Political Philosophy* (Chicago: University of Chicago Press, 1987): 126.

46. Nicholas Greenwood Onuf, "Civitas Maxima: Wolff, Vattel and the Fate of Republicanism," *The American Journal of International Law*, V. 88, N. 2 (April 1994): 287–288.

47. Psalm 144:4 KJV.

48. Niebuhr, *The Nature and Destiny of Man*, 16.

49. Niebuhr, *The Nature and Destiny of Man*, 16.

50. Peter Iver Kaufman, "August and Corruption," *History of Political Thought*, V. 30, N. 1 (Spring 2009): 46.

51. Manuhuia Barcham, "Rule by Natural Reason: Late Medieval and early Renaissance Conception of Political Corruption," in Manuchuia Barcham, Barry Hindess and Peter Larmour, eds., *Corruption: Expanding the Focus* (ANU Press, 2012): 53.

52. Michael Lamb, "Beyond Pessimism: A Structure of Encouragement in Augustine's City of God," *The Review of Politics*, V. 80 (2018): 593.

53. Malcolm P. Sharp, "The Classical American Doctrine of 'The Separation of Powers'," *University of Chicago Law Review*, V. 2, N. 3 (April 1935): 400.

54. Celia Moore, "Moral Disengagement in Processes of Organizational Corruption," *Journal of Business Ethics*, 80 (2008): 131.

55. Adele Berlin and Marc Zvi Brettler, *The Jewish Study Bible* (Oxford: Oxford University Press, 2014): 962.

56. Amos, 6.2-24, Quoted from New Revised Standard Version.

57. R. A. Stern, "'My Station and its Duties': Social Role Accounts in Green and Bradley. In K. Ameriks, ed., *The Impact of Idealism: Volume 1, Philosophy and Natural Sciences* (Cambridge: Cambridge University Press, 2013): 3.

58. Barcham, "Rule by Natural Reason," 65.

59. S. M. Shumer, "Machiavelli: Republican Politics and Its Corruption," *Political Theory*, V. 7, N. 1 (February 1979): 11.

60. Shumer, "Machiavelli, 8.

61. Shumer, "Machiavelli, 27.

62. Adrian Blau, "Hobbes on Corruption," *History of Political Thought*, V. 30, N. 4 (Winter 2009): 616.

63. Blau, 'Hobbes on Corruption," 606.

64. Blau, "Hobbes on Corruption," 616.

65. Onuf, "Civitas Maxima," 291.

66. Onuf, "Civitas Maxima," 281.

67. William Selinger, "Patronage and Revolution: Edmund Burke's 'Reflections on the Revolution in France' and His Theory of Legislative Corruption," *The Review of Politics*, V. 76, N. 1 (Winter 2014): 66.

68. Selinger, "Patronage and Revolution," 66.

69. Lisa Hill, "Ideas of Corruption in the Eighteenth Century: The Competing Conceptions of Adam Ferguson and Adam Smith," in Manuchuia Barcham, Barry Hindess and Peter Larmour, eds., *Corruption: Expanding the Focus* (ANU Press, 2012): 101.

70. Tomas Otahal, "Mises, Hayek and Corruption," *Journal of Business Ethics*, V. 119 (2014): 399.

71. Sharp, "The Classical American Doctrine," 385.

72. Sharp, "The Classical American Doctrine," 406.

73. See, for example, Tina Rosenberg, "Latin America's Magical Liberalism," *The Wilson Quarterly*, V. 16, N. 4 (Autumn 1992): 60.

74. E. Bradford Burns, "The Intellectual Infrastructure of Modernization in El Salvador, 1870-1900," *The Americas*, V. 41, N. 3 (January 1985): 61.

75. Burns, "The Intellectual Infrastructure of Modernization in El Salvador," 59.

76. Huisman and Vande Walle, "The Criminology of Corruption," 127.

77. John Warburton, "Corruption as a Social Process: From Dyads to Networks," in Peter Larmour and Nick Wolanin, *Corruption and Anti-Corruption* (ANU Press, 2013): 222.

78. Huisman and Vande Walle, "The Criminology of Corruption," 128.

79. Shumer, "Machiavelli," 10.

80. Rene Lemarchand and Keith Legg, "Political Clientelism and Development," *Comparative Politics*, V. 4, N. 2 (January 1972): 149.

81. Claude Ake, "Political Integration and Political Stability," *World Politics*, V. 19, N. 3 (April 1967): 489.

82. Lemarchand and Legg, "Political Clientelism and Development," 163.

83. Mark E. Warren, "What Does Corruption Mean in a Democracy?" *American Journal of Political Science*, V. 48, N. 2 (April 2004): 330.

84. Duncan Bell, "What Is Liberalism?" *Political Theory*, V. 42, N. 6 (2014): 684. See, more specifically, Ronald Dworkin, *A Matter of Principle* (Oxford: Clarendon, 1985): 183.

85. Rubinstein and von Maravic, "Max Weber, Bureaucracy, and Corruption," 28.

86. D. Christopher Kayes, "Organization Corruption as Theodicy," *Journal of Business Ethics*, V. 67 (2006): 53.

87. Rubinstein and von Maravic, "Max Weber, Bureaucracy, and Corruption," 34.

88. Rubinstein and von Maravic, "Max Weber, Bureaucracy, and Corruption," 34.

89. Gerald E. Caiden and Naomi J. Caiden, "Administrative Corruption," *Public Administration Review*, V. 37, N. 3 (May-June 1977): 302.

90. Caiden and Caiden, "Administrative Corruption," 303.

91. Rubinstein and von Maravic, "Max Weber, Bureaucracy, and Corruption," 23.

92. David Beetham, "Max Weber and the Liberal Political Tradition," *European Journal of Sociology*, V. 30, N. 2 (1989): 316.

93. Gjalt de Graaf, Pieter Wagenaar and Michel Hoenderboom, "Constructing Corruption," in Gjalt de Graff, Patrick von Maravic and Pieter Wagenaar, eds. *The Good Cause: Theoretical Perspectives on Corruption* (Verlag Barbara Budrich, 2010): 100.

94. B. Honig, "Rawls on Politics and Punishment," *Political Research Quarterly,* V. 46, I. 1 (1993): 118.

95. Caiden and Caiden, "Administrative Corruption," 303.

96. Herbert H. Werlin, "The Roots of Corruption: The Ghanaian Enquiry," *The Journal of Modern Studies*, V. 10, N. 2 (1972): 253.

97. James C. Scott, "Corruption, Machine Politics and Political Change," *The American Political Science Review*, V. 63, N. 4 (December 1969): 1149.

98. "Hinky Dink Kenna is Dead in Chicago," *The New York Times*, 10 October 1946, 27.

99. "Hinky Dink Kenna," 10 October 1946, 27.

100. Moro, "Preventing Systemic Corruption in Brazil," 162.

101. Stephen D. Morris, "Corruption and the Mexican Political System: Continuity and Change," *Third World Quarterly*, V. 20, N. 3 (1999): 623.

102. "Hinky Dink Kenna," 10 October 1946, 27.

103. Marshall Clinard, "Corruptino Runs Far Deeper than Politics," *The New York Times*, 10 August 1952, SM7.

104. Scott, "Corruption, Machine Politics, and Political Change," 150.

105. Daniel Bell, "Crime as an American Way of Life," *The Antioch Review*, V. 50, N. ½ (Winter/Spring 1992): 129.

106. Ake, "Political Integration and Political Stability," 486.

107. Rubinstein and von Maravic, "Max Weber, Bureaucracy, and Corruption," 31.

108. Scott, "Corruption, Machine Politics, and Political Change," 1144.

109. De Graaf, "Causes of Corruption," 55.

110. De Graaf, "Causes of Corruption," 55.

111. Ake, "Political Integration and Political Stability," 486.

112. Alberto Vannucci, "Three Paradigms for the Analysis of Corruption," *Labour and Law Issues*, V. 1 N. 2 (2015): 1.

113. Roberto De Matta, "Is Brazil Hopelessly Corrupt?" *The New York Times*, 13 December 1993.

114. Riordan Roett, "The Transition to Democratic Government in Brazil," *World Politics*, V. 38, N. 2 (January 1986): 379.

115. Samuel H. Barnes, "Group Theory and Political Culture. Joseph La Palombara, Interest Groups in Italian Politics," *The Journal of Conflict Resolution*, V. 9, N. 3 (September 1965): 382.

116. Philip K. Bock, "The Importance of Erving Goffman to Psychological Anthropology," *Ethos*, V. 16, N. 1 (March 1988): 4.

117. See Schieffelin quoted in Bock, "The Importance of Erving Goffman," 4.

118. Carol Brooks Gardner and William P. Gronfein, "Reflections on Varieties of Shame Induction, Shame Management, and Shame Avoidance in Some Works of Erving Goffman," *Symbolic Interaction*, V. 28, N. 2 (Spring 2005): 180.

119. Bock, "The Importance of Erving Goffman," 9.

120. Curtis S. Dunkel and Jon A. Sefcek, "Ericksonian Lifespan Theory and Life History Theory: An Integration Using the Example of Identity Formation," *Review of General Psychology*, V. 13, N. 1 (2009): 15.

121. Samuel P. Huntington, "Political Modernization: America vs. Europe," *World Politics*, V. 18, N. 3 (April 1966): 378.

122. De Matta, "Is Brazil Hopelessly Corrupt?" 13 December 1993.

123. Karl D. Jackson, "Bureaucratic Polity: A Theoretical Framework for the Analysis of Power and Communications in Indonesia," in Karl D. Jackson and Lucian W. Pye, *Political Power and Communications in Indonesia* (Berkeley: University of California, 1978): 35.

124. Jackson, "Bureaucratic Polity," 4–5.

125. Nathan Gilbert Quimpo, "The Philippines: Political Parties and Corruption," *Southeast Asian Affairs* (2007): 277.

126. Quimpo, "The Philippines," 278.

127. Heinz Dieterich, "Enforced Disappearances and Corruption in Latin America," *Crime and Social Justice*, V. 25 (1986): 42–43.

128. Quimpo, "The Philippines," 279.

129. Quimpo, "The Philippines," 278.

130. See, for example, Parker Asmann, "Why the Cachiros Linked Working with Honduras Politicians," *Insight Crime*, 18 July 2018; or his "Criminal Allegations Unravel Honduras President's Crime Fighting Façade," *Insight Crime*, 3 September 2019.

131. Leszek Kolakowski, *Main Currents of Marxism: Its Origins, Growth and Dissolution* (Oxford: Oxford University Press, 1978): 49.

132. Kolakowski, *Main Currents of Marxism*, 105.

133. de Graaf, Wagenaar and Hoenderboom, "Constructing Corruption," 110.

134. Zephyr Teachout, "The Problem of Monopolies and Corporate Public Corruption," *Daedalus* (Summer 2018): 112.

135. Teachout, "The Problem of Monopolies and Corporate Public Corruption," 112.

136. Vannucci, "Three Paradigms for the Analysis of Corruption," 1.

137. Onuf, "Civitas Maxima," 281.

138. Morris, "Corruption and Mexican Political Culture," 674.

139. De Graaf, "Causes of Corruption," 49.

140. Warren, "What Does Corruption Mean in a Democracy?" 328.

141. Michael O. Hardimon, "Role Obligations," *The Journal of Philosophy*, V. 91, N. 7 (July 1994): 335.

142. Ben W. Heineman, Jr., and Fritz Heimann, "The Long War Against Corruption," *Foreign Affairs*, V. 85, N. 3 (May-June 2006): 76.

143. Huisman and Vande Walle, "The Criminology of Corruption," 116.

144. Huisman and Vande Walle, "The Criminology of Corruption," 118.

145. M. E. Newhouse, "Institutional Corruption: A Fiduciary Theory," *Cornell Journal of Law and Public Policy*, V. 23 (2014): 568.

146. Warren, "What Does Corruption Mean in a Democracy?" 330.

147. Neelambar Hatti, Mason C. Hoadley, and James Heimann, "The Corruption Bazaar: A Conceptual Discussion," *Sociological Bulletin*, V. 59, N. 2 (May-August 2010): 219.

148. Warren, "What Does Corruption Mean in a Democracy?" 328.

149. Hatti, Hoadley, and Heimann, "The Corruption Bazaar: A Conceptual Discussion," 219.

150. Alberto Vannucci, "Three Paradigms for the Analysis of Corruption," 1.

151. Newhouse, "Institutional Corruption," 570.

152. Newhouse, "Institutional Corruption," 587–588.

153. Moore, "Moral Disengagement in Processes of Organizational Corruption," 136.

154. Peter D. Feaver, *Armed Servants: Agency, Oversight, and Civil-Military Relations* (Cambridge: Harvard University Press, 2003): 56.

155. Feaver, *Armed Servant,* 57.

156. Caiden and Caiden, "Administrative Corruption," 303.

157. Brooks, "The Nature of Political Corruption," 12.

158. Dennis F. Thompson, "Theories of Institutional Corruption," *Annual Review of Political Science*, V. 21 (2018): 10.

159. Thompson, "Theories of Institutional Corruption," 2.

160. Thompson, "Theories of Institutional Corruption," 1.

161. See the discussion in Eric Breit, Thomas Taro Lennerfors and Lena Olaison, "Critiquing Corruption: A Turn to Theory," *Ephemera: Theory and Politics in Organization,* V. 15, N. 2 (2015): 319–336.

162. Thompson, "Theories of Institutional Corruption," 1.

163. Thompson, "Theories of Institutional Corruption," 5.

164. Thompson, "Theories of Institutional Corruption," 6.

165. Thompson, "Theories of Institutional Corruption," 6.

166. Warren, "What Does Corruption Mean in a Democracy?" 328.

167. Warren, "What Does Corruption Mean in a Democracy?" 328.

168. Teachout, "The Problem of Monopolies and Corporate Public Corruption," 114–115.

169. Teachout, "The Problem of Monopolies and Corporate Public Corruption," 115.

170. Teachout, "The Problem of Monopolies and Corporate Public Corruption," 116.

171. Casey and Zarate, "Corruption Scandals with Brazilian Roots Cascade across Latin America," 13 February 2017.

172. Goni, "South America's Cultural of Graft," 30 December 2015.

173. Goni, "South America's Cultural of Graft," 30 December 2015.

174. Goni, "South America's Cultural of Graft," 30 December 2015.

175. Moises Naim, "The Corruption Eruption," *The Brown Journal of World Affairs*, V. 2, N. 2 (Summer 1995): 251.

176. Quoted in Eduardo Posada-Carbo, "Electoral Juggling: A Comparative History of the Corruption of Suffrage in Latin America, 1830-1930," *Journal of Latin American Studies*, V. 32 (2000): 611.

177. Jeff Ernst, "A Pandora's Box of Corruption in Honduras," *Univision News*, 6 August 2019.

178. Max Fisher and Amanda Taub, "Why Uprooting Corruption Has Plunged Brazil Into Chaos," *The New York Times*, 14 June 2017.

179. Catherine M. Conaghan, "Prosecuting Presidents: The Politics with in Ecuador's Corruption Cases," *Journal of Latin American Studies*, 44 (2012): 649.

180. See Roberto Simon, "Should Latin America Abolish Immunity for Elected Officials?" *Americas Quarterly*, 15 August 2019.

181. See, for example, Aaron Wildavsky, "Choosing Preferences by Constructing Institutions: A Cultural Theory of Preferences," *The American Political Science Review*, V. 81, N. 1 (March 1987): 3–22.

182. See the discussion in Barton Swaim's "'Transaction Man' Review: The Fraying White Collar," *The Wall Street Journal*, 11 September 2019.

183. Luciana Magalhaes and Samantha Pearson, "Brazil to Charge Vale over Deadly Dam Collapse," *The Wall Street Journal*, 11 April 2019. See also the discussion in "Combatting Corruption in Latin America: Congressional Considerations," *Congressional Research Service*, 21 May 2019.

184. Fransisco Sanchez and John Polga-Hecimovich, "The Tools of Institutional Change Under Post-Neoliberalism: Rafael Correa's Ecuador," *Journal of Latin American Studies*, V. 51 (2019): 379.

185. Jorge G. Castaneda, "Latin America's Left Turn," *Foreign Affairs*, V. 85, N. 3 (May–June 2006): 33.

186. Alistair Hennessy, "The New Radicalism in Latin America," *Journal of Contemporary History*, V. 7, N. ½ (January–April 1972): 6.

187. Steve Ellner, "The Contrasting Variants of the Populism of Hugo Chavez and Alberto Fujimori," *Journal of Latin American Studies*, V. 35, N. 1 (February 2003): 161.

188. Bell, "Crime as an American Way of Life," 110.

189. Mitchell A. Seligson, "The Impact of Corruption on Regime Legitimacy: A Comparative Study of Four Latin American Countries," *The Journal of Politics*, V. 64, N. 2 (May 2002): 409.

190. Seligson, "The Impact of Corruption on Regime Legitimacy," 408.

191. Seligson, "The Impact of Corruption on Regime Legitimacy," 408.

192. Hernan Flom, "State Regulation of Organized Crime" Politicians, Police, and Drug Trafficking in Argentina," *Latin American Politics and Society*, V. 61, N. 3 (2019): 104.

193. Flom, "State Regulation of Organized Crime," 120.

194. Flom, "State Regulation of Organized Crime," 120.

195. Shawn C. Smallman, "Shady Business: Corruption in the Brazilian Army before 1954," *Latin American Research Review*, V. 32, N. 3 (1997): 39.

196. Smallman, "Shady Business," 39.

197. Smallman, "Shady Business," 39.

198. Smallman, "Shady Business," 39.

199. Jose Arsenio Torres, "The Political Ideology of Guided Democracy," *The Review of Politics*, V. 25, N. 1 (January 1963): 41–42.

200. Torres, "The Political Ideology of Guided Democracy," 42.

201. Kim Lane Scheppele, "Autocratic Legalism," *The University of Chicago Law Review*, V. 85, N. 2 (March 2018): 548.

202. Scheppele, "Autocratic Legalism," 554.

203. Mark Ungar, "The Rot Within: Security and Corruption in Latin America," *Social Research*, V. 80, N. 4 (Winter 2013): 1188.

204. Luhnow, "Murder Capital," 20 September 2018.

205. Luhnow, "Murder Capital," 20 September 2018.

206. See the discussion in Marie Arana, "Latin Americans Are Souring on Democracy. That's Not Surprising Considering the Region's History," *Time*, 27 August 2019.

207. On "stability maintenance," see Yuhua Wang and Carl Minzner, "The Rise of the Chinese Security State," *The China Quarterly*, V. 222 (2015): 339.

208. Scheppele, "Autocratic Legalism," 547.

209. Posada-Carbo, "Electoral Juggling," 613.

210. Moro, "Preventing Systemic Corruption in Brazil," 158.

211. Miguel Carreras and Sofia Vera, "Do Corrupt Politicians Mobilize for Demobilize Voters?" A Vignette Experiment in Colombia," *Latin American Politics and Society*, V. 60, N. 3 (2018): 77.

212. Carreras and Vera, "Do Corrupt Politicians Mobilize for Demobilize Voters?" 78.

213. Bryan Wilensky, "Guatemala's Anti-Corruption Commission is Ending, But the Fight Will Go On," *Atlantic Council*, 15 August 2019.

214. Conaghan, "Prosecuting Presidents," 652.

215. "Wife of Ex-President of Honduras Convicted in Corruption Case," *Reuters*, 20 August 2019.

216. Gary Reich and Pedro dos Santos, "The Rise (and Frequent Fall) of Evangelical Politicians: Organization, Theology, and Church Politics," *Latin American Politics and Society*, V. 55, N. 4 (2013): 6.

217. See, for example, the discussion in Roberto Simon and Emilie Sweigart, "The Next Frontier in Latin America's Anti-Corruption Drive," *Americas Quarterly*, 22 July 2019 and Charles T. Call, "Can El Salvador's New Anti-Corruption Commission Deliver?" *Americas Quarterly*, 13 September 2019.

218. "Text of La Guardia Talk Announcing He Will Not Be a Candidate," *The New York Times*, 7 May 1945, 11.

219. On purpose and institutions, see Nicholas Onuf, "Institutions, Intentions and International Relations," *Review of International Studies*, V. 28, N. 2 (April 2002): 219.

220. Arana, "Latin Americans Are Souring on Democracy," 27 August 2019.

221. Jorge G. Casteneda, "The U.S. Should Act Before a Global Downturn Destabilizes Latin America," *The New York Times*, 17 September 2019.

Chapter 2

Corruption, Violence, and State Fragility in Mexico

An Examination of the Recent Challenges and Opportunities

Roberto Zepeda and Jonathan D. Rosen

This chapter examines the nexus between corruption,[1] weak institutions,[2] and organized crime in Mexico.[3] Historical legacy has determined the current events of contemporary Mexico, which is characterized by a transition from an authoritarian to a democratic regime. Despite its transition to democracy, Mexico has been plagued by high levels of corruption and impunity. This chapter utilizes data analysis to examine perceptions of corruption and insecurity as well as lack of trust in institutions. This chapter also analyzes organized crime in Mexico and how the country's war on drugs[4] has resulted in increases in violence and instability. It argues that tough on crime policies have failed to address the underlying institutional challenges that the country faces.

DEMOCRATIZATION AND CORRUPTION: FRAGILE INSTITUTIONS

Mexico experienced seven decades of single-party authoritarian rule by the Institutional Revolutionary Party (Partido Revolucionario Institucional—PRI). While the PRI began to lose political control at the state level in the 1980s, this party controlled the federal government until 2000, when for the first time in history, the National Action Party (Partido Acción Nacional—PAN) assumed power with the election of Vicente Fox Quesada to the presidency.[5]

Despite the transition to democracy, Mexico remains plagued by high levels of corruption[6] and impunity.[7] According to Transparency International's Corruption Perceptions Index (CPI), Mexico has become more corrupt over time. From 2000 to 2015, Mexico moved from the 57th to the 106th position on the corruption ranking, with one being the least corrupt country and 180 being the most corrupt country.[8] In 2018, Mexico ranked 135 out of 180 countries, with the higher the number the more corruption.[9] The levels of corruption between 2015 and 2018 escalated notably, which is paradoxical as this period marked the democratic transition in the country.

Furthermore, organized crime groups are infiltrating government structures, especially in local governments. High level officials, including governors, from various states like Michoacán, Nayarit, Tamaulipas, and Quintana Roo have been involved in cases of corruption and linkages to drug cartels.[10] The complex relationship between states and organized crime groups presents major challenges when attempting to implement strategies to combat drug trafficking and organized crime. During the period 2007–2017, at least seventeen Mexican governors have either been under investigation, captured, or are fugitives of an array of crimes and felonies.[11]

One of the institutions that has been plagued by corruption is the police.[12] Prior to the implementation of the national guard, there were different police bodies at various levels (i.e., federal, state and local police). The police, especially the local police, are perceived as one of the most corrupt institutions in the country. At the national level, the municipal preventative police forces accounted for nearly 40 percent of the police force, while the federal ministerial police, accounted for only 1.6 percent of the total police forces. Working as a police officer is very dangerous and many individuals have died while in the line of duty. Police are not well paid, which also makes them vulnerable to accepting bribes from organized crime groups.

Vanderbilt University's Latin American Public Opinion Project (LAPOP) 2017[13] Mexico survey reveals that 32.02 percent of the survey participants responded, "not at all" when asked their levels of trust in the national police. On the other hand, only 5.12 percent answered that they had "a lot" of trust in the national police. Regression analysis helps determine what factors influence levels of trust in the national police, which is coded one for "not at all" and seven for "a lot." The independent variables are sex, urban, years of schooling, ideology, and victim of a crime in the last twelve months. The age variable is from eighteen to eighty-eight, but it has been recoded into six categories. The sex variable is coded male and female. The urban variable is coded urban and rural, while household monthly income is from no income to more than $11,050. Moreover, the victim of crime variable is coded yes and no. Finally, ideology is coded one for left and ten for right.

The regression analysis reveals[14] that ideology and having been a victim of a crime in the last twelve months are statistically significant at the 95 percent confidence interval. A one-unit shift in ideology (i.e., moving from left to right) leads to a .110 shift in the dependent variable. This means that people who are farther right, on average, have more trust in the national police.

In addition, a one-unit increase in being a victim of crime in the last twelve months (i.e., moving from yes to no) leads to a .590 shift in the dependent variable. Therefore, people who have not been a victim of the crime during the last year, on average, have more trust in the national police (see table 2.1).

Furthermore, Mexico faces major challenges with high levels of impunity generated by an inefficient judiciary system. In 2016, for example, Mexico had an impunity rate of 99 percent.[15] The high levels of impunity in the country persist despite major reforms to the judicial system that began in 2008. According to a Washington Office on Latin America (WOLA) report, there remains much "to be done for Mexico to enjoy a system that holds perpetrators accountable for crimes while ensuring respect for human rights."[16] There are various obstacles that must be addressed, such as the need to change entrenched practices, pass new laws, and train personnel. Ultimately, reforming a judicial system is a decades-long process.

Table 2.1   Factors Influencing Trust in the National Police

	Coeff	
Variables	*(SE)*	*t-test*
Sex	0.030	0.29
	(0.103)	
Urban	0.062	0.46
	(0.135)	
Education	–0.012	–0.90
	(0.013)	
Monthly Household Income	–0.016	–1.48
	(0.011)	
Ideology	0.110***	5.24
	(0.021)	
Victim of Crime last 12 months	0.590***	5.66
	(0.104)	
Constant	1.536***	4.60
	(0.334)	
Observations	1,244	
R-squared	0.063	

Robust standard errors in parentheses.
*** $p < 0.01$, ** $p < 0.05$, * $p < 0.1$.
Source: Created by authors with data from LAPOP 2017.

TRUST IN INSTITUTIONS AND DEMOCRACY

The high levels of corruption and impunity have contributed to Mexicans being very distrustful of institutions. For example, 46.5 percent of Mexicans responded "not at all" in the 2017 LAPOP survey when asked their level of trust in political parties. On the other hand, only 2.20 percent of respondents contended that they had "a lot" of trust in political parties. Meanwhile, 46.62 percent of respondents in the LAPOP survey answered "not at all" when asked their level of trust in the executive. Only 5.01 percent of respondents answered that they have "a lot" of trust in the executive.

Mexicans also have very low levels of trust in politicians, likely because of the seemingly endless number of corruption scandals involving politicians in all branches of government. In fact, 41.16 percent of Mexicans in 2017 believed that "all" politicians are corrupt, while 36.76 percent believed that "more than half of them" are corrupt. On the other hand, only 5.20 percent answered that "less than half of them" are corrupt.

Moreover, survey research demonstrates that Mexicans are very dissatisfied with democracy. According to the 2017 Mexico survey conducted by LAPOP, only 3.46 percent of the population responded that they are "very satisfied" with democracy. On the other hand, 49.53 percent of the survey contended that they are "dissatisfied," while 23.97 argued that they are "very dissatisfied (see figures 2.1 and 2.2)."

Regression analysis helps determine the factors that influence satisfaction with democracy in Mexico. The dependent variable is coded "very satisfied," "satisfied," "dissatisfied," and "very dissatisfied." Age is from eighteen to eighty-eight, but it is recoded into six categories.[17] The independent variables sex, urban, monthly household income, and ideology are

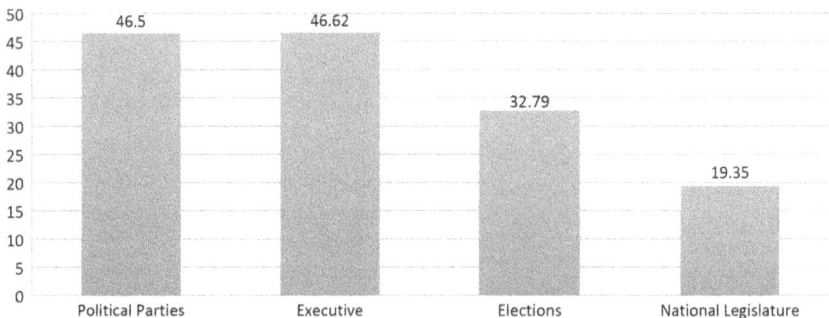

Figure 2.1   Percentage of Mexicans who have no Trust in the Following Institutions (2017). Created by authors with data from LAPOP 2017. Note: The respondents in this question answered "not at all" when asked their levels of trust in these institutions.

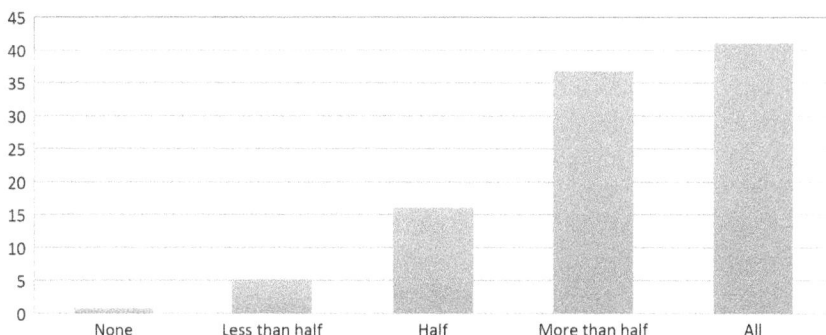

Figure 2.2 Amount of Corruption among Mexican Politicans (2017). Created by authors with data from LAPOP 2017.

Table 2.2   Factors Influencing Satisfaction with Democracy

Variables	Coeff. (SE)	t-test
Age	0.026 (0.016)	1.58
Sex	0.062 (0.046)	1.35
Urban	−0.055 (0.062)	−0.89
Monthly Household Income	0.014*** (0.005)	2.91
Ideology	−0.033*** (0.009)	−3.53
Constant	2.904*** (0.141)	20.63
Observations	1,229	
R-squared	0.022	

Robust standard errors in parentheses.
*** p < 0.01, ** p < 0.05, * p < 0.1.
Source: Created by authors with data from LAPOP 2017.

coded as described earlier. The regression model[18] indicates that monthly household income and ideology are statistically significant at the 95 percent confidence interval. The interpretation of the model is that a one-unit shift in monthly household income leads to a .014 shift in the dependent variable. This means that people who make more money, on average, are more dissatisfied with democracy. Moreover, a one-unit shift in ideology (i.e., moving from left to right), leads to a -.033 shift in the dependent variable. Therefore, people who are farther right, on average, are more satisfied with democracy (see table 2.2).

FELIPE CALDERÓN'S DRUG WAR

President Felipe Calderón (2006–2012) assumed the presidency after a contested election against Andrés Manuel López Obrador of the Party of the Democratic Revolution (Partido de la Revolución Democrática—PRD). Thousands of protestors hit the streets to protest the massive levels of fraud that allegedly occurred during the elections. Given this context, Calderón, who assumed power as a relatively weak president, sought to increase his power and demonstrate his toughness by launching a war on drugs against the major drug cartels and organized crime groups operating in the country. As stated by Rubén Aguilar and Jorge Castañeda, the main reason that Calderón declared the war on drugs was political to gain the legitimation, supposedly lost in the 2006 presidential elections, in the middle of the protests in the streets of Mexico City.[19] Other scholars also observe that the war on drugs[20] was launched immediately after Calderón was sworn in and sought to draw attention away from the highly controversial 2006 election.[21]

President Calderón desired to weaken the increasing power of the cartels in the country and elevated the threat of drug trafficking and organized crime groups to the top national security threat. Drug trafficking and violence increased during the Calderón government.[22] First, organized crime groups battled among each other for control of territory and drug routes.[23] These activities resulted in increase in violence over time. Second, drug trafficking organizations fought with the government, who deployed the military to combat these criminal groups. President Calderón used the military instead of the police because he did not have high levels of confidence in the police forces due to corruption. The Mexican military is also better trained than the police.[24]

The militarization of the drug war led to high levels of violence in Mexico. Drug-related killings spiked from 2,120 in 2006 to 5,153 in 2008. In 2009, 6,587 drug-related killings occurred.[25] According to data from *Reforma*, Chihuahua accounted for 31 percent of the total drug-related killings in 2009. Other states also had high percentages of drug-related homicides: Sinaloa (12 per cent); Guerrero (10 per cent); and Durango (10 per cent).[26]

According to various official sources, the number of narco-executions increased notably from 2007 to 2011, when violence reached its peak.[27] In 2012, violence started to decline as the number of narco-executions related to organized crime reduced notably compared with the previous year. Furthermore, between 2006 and 2012 approximately 26,000 people disappeared.[28] In addition, at least 10,000 individuals were murdered and buried in "narco-graves" over the same period.[29] In summary, estimates reveal that more than 100,000 murders occurred during the Calderón government as a result of the war on drugs.

VIOLENCE DURING THE PEÑA NIETO GOVERNMENT

Enrique Peña Nieto assumed the presidency in 2012.[30] The new president distinguished himself from the previous government by focusing less on the discourse of the drug war and more on various reforms.[31] Peña Nieto passed educational and energy reforms, although they have been quite controversial in nature. In addition, the new president spent less effort marketing the victories of the war on drugs, which is a stark contrast from the Calderón government, which invested tremendous resources touting the successes of the drug war.[32] For instance, Mexican television stations would routinely show the capture of major kingpins who were paraded in front of the public. Thus, while the discourse regarding drug strategies might be different, the drug policies have remained quite similar.

The Peña Nieto *sexenio* had more homicides than the one of his predecessor Felipe Calderón. According to data provided by The National System of Public Security (El Sistema Nacional de Seguridad Pública—SNSP), 104,794 homicides occurred between 2006 and 2012. However, relying on the same source, during the Peña Nieto *sexenio*, there have been 106,817 homicides—from January 1, 2013, to April 30, 2018. Mexico is confronting the highest levels of violence in recent decades. In 2017, there were 25,339 intentional homicides. The homicide rate per 100,000 inhabitants in 2017 was 20.5, the highest in the last 20 years. At the subnational level, the rates were even more drastic. Colima registered the highest rate in 2017 for this crime (93.6), followed by Baja California Sur (69.2), and Guerrero (64.3). In sum, twenty-eight out of the thirty-two subnational states registered an increase in the number of intentional homicides in 2017 with regard to the previous year, according to the security analyst Alejandro Hope.[33]

The Peña Nieto government had some "successes" in the war on drugs. When the country's most wanted drug lord Joaquín "El Chapo" Guzmán was recaptured in January 2016, President Peña Nieto tweeted: "Mission accomplished." Yet this victory in the war on drugs has not led to a reduction in crime, as Guzmán's extradition to the United States in January 2017 has triggered more violence in Mexico. At the same time, other rival cartels such as the Jalisco New Generation cartel—a powerful organization specializing in methamphetamines and excessive violence—has expanded along the Pacific coast, which is a region formerly controlled by the Sinaloa cartel.[34]

The impacts of organized crime and illicit activities have also reached the business community. On May 3, 2018, Grupo Lala, one of the most important private companies in Mexico, closed operations in one of its distribution centers located in Southern Tamaulipas, due to insecurity and high levels of violence. The firm argued that security conditions were not adequate to continue operating. This company controls almost 50 percent of the milk market in Mexico, but the distribution center was shut down after one of the company's trucks were torched in a nearby locality.[35] Tamaulipas is one of Mexico's most violent states, mainly due to the fighting between the Gulf cartel and the Zetas for the control of the Northeast of Mexico.[36]

Not only has Grupo Lala suffered due to organized crime groups, but also companies such as Coca Cola–FEMSA and Grupo Mexico Transportes, which have either relocated their plants or suffered significant robberies. In May 19, 2018, organized crime groups caused the derailment of thirty-nine train cars and four locomotives in Orizaba, Veracruz. According to Grupo México Transporte, this event generated losses valued at $312 million pesos, considering the costs from sales, theft of goods and restoration of roads and equipment.[37] Veracruz has been one of the most violent states in recent years as a result of the disputes of criminal groups for the control of drug trafficking routes. These criminal groups have also diversified their illicit activities to include the theft of oil and gas from pipelines.

According to official sources, the theft of fuel, also known as *huachicoleo*, generated losses to PEMEX (the major oil company in Mexico) of around 30,000 million pesos (approximately US$1.5 billion). This kind of theft has increased around 35 percent during the Peña Nieto's *sexenio*. In 2006, the number of illegal taps detected in the company's pipelines was 213, climbing to 691 in 2010 and to 6,249 in 2015. This figure reached 10,363 in 2017.[38] The majority of Mexican drug cartels participate in fuel theft.[39]

CORRUPTION, IMPUNITY, AND HUMAN RIGHTS

The Peña Nieto administration faced an international scandal with the killing of forty-three students from a local teachers college in Ayotzinapa, Guerrero, who were murdered in the city of Iguala. Hannah Stone argues, "A crime of this scale—the abduction and killing of 43 people—could not be carried out in secret. It required a culture of fear and complicity to prevent other authorities in Iguala from intervening, and keep the residents silent."[40] The police allegedly handed over the students to a local gang in Guerrero, Guerreros Unidos, who helped dispose the bodies. Investigations demonstrate that the government played an important role in the cover-up of such horrific events. Maureen Meyer of WOLA asserts that "[t]his is one of the worst cases of human rights violations seen in Mexico's recent history. Two years later, the Mexican government has done very little to help these wounds heal. It is shocking that, despite dedicating significant resources, the Mexican government has not found the students, and that its own officials have obstructed the investigation."[41] The events that occurred in Guerrero have harmed Mexico's international reputation and called into question the ability of the Peña Nieto government to maintain law and order in the country.

Moreover, the police and military have been involved in major human rights abuses, which are examples of state fragility. Upon assuming office, President Peña Nieto sought to make significant changes to the nature of internal security in the country. First, he launched the National Gendarmerie, which served as a special unit within the Mexican Federal Police. The government planned for the National Gendarmerie to initially have 50,000 members, but this unit ended up with 10,000 members. Second, the Peña Nieto government passed its Internal Security Law, which increased the power of the military, specifically their role in internal policing, and made it more difficult for civilian oversight of the institution.[42] Despite the Mexican Congress approving the law in 2017, a year later the Supreme Court ruled that this law violated the Mexican constitution. Human rights experts viewed this as a victory. According to Maureen Meyer, an expert on Mexico,

> This Supreme Court ruling is one of the most important of recent years: it's an acknowledgement that civil institutions are responsible for providing security to a country's citizens, and that the military is not a police force. Soldiers should not be used as a substitute for police and Mexico's armed forces shouldn't be in charge of the country's domestic security. This law would have cemented the military's role in patrolling the streets and would have granted them broad power over civil institutions.[43]

Despite human rights advocates celebrating the Supreme Court ruling, Mexico has faced many challenges regarding human rights abuses by authorities. According to Mexico's National Human Rights Commission (Comisión Nacional de los Derechos Humanos—CNDH), this organization has been flooded with complaints—10,000 to be exact—of human rights violations of the armed forces.[44] Yet the number of investigations by Mexican authorities have been significantly less, demonstrating that impunity remains rampant. For instance, between 2012 and 2016, 268 investigations existed regarding cases of torture and crime committed by soldiers. During the same period, official figures show that there were 121 investigations into abuse of authority by soldiers as well as 37 investigations of forced disappearances. The number of investigations of other crimes committed by soldiers during the same period is significantly less: thirty-one investigations of crimes related to sexual violence, seventeen investigations into homicides, three cases of extortion, three investigations of false imprisonment, and two cases of robbery.[45]

Despite the plethora of complaints, the number of convictions against Mexican soldiers for human rights violations and other crimes remains astonishingly low. It also is important to note that the Mexican government is not transparent about such information. This is a strategic move on the government to hide information from civilians by decreasing the levels of transparency and accountability. According to Ximena Suárez-Enríquez, "There is little available information about convictions of soldiers in the civilian justice system for crimes and human rights violations. Such information is not public, and it is fragmented among the hundreds of thousands of cases that the Federal Judiciary tries each year. Obtaining information about convictions of soldiers is a complicated endeavor, demanding great monitoring efforts."[46] Based on official data, only seven convictions have occurred for covering up crimes and destroying corpses between 2012 and 2016. Moreover, only three convictions existed for forced disappearances and three for homicides. There have also been two convictions for "injuries and trespassing" and one conviction for rape. In summary, there have only been sixteen convictions between 2012 and 2016 despite the rampant number of reported human rights abuses by soldiers.[47]

EXTORTION AND PERCEPTIONS OF INSECURITY

According to the 2016/2017 LAPOP survey data in Mexico 19.69 percent of respondents contended that they have had a family member who has been a victim of extortion. Who is more likely to be a victim of extortion?[48] Regression analysis helps explain the relationship between the dependent variable and different control variables. In this model, the dependent variable, family members who have been extorted, is coded no and yes. The independent variables are age, sex, urban, and monthly household income. The age variable is from eighteen to eighty-eight, but it has been recoded into six categories.[49] The urban variable is coded urban and rural, while monthly household income is from no income to more than $11,050.[50]

The regression model shows that age and urban as statistically significant variables at the 95 percent confidence level. A change in age leads to a -.019 shift in the dependent variable. This means that, on average, older people are less likely to have had a family member who has been a victim of extortion. Furthermore, a one-unit change in urban (i.e., moving from urban to rural) results in a -.060 shift in the dependent variable. This means, on average, people living in rural areas are less likely to have had a family member extorted (see table 2.3).

The result of the high levels of violence has been that Mexicans feel unsafe. According to the 2017 LAPOP data, 17.69 percent of Mexicans have "a lot of fear" of being a homicide victim, while 30.96 percent have "some fear" of being a homicide victim.

Table 2.3   Factors Influencing Having a Family Member Having been a Victim of Extortion

Variable	Coeff. (SE)	t-test
Age	−0.019***	−2.65
	(0.007)	
Sex	0.022	1.00
	(0.022)	
Urban	−0.060**	−2.41
	(0.025)	
Monthly Household Income	0.003	1.28
	(0.002)	
Constant	0.260***	4.37
	(0.059)	
Observations	1,382	
R-squared	0.011	

Robust standard errors in parentheses.
*** $p < 0.01$, ** $p < 0.05$, * $p < 0.1$.
Source: Created by authors with data from LAPOP 2017.

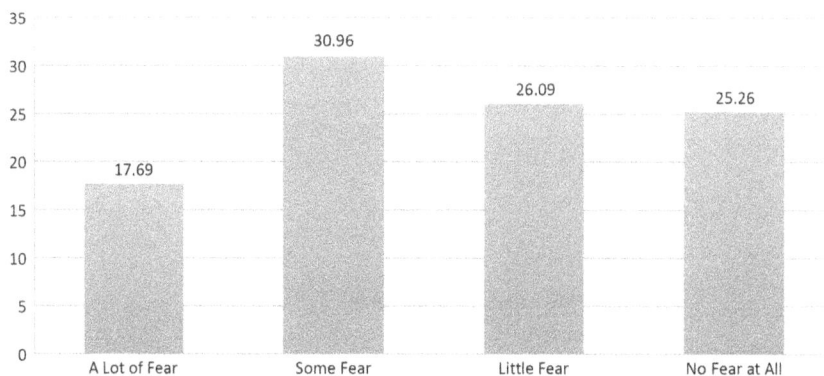

Figure 2.3   Fear of Being a Murder Victim (2017). Created by authors with data from LAPOP 2017.

Regression analysis helps determine what variables impact the fear of being a victim of homicide, which is coded "a lot of fear," "some fear," "little fear," and "no fear at all." The independent variables are age, sex, urban, education, victim of a crime in the last twelve months, and ideology. The variables are the same as defined in the previous sections.

The regression analysis reveals[51] that sex and having been a victim of a crime in the last twelve months are statistically significant at the 95 percent confidence level. Furthermore, a one-unit shift in age (i.e., male to female) results in a -.356 shift in the dependent variable. This means that females,

Table 2.4 Factors Influencing Fears of Being a Murder Victim

Age	0.042*	1.79
	(0.023)	
Sex	−0.356***	−6.07
	(0.059)	
Urban	−0.054	−0.73
	(0.074)	
Education	0.006	0.63
	(0.009)	
Victim of Crime in Last Twelve Months	0.337***	6.1
	(0.055)	
Ideology	0.015	1.38
	(0.011)	
Constant	2.376***	10.28
	(0.231)	
Observations	1,385	
R-squared	0.057	

Standard errors in parentheses.
*** $p < 0.01$, ** $p < 0.05$, * $p < 0.1$.
Source: Created by authors with data from LAPOP 2017.

on average, have higher levels of fear of being victims of homicide. Finally, a one-unit shift in someone being a victim of crime in the last twelve months (i.e., moving from yes to no) leads to a .337 shift in the dependent variable. This means that people who have not been victims of crime in the last twelve months, on average, have less fear of being a victim of homicide (see table 2.4).

AN UNCERTAIN FUTURE

Andrés Manuel López Obrador (AMLO) won the presidential elections in July 2018 in a landslide victory. López Obrador has a different perspective on how to combat drug trafficking and organized crime. For example, he has stressed that reducing poverty and fighting corruption will be two major actions of his government to counter violence and crime. He has highlighted the problem of the youth who neither work nor study. AMLO believes that providing more employment and education opportunities will reduce the recruitment of disconnected youth by organized crime groups. Similarly, creating economic prosperity and more opportunities for the poorest will reduce the levels of violence in Mexico.

Yet the AMLO government has continued to face major challenges with violence and insecurity. Causa en común released a report in 2019 to contest the official governmental statistics and demonstrate that many indicators of violence have increased in 2019 compared to 2018.[52] Mexico has had more than 820 intentional homicides in the first seven months of 2019 compared to the same seven-month period in 2018,[53] revealing that violence has continued unabated despite the promises of the AMLO government. There also have been increases in the number of reported victims for certain crimes. For instance, there have been 133 more reported kidnapping victims in the first seven months of this year when compared to the same time period in 2018 during the AMLO administration,[54] demonstrating the high levels of human insecurity that exist in Mexico despite the governments focus on reducing levels of violence. Researchers also note that Mexico has witnessed 5,593 more robberies with the use of violence during the first seven months of 2019 compared to the available data from the previous year.[55] In summary, the AMLO government faces many challenges as it seeks to reduce violence. Decreasing violence in Mexico will not happen overnight, but the current data reveals that the AMLO government has not witnessed reductions in insecurity levels as of September 2019. President López Obrador will continue to face pressure to increase levels of citizen security and reduce the levels of violence plaguing the country.

Moreover, President López Obrador began his administration with a struggle against oil theft. According to data from his government, during 2018 the economic losses for this criminal activity amounted to 65 billion pesos. Before taking office in December 2018, around 80,000 barrels per day were stolen, but by April 2019, this figure had been reduced to 5,000 barrels per day. In other words, the efforts of the AMLO government contributed to the reduction of this type of crime, but, as mentioned earlier, overall levels of violence in the country have increased.[56]

The AMLO administration has implemented a new security strategy. Previously, the insecurity problem generated by organized crime was considered to be the result of political-institutional factors, but the relevance of factors related to the economy, the labor market, poverty, as well as inequality and social marginalization were overlooked. These have become factors that encourage the illicit activities of organized crime groups.

AMLO's security strategy is different perspective from that of his predecessors Peña Nieto and Calderón. The fight against corruption and the reduction of poverty are two of the main actions of his government to counteract violence and organized crime. There has been a serious commitment to tackle corruption in all levels of the public administration as various union leaders, lawyers, and high-level officials of previous governments have been prosecuted for a diverse array of crimes. AMLO has also highlighted the problem of young people who neither study nor work (ninis);[57] he believes that, if more employment and education opportunities are offered to these people, recruitment by organized crime groups will be reduced. AMLO considers that the government should promote economic prosperity and greater job opportunities to reduce levels of violence in Mexico.

CONCLUSION

Violence and bloodshed have plagued Mexico during the Calderón and Peña Nieto administrations. While violence initially decreased during the Peña Nieto government, violence has increased over time. Peña Nieto was inundated with various scandals.[58] His administration did not combat the levels of drug-related violence. In addition, human rights abuses remain rampant. Drug trafficking, organized crime, and violence will continue if the Mexican government does not reform the institutions and combat the high levels of corruption and impunity.

Democratization has affected attempts to combat drug trafficking and organized crime as a result of differences between state governments and the federal government. State governments do not always cooperate with the federal government, particularly when governors are from a different political party than the party in power at the federal level. Thus, there has not been effective collaboration between the different levels of government because of political interests and rivalry. It is important to create a robust institutional framework of coordination for security-related issues between the different levels of government. This framework must go beyond political interest and should prioritize national and public security.

Finally, Mexico must advance in the consolidation of democracy and the strengthening of the judiciary system to reverse the high levels of impunity.[59] Despite the judicial reforms that occurred in 2008,[60] the impunity rate remains over 90 percent. More needs to be done to increase the levels of transparency in the government and combat the high levels of corruption. In sum, reforms to institutions cannot only happen at one part of the government, but instead must occur at all three branches of government: the executive, legislative, and judiciary.

NOTES

1. For more, see: Stephen D. Morris, "Corruption, drug trafficking, and violence in Mexico," *The Brown Journal of World Affairs* 18, no. 2 (2012): pp. 29–43; Peter Andreas, "The political economy of narco-corruption in Mexico," *Current History* 97, no. 618 (1998): p. 160; Viridiana Rios, "How government coordination controlled organized crime: The case of Mexico's cocaine markets," *Journal of Conflict Resolution* 59, no. 8 (2015): pp. 1433–1454.

2. For more, see: Stephanie Brophy, "Mexico: Cartels, corruption and cocaine: A profile of the Gulf cartel," *Global Crime* 9, no. 3 (2008): pp. 248–261; Jerjes Aguirre and Hugo Amador Herrera, "Institutional weakness and organized crime in Mexico: The case of Michoacán," *Trends in Organized Crime* 16, no. 2 (2013): pp. 221–238.

3. A few sections of this chapter are from Roberto Zepeda and Jonathan D. Rosen, "Violence in Mexico: An examination of the major trends and challenges," in *Violence in the Americas*, eds. Hanna S. Kassab and Jonathan D. Rosen (Lanham, MD: Lexington Books, 2018), pp. 109–124; Roberto Zepeda and Jonathan D. Rosen, "The Dimensions of Violence in Mexico," in *The Criminalization of States: The Relationship Between States and Organized Crime*, eds. Jonathan D. Rosen, Bruce Bagley, and Jorge Chabat (Lanham, MD: Lexington Books, May 2019), pp. 55–80. Thanks to Lexington Books for giving us permission to use these sections.

4. For more, see: Ted Galen Carpenter, *The Fire Next Door: Mexico's Drug Violence and the Danger to America* (Washington, DC: CATO Institute, 2012).

5. For more on Mexican politics, see: Emily Edmonds-Poli and David A. Shirk, *Contemporary Mexican Politics* (Lanham, MD: Rowman & Littlefield, 2016, third edition); David A. Shirk, *Mexico's New Politics: The PAN and Democratic Change* (Boulder, CO: Lynne Rienner Publishers, 2005).

6. For more on corruption, see: Stephen D. Morris and Joseph L. Klesner, "Corruption and trust: Theoretical considerations and evidence from Mexico," *Comparative Political Studies* 43, no. 10 (2010): pp. 1258–1285; Andreas, "The political economy of narco-corruption in Mexico," p. 160; Louise Shelley, "Corruption and organized crime in Mexico in the post-PRI transition," *Journal of Contemporary Criminal Justice* 17, no. 3 (2001): pp. 213–231; Stephen D. Morris, *Political Corruption in Mexico: The Impact of Democratization* (Boulder, CO: Lynne Rienner Publishers, 2009).

7. Jonathan D. Rosen and Roberto Zepeda, *Organized Crime, Drug Trafficking, and Violence in Mexico: The Transition from Felipe Calderón to Enrique Peña Nieto* (Lanham, MD: Lexington Books, 2016).

8. For more, see Transparency International's Corruptions Perceptions Index, https://www.transparency.org/country/MEX, accessed September 2019.

9. "Corruption Perceptions Index 2014: Results," *Transparency International*, http://www.transparency.org/cpi2014/results, accessed September 2016.

10. For more, see: Ioan Grillo, "After vigilante war, drug trafficking returns to Michoacan, Mexico," *InSight Crime*, October 13, 2014, http://www.insightcrime.org/news-analysis/vigilante-war-drug-trafficking-michoacan-mexico, accessed April 2017; Salvador Maldonado Aranda, "Drogas, violencia y militarización en el México rural: el caso de Michoacán," *Revista mexicana de sociología* 74, no. 1 (2012): pp. 5–39.

11. Jacobo García, "La corrupción de los gobernadores sacude México y cerca a Peña Nieto," *El País*, April 12, 2017.

12. For more on the police, see: Diane E. Davis, "Undermining the rule of law: Democratization and the dark side of police reform in Mexico," *Latin American Politics and* Society 48, no. 1 (2006): pp. 55–86; Benjamin Reames, "Police forces in Mexico: A profile," *Center for US-Mexican Studies* (2003); Nelson Arteaga Botello

and Adrián López Rivera, "'Everything in This Job Is Money': Inside the Mexican Police," *World Policy Journal* 17, no. 3 (2000): pp. 61–70; Guillermo Zepeda Lecuona, "Mexican police and the criminal justice system," in *Police and Public Security in Mexico*, eds. Robert A. Jr. Donnelly and David A. Shirk (San Diego, CA: University Readers, 2009): pp. 39–63; Wayne A. Cornelius and David A. Shirk, eds., *Reforming the Administration of Justice in Mexico* (Notre Dame, IN: University of Notre Dame Press, 2007).

13. Vanderbilt's LAPOP team indicates that the following command will set the data: svyset upm [pw=wt], strata (estratopri).

14. The regression model is tested for specification, multicollinearity, and heteroscedasticity. The linktest produces a hatsq of 0.380, which indicates that the model does not have issues with specification. The model has a Mean Variance Inflation Factor (VIF) of 1.10, which indicates that there are no issues of multicollinearity. Finally, the Breusch-Pagan/Cook-Weisberg test for heteroscedasticity produces at prob > ch2 of 0.00, indicating that the model has issues with heteroscedasticity. The model is adjusted using the vce (robust) command.

15. James Bargent, "Mexico Impunity levels reach 99%: Study," *InSight Crime*, February 4, 2016, http://www.insightcrime.org/news-briefs/mexico-impunity-levels-reach-99-study, accessed April 2016.

16. Maureen Mayer and Ximena Suarez Enriquez, *WOLA Report: Mexico's New Judiciary System* (Washington, DC: Washington Office of Latin America, 2016).

17. recode q2 (18/28=1) (29/39=2) (40/50=3) (51/61=4)(62/72=5) (73/88=6), gen (age)

18. This regression is tested for model specification, multicollinearity, and heteroscedasticity using Stata 15.1 The linktest produces at hatsq of 0.752, which is not statistically significant at the 95 percent interval. This means that the model does not have issues with specification. The model also has a Mean Variance Inflation Factor (VIF) of 1.04, which indicates that the model does not have issues with multicollinearity. Finally, the Breusch-Pagan/Cook-Weisberg test for heteroscedasticity produces at prob > ch2 of 0.00, which indicates that the model needs to be adjusted for heteroscedasticity. The model is adjusted using the vce (robust) command.

19. Rubén Aguilar and Jorge Castañeda, *El narco: la guerra fallida* (México: Punto de Lectura, 2009).

20. For more on this topic, see: Jorge Chabat, "La respuesta del gobierno de Calderón al desafío del narcotráfico: entre lo malo y lo peor," *Centro de Investigación y Docencia Ecónomicas (CIDE)*, División de Estudios Internacionales, 2010.

21. Peter Watt and Roberto Zepeda, *Drug War Mexico: Politics, Neoliberalism and Violence in the new Narcoeconomy.* (London: Zed Books, 2012), p. 2.

22. Carpenter, *The Fire Next Door: Mexico's Drug Violence and the Danger to America*; Ioan Grillo, *El Narco: Inside Mexico's Criminal Insurgency* (New York, NY: Bloomsbury Press, 2012).

23. Watt and Zepeda, *Drug War Mexico*; see also Nathan P. Jones, *Mexico's Illicit Drug Networks and the State Reaction* (Washington, DC: Georgetown University Press, 2016).

24. For more on this topic, see: Marcos Pablo Moloeznik, "The militarization of public security and the role of the military in Mexico," in *Police and Public*

Security in Mexico eds. Robert A. Jr. Donnelly and David A. Shirk (San Diego, CA: University Readers, 2009): pp. 65–92; Angel Gustavo López-Montiel, "The military, political power, and police relations in Mexico City," *Latin American Perspectives* 27, no. 2 (2000): pp. 79–94; Shannon O'Neil, "The real war in Mexico: How democracy can defeat the drug cartels," *Foreign Affairs* (2009): pp. 63–77.

25. David A. Shirk, *Drug Violence in Mexico: Data and Analysis from 2001-2009* (San Diego, CA: Trans-Border Institute: Joan B. Kroc School of Peace Studies, 2010), p. 4.

26. Shirk, *Drug Violence in Mexico: Data and Analysis from 2001-2009*, p. 7.

27. Rafael López and M. del Pozo, "27 ejecutados al día," *Milenio*, December 1, 2012.

28. Notimex, "Segob da a conocer lista de 26,000 desaparecidos," *El Financiero*, December 12, 2014.

29. Veronica Macias, "Han encontrado 246 narcofosas, en tres años," *El Economista*, June 11, 2014; see also "Narcofosas en 13 estados: el saldo del horror," *El Informador*, April 6, 2014.

30. Kate Linthicum, "Even before Trump's visit, Peña Nieto was Mexico's least popular president ever. Too late to change that?" *Los Angeles Times*, September 2, 2016, pp. 2–3.

31. David Bacon, "Why are Mexican teachers being jailed for protesting education reform?" *The Nation*, June 17, 2016; Diana Villiers Negroponte, "Mexico's energy reforms become law," *The Brookings Institution*, August 14, 2014, https://www.bro okings.edu/articles/mexicos-energy-reforms-become-law/, accessed September 2016.

32. Rosen and Zepeda, *Organized Crime, Drug Trafficking, and Violence in Mexico: The Transition from Felipe Calderón to Enrique Peña Nieto.*

33. "México rompió record de asesinatos en 2017," *The Huffington Post*, January 22, 2018.

34. David Agren, "Mexico maelstrom: How the drug violence got so bad," *The Guardian*, December 26, 2017.

35. Christopher Woody, "Another major Mexican company is shutting down some of its operations amid record levels of violence," *Business Insider*, May 24, 2018.

36. Woody, "Another major Mexican company is shutting down some of its operations amid record levels of violence."

37. Milenio, "Descarrilamiento de trenes en Veracruz dejó pérdidas por 312 millones de pesos," May 26, 2018.

38. "Robo de gasolinas a Pemex se incrementa," *El Economista*, April 12, 2018.

39. Christopher Woody, "Mexico's oil company is losing more than a billion dollars a year to cartels — and its own employees are helping them out," *Business Insider*, April 13, 2018.

40. Hannah Stone, "The disappeared of Iguala, Mexico: A crime foretold," *InSight Crime*, November 20, 2014, http://www.insightcrime.org/news-analysis/mexico-d isappeared-iguala-crime-foretold-students, accessed September 2016, p. 2.

41. Maureen Meyer quoted in "On the Eve of the 2nd Anniversary of the 43 Students' Disappearance, the Mexican Government Still Holds on to Already Disproven 'Historic Truth,'" *Washington Office on Latin America*, September

22, 2016, https://www.wola.org/2016/09/eve-2nd-anniversary-43-students-disappear ance-mexican-government-still-holds-already-disproven-historic-truth/, accessed September 2016.

42. Maureen Meyer, "Mexico's Proposed National Guard Would Solidify the Militarization of Public Security," *Washington Office on Latin America*, January 10, 2019, https://www.wola.org/analysis/mexico-national-guard-military-abuses/, accessed May 16, 2019.

43. *Washington Office on Latin America* (WOLA), "Mexico Supreme Court Overturns Controversial Security Law," *WOLA*, November 15, 2018, https://ww w.wola.org/2018/11/mexico-supreme-court-overturns-controversial-security-law/, accessed May 15, 2019, p. 1.

44. Meyer, "Mexico's Proposed National Guard Would Solidify the Militarization of Public Security."

45. Ximena Suárez-Enríquez, with contributions from Maureen Meyer, *Overlooking Justice: Human Rights Violations Committed by Mexican Soldiers against Civilians are Met with Impunity* (Washington, DC: WOLA, 2017).

46. Ximena Suárez-Enríquez, with contributions from Maureen Meyer, *Overlooking Justice: Human Rights Violations Committed by Mexican Soldiers against Civilians are Met with Impunity*, p. 17.

47. Ximena Suárez-Enríquez, with contributions from Maureen Meyer, *Overlooking Justice: Human Rights Violations Committed by Mexican Soldiers against Civilians are Met with Impunity*.

48. The LAPOP data requires you to preform the following command in STATA to weight the data. As per the LAPOP instruction, I used the following command: svyset upm [pw=wt], strata (estratopri).

49. The recode command is as follows: recode q2 (18/28=1) (29/39=2) (40/50=3) (51/61=4)(62/72=5) (73/88=6), gen (age).

50. The model is test for specification, multicollinearity, and heteroscedasticity. The linktest is State 15.1 produces a hatsq of 0.904, indicating that the model does not have specification issues. The model has a mean Variance Inflation Factor (VIF) of 1.05, revealing that it does not have issues with multicollinearity. Finally, the Breusch-Pagan/Cook-Weisberg test for heteroscedasticity results in Prob > chi2 of 0.00, indicating that the model has issues with heteroscedasticity. The model is corrected by running the vce (robust) command in state.

51. The regression is tested for specification, multicollinearity, and heteroscedasticity. The linktest indicates that the model does not have issues with specification. The model has a VIF of 1.10, indicating that there are no issues of multicollinearity. Finally, the Breusch-Pagan/Cook-Weisberg test for heteroscedasticity produces at prob > ch2 of 0.55. Thus, the model does not have issues with heteroscedasticity.

52. Causa en común, *Elementos para un verdadero informe sobre seguridad con motivo del primer informe de gobierno* (México: Causa en común, 2019).

53. Causa en común, *Elementos para un verdadero informe sobre seguridad con motivo del primer informe de gobierno*.

54. Causa en común, *Elementos para un verdadero informe sobre seguridad con motivo del primer informe de gobierno*.

55. Causa en común, *Elementos para un verdadero informe sobre seguridad con motivo del primer informe de gobierno.*

56. For more, see: Kirk Semple, "Mexico declares victory over fuel thieves. But is it lasting?" *The New York Times*, May 5, 2019; "Murders in Mexico surge to record in first half of 2019," *Reuters*, July 21, 2019.

57. For more on this topic, see: Teresa Moreno, "'Ninis' are growing problem in Mexico," *El Universal*, April 7, 2018.

58. Eric Martin, "Mexican President's Support Plumbs New Low as Gasoline Soars," *Bloomberg,* January 18, 2017.

59. Chappell Lawson, "Mexico's unfinished transition: democratization and authoritarian enclaves in Mexico," *Mexican Studies/Estudios Mexicanos* 16, no. 2 (2000): pp. 267–287; Jonathan T. Hiskey and Shaun Bowler, "Local context and democratization in Mexico," *American Journal of Political Science* 49, no. 1 (2005): pp. 57–71; Morris, "Corruption, Drug Trafficking, and Violence in Mexico," pp. 29–43.

60. Silvia Inclán Oseguera, "Judicial reform in Mexico: Political insurance or the search for political legitimacy?" *Political Research Quarterly* 62, no. 4 (2009): pp. 753–766.

Chapter 3

Guatemala, a Captured State

Adriana Beltrán

For over a decade, Guatemala championed an unprecedented crusade against corruption.[1] The work of a unique, UN-led anti-impunity commission, brought Guatemalans hope that corrupt elites and powerful criminals could finally be brought to justice. The impact of the International Commission against Impunity in Guatemala, commonly known as CICIG, was unprecedented and opened up a new era of rule of law reform in a country mired in poverty and violence.

In its twelve years of operations, the Commission helped equip Guatemalan institutions with investigative techniques and contributed to purging institutions. Its partnership with the Public Prosecutor's Office and other institutions garnered praise for its prosecution of high-profile cases. This was particularly the case in 2015, when the CICIG helped uncover a multimillion dollar corruption scheme within the country's customs agency, known as *La Línea*, which led to the resignation and imprisonment of then-president Otto Pérez Molina and Vice President Roxanna Baldetti.[2] Guatemala became the first country in the region to send a president to jail on corruption charges before the end of their term.[3]

La Línea case ignited massive peaceful demonstrations that brought together Guatemalans from all walks of life to demand greater government accountability.[4] The mobilizations invigorated the fight against corruption as the Commission and Public Prosecutor's Office continued to unveil scandals that implicated powerful members of the country's political and economic elite, military and police, and judiciary. The events that unfolded in Guatemala triggered calls for the creation of similar mechanisms in neighboring countries.[5]

Through the investigations, the CICIG exposed the depth and breadth of political corruption in Guatemala and the level of co-optation of the state.

The investigations revealed the nature of power in the country, and how networks of powerful and influential individuals have colluded to co-opt all branches of state power to use public institutions for their own interest and impunity.[6]

But, as the Commission helped present more cases, it gained more enemies. Targets of its investigations unified to oppose and ultimately get rid of the Commission and the gains achieved. In September of 2019, the Commission had to prematurely close its doors.

The fierce backlash underscored that sustaining the progress against corruption requires profound political and institutional reforms to the machinery that has enabled illicit structures to operate unimpeded. Developments over the last two years have shown that the desire to end the Commission's involvement in the country had less to do with selective prosecutions and sovereignty concerns and more with the desire of the political and economic elite to revert to "business as usual."

A BOLD ANTICORRUPTION EXPERIMENT

Faced with a spiraling problem of violence and infiltration of organized crime, the Óscar Berger administration sought the assistance of the international community, and in 2007 signed an agreement with the United Nations to set up the CICIG. The Commission was tasked with helping Guatemalan institutions investigate and dismantle illicit criminal groups that had co-opted state institutions since the end of the country's armed conflict in the 1990s.[7]

The Commission was established as an innovative, hybrid mechanism for strengthening the rule of law. Its novelty lied in the fact that the Commission functioned as an independent investigative body but operated under Guatemalan law and within the local justice system. Thus, Guatemala was relying on the expertise of the Commission to work hand in hand with the country's prosecutors and investigators, helping to build their capabilities in the process.[8] Unlike other international mechanisms, the Commission's aim was to go after criminal networks that emerged from the war and were linked to the state.[9]

To carry out its mandate, the Commission was granted the authority to investigate a select number of emblematic cases, collect information from any person, public official or entity, and enter into agreements with the Attorney General's Office, the police, and other state institutions.[10] Vital to the CICIG's efforts was its relationship with the Public Prosecutor's Office, and in particular with the FECI, a specialized prosecutorial unit created to work exclusively with the CICIG, and whose members were selected and trained by the Commission.[11]

The Commission did not have prosecutorial powers, nor could it independently carry out raids, arrests, or wire taps. Upon obtaining the approval of the judiciary, it was able to initiate and collaborate in investigations and participate as a co-plaintiff (*querellante adhesivo*)[12] in the cases within its mandate that the attorney general decided to pursue in court.[13]

CICIG's collaboration with the Attorney General's Office resulted in the arrest and prosecution of powerful criminals and corrupt officials who were once considered untouchable. Aside from Pérez Molina and Baldetti, the Commission helped indict two former presidents, high-ranking security officials, police chiefs, ministers, and members of the country's traditional economic elite.[14] Its investigations dealt major blows to networks of corruption embedded in every branch of government, political parties, and local politics. By September 2019, the CICIG had collaborated in identifying over 70 criminal networks, prosecuting some 120 cases resulting in 1,540 indictments and over 400 convictions.[15] According to the CICIG, this represents an 85 percent success rate in resolving cases.[16]

While better known for investigating high-impact cases, the Commission also played an important role in promoting the adoption of public policies and legal and institutional reforms. Chief among these were legal reforms, which equipped local investigators with modern investigative techniques such as plea bargaining, lawful surveillance and wiretapping, and video conferencing to allow remote witness testimony, among other tools.[17] Its contributions to the Public Prosecutor's Office also included the implementation of a new methodology for pursuing group investigations of criminal networks as opposed to case-by-case investigations, as well as the restructuring of the criminal analysis unit and witness protection program.[18] Within the judiciary, the Commission helped establish high-risk tribunals in the capital where judges, prosecutors, and witnesses can be better protected.[19] These special courts oversee complex criminal cases, including those related to corruption, drug trafficking, war crimes, and crimes against humanity, among others.

THE NATURE OF GUATEMALA'S CORRUPTION

In 2017, CICIG commissioner Velásquez noted during an interview that the problem of corruption in Guatemala was not "episodic, temporary, a one-off."[20] Instead, "it's structural and systematic. It's corruption that has led to a complete capture of the state; that's how it perpetuates itself and that's why it continues despite the arrest and prosecution of the leaders of these structures."[21]

Indeed, the CICIG and Attorney General's Office revealed the existence of illicit groups that operate at the national, state, and municipal levels in all branches of government with power that extends beyond any one administration.[22] Consequently, the state has ceased to focus on the common good in order to make policies that benefit individual people and groups.[23]

> "At the crux of the fragility of the Guatemalan state is a clientelistic, elite-based political system that has remained largely intact since the signing of the 1996 peace accords. Throughout the long-period of military rule, an informal alliance between the military and the country's economic elite concentrated power in the hands of a few. This arrangement facilitated their privileged access to land, labor, and other resources and generated a widespread culture of impunity. The peace process sought to bring an end to this partisan and exclusionary system but several constraints within the post-conflict settlement left the underlying power structures largely untouched. Thus, Guatemala acquired the features of formal democratic institutions but underneath, participation is mediated through a web of personal, business or criminal relationships and understandings, generating a state that is porous, corroded, and criminalized."[24] The principal effect of this arrangement has been the perpetuation of de facto criminal structures that have co-opted the state and feed off the national budget, excluding the majority of the population and limiting the state's ability to address the high levels of inequality, poverty, and violence in the country. "Corruption is the livelihood of this system."[25]

GUATEMALA'S ORIGINAL SIN

One of the factors that helps explain the capture of Guatemala's institutions is the financing of political parties.[26] Since 1984, Guatemala has been characterized for having weak, exclusive, and volatile political institutions. Centered mainly around personalities, rather than political ideologies and policies, they have served as vehicles to get certain politicians in public office. The average political party is only six years old. In fact, since the return to democracy, no party has won the presidency more than once.[27] Many, including the two largest parties since 1999, have disappeared. As described by a local academic, "Guatemala is a cemetery of political parties."[28]

Political parties neither represent the interests of voters nor have they been able to effectively mediate between the state and the citizenry. Rather, they have served the interest of powerful political, business, and criminal interests that finance the campaigns. Electoral campaigns require candidates to mobilize considerable sums. Although the system allows for a combination of public and private financing, most comes from private sources. Many donations come from contractors who do business with the state or from organized crime, while political parties exceed the legal spending limits and tend to spend more money than they report to the electoral authorities.[29] A 2015 report by the CICIG found that 50 percent of campaign donations come from contractors doing business with the state and another 25 percent from organized crime.[30] Political parties and candidates, the report concluded, used various mechanisms to illegally finance their campaigns. In Guatemalan politics, elites and powerful groups finance elections expecting to receive returns on their investment in the form of contracts, benefits, influence over policy or jobs in key ministries.[31] This dynamic shapes a political party system that incentivizes corruption and erodes democracy.[32] As Commissioner Velásquez described, illegal campaign financing is the "original sin of Guatemalan democracy, it is the doorway to the vicious circle of corruption."[33] It has enabled the private sector, criminals, and the political elite to have a disproportionate degree of influence over decisions, policies, and public resources.[34]

The case of the cooptation of the state (*Cooptación del Estado*) is emblematic of the methods utilized by corrupt elites to co-opt the state and changed the rules of the game for their personal benefit to perpetuate themselves in power.[35] According to investigators, Pérez Molina and Baldetti had set up a scheme to ensure the party's victory in the 2011 elections by promising preferential treatment for state contracts in exchange for illegal campaign contributions.[36] Through shell companies, the network accepted funds from various donors, laundered it, and transferred it to the party's campaign coffers without reporting it to the electoral tribunal.[37] Members of the private sector and other donors contributed money, as well as goods and services, including travel arrangements, cell phone usage plans, and high-end vehicles. Contributions came from various sources. Two of the companies that contributed to the campaign, for example, were TV channels owned by Alba Elvira Lorenzana Cardona, wife of businessman and media mogul Ángel González,[38] which contributed nearly $2.5 million through at least four companies owned by Baldetti. According to prosecutors, nearly 95 percent of the funds were never reported.[39]

Once in office, the Pérez Molina administration rewarded their contributors by signing contracts in exchange for bribes, interfering in court cases to benefit donors, and appointing friends and allies to key positions.[40] The evidence suggests that the corruption network received at least $67 million through more than 450 government contracts.[41] Molina and Baldetti obtained 60 percent of the bribes and the rest was distributed among other members of the network.[42]

The scheme was devised to repeat itself once Alejandro Sinibaldi, the Patriot Party's 2015 candidate, assumed the presidency. But Sinibaldi resigned his candidacy in April 2015 and was later implicated in the Cooperacha case.[43] He was later accused of money laundering and illicit association in a separate case during his time as minister of infrastructure, housing, and communications.[44] Sinibaldi is currently a fugitive from justice. In December 2019, the US Department of State publicly designated Sinibaldi, his wife, and children for their engagement in significant corruption.[45]

The problem of illicit campaign financing was not limited to Pérez Molina and the Patriot Party. From the Convergence Front (Frente de Convergencia Nacional—FCN) to the National Unity of Hope (Unidad Nacional de la Esperanza—UNE),[46] and the Renewed Democratic Liberty (Libertad Democrática Renovada—Líder),[47] accusations of campaign financing wrongdoing have touched every political party in the country.

Similar corrupt practices also play out at the local level. A study by the Myrna Mack Foundation, Nómada and CICIG used Congressional party and voting information to identify a "hard nucleus" of members of Congress that vote together to oppose or distort key judicial reforms in order to maintain the status quo. Unbeholden to political ideology or local issues, the nucleus controls a narrow set of legislative actions driven by the motivation to protect themselves, their allies, and financiers from prosecution.[48] These power dynamics are a product of corrupt practices in the Congress such as *transfugismo* (switching from one political party to another without holding new elections first), and unreported illicit campaign financing practices that allow networks of power to be perpetuated through negotiations and financial rewards despite the results of the elections. Legal actions taken to do away with these practices has prevented the reelection of some powerful operatives in Congress. However, even after new elections in 2019, Congress maintains its corrupt allegiances through new conservative alliances.

A CO-OPTED JUDICIARY

Historically, the criminal justice system has suffered from poor leadership, absence of independence and impartiality, inadequate funding, and limited access to justice for many sectors of society.[49] In recent years, important steps have been taken to expand the justice system's reach across the country and increase the number of prosecutors, judges, and technical staff. Nonetheless, significant gaps in coverage remain, particularly in rural areas of the country. By the end of 2017, for example, the Public Prosecutor's Office only had offices in 20 percent of the country's municipalities.[50] Moreover, between 2014 and 2017, there was an average of about six judges for every 100,000 people in the country, well below the national global average of 17. During that same period, there was an average of 13.5 prosecutors and two forensic experts per 100,000 people, and an equally low number of public defenders.[51]

Equally debilitating has been the exploitation by defense attorneys of due process protections to trigger prolonged delays in criminal proceedings.

Guatemalan law provides several protections for criminal defendants, including the *amparo* or right to appeal for protection of any Constitutional right at any point of criminal proceedings, as well as the right to petition for the removal of a judge from a case (*recusación*) or to request that a judge recuse him or herself (*excusa*) on grounds of alleged conflict or bias.[52] While these safeguards are important to protect fundamental rights, the manipulation and repeated use of these petitions have brought many emblematic corruption and human rights cases to a standstill.[53] For instance, in *La Línea* case, the defense has filed at least forty-nine appeals.[54] As a result, the trial was scheduled to start in March 2020, more than five years after the initial arrests.

But, as Human Rights Watch rightfully notes, while defense lawyers have figured out how to exploit the law, the derailing of justice is only possible because the courts allow frivolous delays.[55] Although allowed, judges rarely decline unfounded appeals or opt to continue with proceedings while petitions are pending so long as there is no risk of irreparable harm.[56] Reform of the *amparo* law was among the proposals that the CICIG promoted, but it stalled in the Guatemalan Congress due to a lack of political will.

The persistent attempts by powerful sectors, both licit and illicit, to infiltrate criminal justice institutions is another obstacle that has threatened the guarantee of an independent and impartial justice system. In this regard, the CICIG cautioned that networks operating from within and outside the justice system have sought to influence court decisions, and in some cases offered impunity through their contacts within justice institutions.[57] One of the most revealing examples of these illicit networks is the case of Supreme Court magistrate Blanca Stalling, who was detained in February 2017 on charges of influence peddling.[58] According to the attorney general and CICIG's investigation, in 2016, Stalling sought to use her position to pressure the judge who was presiding over a case that her son was involved in.[59] Stalling had already been linked to several criminal investigations, including an attempt to block the impeachment proceedings against former president Otto Pérez Molina and an attempt to influence the *La Línea* case.[60]

In the case of the courts and in contrast to other countries in the region, only lower court judges are given tenure in Guatemala.[61] Appellate Court judges and Supreme Court magistrates are elected every five years. Although Congress appoints Supreme Court and Appellate Court judges, the process involves special selection commissions made up of representatives from the Guatemalan Bar Association, law school deans, and appellate judges.

A law adopted in 2009 attempted to make the selection commission more transparent and regulated, and allow for civil society participation and oversight.[62] In practice, however, the selection process has been mired by political, private, and illicit interests seeking to control the makeup of the commissions or negotiate quotas of final candidates.[63] The competition for influence in the process has resulted in the establishment and funding of law schools as a vehicle for guaranteeing a seat at the table. According to a 2019 study, the number of law schools has increased from four to over ten since the adoption of the law.[64] At the same time, conflicts of interest have debilitated the process as members of the Supreme Court Nominations Commission are eligible to apply as candidates for the Appellate Courts and vice versa.[65] Candidates often compete for political support in order to be elected or maintain their position.[66] Selection commissions are also used to select other key judicial posts, including the attorney general, the Constitutional Court, and the director of the Institute of Criminal Public Defense.[67]

The case of Roberto López Villatoro, known as the "Tennis Shoe King," best illustrates how networks of power seek to influence the nomination process. A lawyer and businessman who made his wealth selling imported shoe knockoffs,[68] and gained influence from having a brother in the Senate and marrying Zury Ríos Montt (daughter of military dictator Efrain Ríos Montt), Villatoro used his connections and wealth to gain control over the Guatemalan Bar Association and ensure the election of loyal candidates to the Supreme Court and Court of Appeals during the 2014 process. In February 2018, Villatoro was arrested, along with Judge Giovanni Orellana Donis, who served as a member of the 2014 Supreme Court Nominations Commission.[69] According to the Public Prosecutor's Office and the CICIG, Villatoro had gifted Donis a luxury apartment in exchange for Donis' vote in favor of Villatoro's candidates who were eventually appointed to the Supreme Court.[70] In 2017, one of Villatoro's candidates was elected as president of the Supreme Court and played a key role in the election of the current attorney general.[71]

The numerous irregularities and controversies of the 2014 selection process demonstrated the need for a profound reform. In 2016, taking advantage of the political opening created by the 2015 protests, the CICIG worked with the Attorney General's Office and other branches of government to press for far-reaching reforms of the Constitution and ordinary laws to improve the functioning of the justice system. In April 2016, the heads of the three branches of government began the reform process by launching a national dialogue. Through the dialogue, regional meetings were held involving broad sectors of civil society, the private sector, and indigenous authorities that resulted in a draft bill of Constitutional and legal reforms.[72] The reform proposal included measures to improve access to justice, strengthen the independence of the judiciary, reform the selection process of judicial officials, and recognize indigenous legal jurisdiction.[73] Pending approval of the Constitutional reforms, Congress passed amendments to reform the organic law of the Attorney General's Office in order to further professionalize the institution, as well as the law on judicial career, which ensured a clearer separation between the administrative and legal functions of the Supreme Court, improved the career track, and evaluation and disciplinary procedures.[74] However, debates on the Constitutional reforms stalled in Congress due to the lack of consensus and political will, eventually breaking down. What promised to bring about sweeping reforms to strengthen the independence of the justice sector, in the end was met with resistance and failed to achieve substantial changes.

THE DEMISE OF THE ANTICORRUPTION AGENDA

Despite advancements in emblematic cases and a 70 percent approval rating of the population,[75] by late 2016 the Commission began experiencing a severe backlash. As the investigations began to implicate and threaten multiple centers of political and economic power in Guatemala, the Commission and the anticorruption agenda began gaining more enemies. Targets (and potential targets) of investigations colluded to put an end to the probes and shut down the Commission itself.

In October 2015, Jimmy Morales, a former comedian who rose to power on an anticorruption platform, won the presidency with backing from a political party founded by military veterans implicated in wartime atrocities.[76] Still, as Morales took office in January 2016, he extended the CICIG's mandate until 2019 and vowed to extend it again until 2021.[77]

By late 2016, however, Morales' support for the anticorruption agenda began to wane after the Commission and the Public Prosecutor's Office started pursuing cases of illicit campaign financing,[78] including against his party and Morales himself. The relationship deteriorated even further after Morales' son and brother were detained in January 2017 for facilitating false receipts used to defraud the national property registry in 2013.[79]

On August 27, 2017, two days after the Commission and the Public Prosecutor's Office filed the first of three requests to lift President Morales' political immunity so he could be investigated for illicit campaign financing, the government declared CICIG commissioner Iván Velásquez persona-non-grata in an attempt to expel him from the country. Following massive protests, Guatemala's highest court reversed the declaration,[80] but Morales continued attacks.

At the outset of 2018, the Morales administration ousted several high-level government officials who had been known to support anticorruption efforts, including the head of the Internal Revenue Service (Superintendencia de Administración Tributaria—SAT) and the minister of the interior. Shortly after assuming office, the new minister of the interior Enrique Degenhart began removing or relocating senior police officers and detectives without justification and due process guarantees.[81] Many had ten to twenty years of experience and were trained in criminal investigations, anti-narcotics and other specialized areas.[82] The overhaul at the Interior Ministry also marked an important shift in the government's official narrative from prioritizing the fight against corruption toward a focus on the fight against gangs.[83] Degenhart eventually stopped cooperating with the Public Prosecutor's Office and the CICIG, obstructing the capacity of prosecutors to carry out search warrants, something that had never happened since CICIG began operations in the country.[84]

In August of that same year, in a scene reminiscent of the wartime era, Morales, surrounded by military officials, declared that Guatemala would not be renewing the Commission's mandate (see figure 3.1).[85] Earlier that day, the US-donated military-grade vehicles were deployed outside of the CICIG offices, as well as several embassies including that of the United States.[86] Commissioner Velásquez, who at the time was out of the country, was declared a "public threat" and banned from returning to Guatemala. The Constitutional Court, in line with its ruling the previous year, reversed the president's decision and ordered that the commissioner be allowed to reenter the country. Despite the court's rulings, the commissioner's visa expired, and vhe never returned to Guatemala. Velásquez led the Commission from abroad until its closure.

Figure 3.1 Guatemalan President Jimmy Morales Speaks to the Nation Flanked by Military Officers, in Guatemala City, Friday, August 31, 2018. *Source*: AP Photo/Oliver de Ros.

By year's end, the Guatemalan Ministry of Foreign Affairs had revoked the visas and diplomatic credentials of eleven CICIG investigators and gave them seventy-two hours to leave the country or face expulsion.[87] The country's highest court intervened and ordered the Foreign Ministry to abstain from obstructing the Commission's work. Nonetheless, in January 2019, in flagrant disobedience of the court ruling, the authorities detained CICIG investigator Yilen Osorio at Guatemala City's Aurora airport for over twenty-four hours.[88] Osorio was finally able to leave the airport after the Constitutional Court gave the head of the migration department one hour to allow Osorio's entry into the country.

Two days later, on January 7, the government announced that it was immediately terminating the CICIG mandate and gave the Commission's international staff twenty-four hours to leave the country. During the announcement, President Jimmy Morales cited "illegal actions taken by the CICIG as well as its officials who violated the human rights of Guatemalans and foreigners." Furthermore, Morales stated that the Commission "has put the national security, public order, governability, respect for human rights, and above all the sovereignty of the state of Guatemala at risk."[89] The decision to unilaterally end the CICIG's mandate violated both Guatemala's domestic laws and its obligations under international law, as well as the agreement between Guatemala and the United Nations that established the Commission. The Constitutional Court reversed the president's decision. While the Commission continued operating until its departure on September 3, 2019, the government sought repeatedly to continue obstructing its work.[90]

The backlash went beyond attacks against the Commission. Misinformation and defamation campaigns also targeted judges, prosecutors, journalists, and civil society actors actively engaged in the fight against corruption. Reported threats and attacks against judges increased by 22 percent between 2017 and 2018, and little political will exists to investigate these threats.[91] Defamation campaigns against those aligned with the anticorruption camp are prevalent on social media in Guatemala, and are circulated by government-aligned accounts with significant influence or boosted by "net centers," or centers where many accounts are managed at a time to amplify certain messages.[92]

The Elite Push Back

The Morales administration was not alone in his fierce criticism of the Commission. The CICIG and attorney general's decision to investigate illicit electoral finances inevitably implicated the business community. Fearing risk of criminal prosecution, members of the economic elite, once supportive of the anticorruption efforts, also turned against the Commission.

To that end, in February 2017, Guatemalan business leaders and politicians came together to devise a plan to diminish US support for the commissioner.[93] Within a few months, they contracted US lobbying firms with connections to the Trump administration and influential Republicans in Washington, according to a report by Guatemalan online newspaper *Nómada*.[94] One firm, Barnes and Thornburg, an employer of several Republicans who worked for Vice President Mike Pence, received a $80,000 monthly contract from one of Morales' main campaign fundraisers,[95] and later signed another $80,000 monthly contract with four Guatemalan congressmen notorious for their criticism of CICIG.[96] Barnes and Thornburg would go on to sign a new $480,000 six month contract with Batab Coalition, a coalition of businesses run by Guatemalan businessman Fernando Saenz.[97] The other firm contracted by the Guatemalans, Greenberg Traurig, is a Florida-based firm that, according to *Foreign Policy*, contributes political donations to Senator Marco Rubio.[98]

The lobby failed to remove the commissioner but did manage to weaken bipartisan support for the CICIG within the halls of the US Congress. By the summer of 2018, a handful of Republican members were holding congressional hearings on presumed abuses committed and issuing tweets in support of the Morales administration's decision to terminate CICIG's mandate citing sovereignty concerns.[99] As one congressional aide explained, "the fact is that most people don't know a great deal about Central America. The commission's enemies have pursued a strategy that boils down to throw everything at the wall and see what sticks. And different stuff stuck."[100]

In early 2018, the anti-CICIG lobby also gained support from an unexpected quarter, Bill Browder, an American-born British hedge fund manager and CEO of Hermitage Capital Management, one of the largest investors in Russia, who led efforts behind the Magnitsky Act.[101] Browder took on the case of a wealthy Russian family who had presumably fled to Guatemala in 2009 to escape persecution from the Russian government. They were then implicated in a case involving a massive fraud ring within the Guatemalan migration department, which the CICIG joined in investigating in 2013.[102] The family was charged with identity fraud for buying fake passports, birth certificates, and other documents and was given lengthy sentences. Convinced that the case was proof of a Kremlin-CICIG connection, Browder joined the campaign in the US Congress against the CICIG.[103] Although no evidence of Russian interference was ever provided, and the State Department stated during a hearing that neither the Embassy in Guatemala nor the department had found proof of collusion,[104] the accusations were echoed by a handful of members of Congress. Senator Marco Rubio went as far as suspending the US annual contribution of $6 million to the CICIG; a third of the Commission's overall budget. The aid was eventually restored after several months.

A Weak Separation of Powers

The Guatemalan legislature has been one of the primary parties seeking retribution against those affiliated with the CICIG and looking to roll back progress in the fight against corruption. This was to be expected given that 20 percent of its members faced corruption charges.[105] Headed by a group of members who became known as the *pacto de corruptos*, one of the initial actions carried out in September of 2017 with the support of the majority of the Congress was to severely reduce the penalties for about 400 crimes, including corruption crimes, by reforming the country's penal code.[106] Due to pressure from civil society and international actors, the reforms were not signed into law. However, the *pacto* continued in its attempts to legislate impunity. At the tail end of their term, Congress approved reforms to the country's penal code that allowed those accused of corruption and organized crime to reduce their penalties by as much as 50 percent should they accept the charges. Some of the crimes that this law would affect include money laundering and bribery.[107]

Congress continued its offensive against the CICIG even after its mandate expired by creating its own commission to investigate and sanction the work of the CICIG. The Constitutional Court ruled in favor of a complaint submitted by the Public Prosecutor's Office that the anti-CICIG commission usurped investigative functions deemed only for that office, and ordered the suspension of said commission.[108] However, a new commission formed under a new name that held multiple hearings on behalf of "victims" of the CICIG; those accused of corruption and their family members were given a platform to tell their stories in the Congress.[109] The commission, established by several members of Congress, many of which are under investigation for corruption, was viewed as a space created to attack those who have publicly supported the CICIG and denounce those dedicated to tackling corruption.

Throughout the backlash, the Constitutional Court consistently ruled to abide by Guatemala's national and international agreements and allow the Commission to operate without interference. Up until the Morales administration the court's authority has always held ground. However, as described earlier, the Morales administration defied the court's ruling on repeated occasions further debilitating the country's fragile democracy.

In retaliation, members of Congress, as well as other backers of the Morales administration in government, spearheaded multiple attempts to remove justices from the country's Constitutional Court.[110] In one attempt, the executive petitioned the Supreme Court to bring criminal charges against three magistrates, an unprecedented action that was seen as a serious threat to judicial independence in the country.[111]

The US Betrayal

Morales' efforts to dismantle anticorruption initiatives would not have advanced had US policy not suffered a dramatic shift. Unlike past Republican and Democratic administrations, the Trump administration failed to provide consistent, strong support for efforts to combat corruption and strengthen the rule of law in Guatemala.[112] A telling example was Secretary of State Mike Pompeo's response to the Guatemalan government's misuse of US-donated military vehicles to intimidate the CICIG and Embassies.[113] Rather than condemning the Guatemalan government's actions, he issued a tweet stating that the US "relationship with Guatemala is important. We greatly appreciate Guatemala's efforts in counternarcotics and security."[114] Another telling example was the lukewarm US response to Morales' announcement in early January of plans to terminate the Commission.[115]

According to several analysts, the shift in the United States' strong support of Guatemala's anticorruption efforts is linked to Guatemala becoming the second country in the world to move its Embassy in Israel to Jerusalem. The move earned Morales access to officials close to President Trump, including then US ambassador to the United Nations, Nikki Haley, who visited Guatemala to thank Morales and supported efforts to reign in the Commission.[116] Morales was further able to curry favor with the White House by collaborating with the Trump administration in stopping irregular migration from Central America. In fact, in July 2019, Guatemala became the first country in the region to sign a controversial migration agreement with the United States, which allows the US government to send non-Guatemalan asylum seekers to Guatemala.[117]

The loss of support from the United States, Guatemala's main political and economic ally, emboldened President Morales and his allies and created the space needed for Guatemala's old political order to reassert themselves.[118]

THE 2019 ELECTIONS—MORE OF THE SAME

In 2019, Guatemala held elections for president, vice president, Congress, municipal authorities, and representatives to the Central American Parliament. The elections were the first to be held under the 2016 electoral reforms which intended to address some of the key aspects of corruption in Guatemalan politics.[119] The electoral process was an opportunity to usher in a new era of political governance, as support for the CICIG and continuing the fight against corruption topped the list of the electorate's concerns. However, the election was also an opportunity for the old guard, backed by powerful economic and political interests, to maintain their control. The intensity of the political moment led to a process marred with irregularities, threats to democratic processes, and confusion.

The lack of resources and other obstacles led to numerous delays and inconsistencies on the part of the electoral tribunal when vetting candidates. Zury Ríos, the conservative Valor candidate, was barred from the race due to the Constitutional prohibition against coup leaders and their family members running for public office. However, at least 150 candidates running for national office had questionable credentials, according to civil society groups. The charges against them ranged from receiving suspicious government contracts to drug trafficking.[120]

Among the most worrisome controversies was the cancellation of former attorney general and anticorruption crusader, Thelma Aldana's candidacy. Aldana was the only top contender who had vowed to reinstate the CICIG and continue anticorruption efforts. Aside from defamation campaigns and threats, Aldana had eighteen accusations filed against her, many from groups and individuals who came under investigation during her time as attorney general.[121] Ultimately, her detractors succeeded and the electoral authorities blocked her candidacy based on a politically motivated accusation of misuse of public funds.[122] The Supreme Court denied her request for an injunction and in mid-May 2019 the Constitutional Court denied her final appeal.[123] An arrest warrant was issued the day before her official registration as a candidate. The judge responsible was reportedly under investigation for allegedly taking a bribe in exchange for issuing the warrant.[124] Aldana is now living in exile.

Powerful criminal organizations also influenced the presidential election. In April 2019, UCN presidential candidate Mario Estrada was arrested in Florida on drug trafficking charges. According to the Department of Justice, Estrada had conspired to solicit campaign funds from the Sinaloa cartel.[125] In return, Estrada offered the drug cartel cabinet positions and access to ports and airports. To ensure his victory, he allegedly offered to hire hitmen to kill political rivals, including Aldana.[126]

In the end, voters had to choose between two traditional politicians both of whom were investigated by the CICIG. Sandra Torres, former first lady and longtime political persona running on the UNE ticket, who was implicated in an investigation for allegedly receiving an estimated $2.5 million in unreported campaign donations during the 2015 process. However, the Attorney General's Office refrained from officially charging Torres until after she was registered to run granting her immunity. The other was Alejandro Giammattei, a doctor, the former director of the penitentiary system, and a four-time presidential candidate. Giammattei was also prosecuted for his involvement in the extrajudicial killing of inmates during his time as director of prisons, though was acquitted by a judge due to lack of evidence.[127]

The series of legal actions against candidates, as well as inconsistencies in the TSE's decisions led to confusion and distrust in the political system. For the most part, the elections produced more of the same: candidates deep in well-established political circles that were unlikely to prioritize the much-needed justice reforms in Guatemala. In the final round of votes, Giammattei won 57 percent of the votes while Sandra Torres trailed at 41 percent. Turnout was low, with only 42 percent of registered voters participating, a 14 percent drop compared to the 2015 election and illustrative of Guatemalans' lack of interest for the two finalists.

THE GIAMMATTEI ADMINISTRATION AND THE FUTURE OF THE ANTICORRUPTION AGENDA

In January 2020, Alejandro Giammattei entered the presidency after touting a hardline on public security and a development plan that would focus on the country's high rates of poverty and malnutrition. Many of his backers come from the same former military guard and economic elite as those of President Morales and are staunch opponents of anticorruption efforts and initiatives like the CICIG.[128]

During Giammattei's term, there will be many opportunities for the administration and Congress to regain control over certain institutions that have been at the forefront of the rule of law in Guatemala and beat back anticorruption progress. In addition to the physical absence of the CICIG, Guatemala now faces emboldened networks of traditionally corrupt actors that were successful in bringing down the CICIG and preventing a reform-minded candidate from leading the country.

In this context, it is likely that the new congressional leadership will resume attempts to pursue a regressive agenda to roll back the rule of law gains achieved over the last decade, adding the final nails in CICIG's coffin. Already the new Congress has approved a controversial law that strictly regulates nongovernmental organizations[129] and elected new magistrates to the electoral authorities via secret vote.[130] Their actions signal that Congress will continue to be a major obstacle to the rule of law and fight against corruption in Guatemala.

In the meantime, a number of high-impact corruption investigations once supported by the CICIG are at risk of unraveling due to lack of resources and political will. Some of CICIG's emblematic corruption investigations are just now going to trial. These cases no longer benefit from the backing of CICIG experts and prosecutors. Furthermore, many of the judges deciding these complex corruption cases face increased pressure and threats as opponents of the CICIG see the High Risk Tribunal judges as part of the CICIG's legacy.[131]

It is under these high stake conditions that the election of magistrates and appellate court judges is currently taking place. This year's process has not been exempt from similar obstacles faced in the past. Members of the nominating commission are co-opted by interest groups in order to select judges that can be more easily manipulated.[132] A recent audio leaked to the public revealed a conversation between a judge imprisoned for bribery and a former presidential advisor and political operator accused on various criminal counts, Gustavo Alejos, discussing their attempt to manipulate the selection process. Of equally high stakes are next year's Constitutional Court elections that will determine a new set of magistrates for a four-year period. If manipulation persists, the results of these processes may have a long-term chilling effect on the rule of law and democracy in Guatemala.

NOTES

1. Research assistance provided by Adeline Hite.

2. Brendan O'Boyle, "The Rise and Fall of CICIG: LatAm's Biggest Stories of the 2010s," *Americas Quarterly*, December 11, 2019, https://www.americasquarterly. org/content/rise-and-fall-cicig-latams-biggest-stories-2010s

3. Patricia Navia, Lucas Perello, and Vaclav Masek, "The Determinants of Perception of Corruption in Guatemala, 2006-2016," *Public Integrity* (2019).

4. The Public Prosecutor's Office and the CICIG uncovered evidence that the Otto Pérez Molina's administration was operating a corruption scheme out of its customs agency, in which agency agents would give importers reduced tax rates in exchange for bribes. The bribes went to the then president Pérez Molina and vice president Roxana Baldetti and amounted to millions of dollars, according to the judge overseeing the case. The *La Línea* investigation alone involved 88,920 wiretaps, 5,900 intercepted emails and 175,000 documents.

5. In 2015, the Organization of American States and the government of Honduras signed an agreement to create a similar entity. The Mission to Support the Fight against Corruption and Impunity in Honduras (MACCIH). The MACCIH's mandate came to an end in January 2020 after facing backlash from the Honduran political and economic elite.

6. Washington Office on Latin America, *The CICIG: An Innovative Instrument for Fighting Criminal Organizations and Strengthening the Rule of Law* (Washington Office on Latin America, 2015).

7. Adriana Beltrán, "Will the Rebellion for the Rule of Law Prevail in Guatemala?" in *Fragile States in the Americas*, eds. Jonathan D. Rosen and Hanna S. Kassab (Lexington Books, 2016), pp. 36–60.

8. Washington Office on Latin America, "Fact Sheet: The CICIG's Legacy in Fighting Corruption in Guatemala," *Washington Office on Latin America*, August 27, 2019, https://www.wola.org/analysis/cicigs-legacy-fighting-corruption -guatemala/.

9. Andrew Hudson and Alexandra Taylor, "The International Commission against Impunity in Guatemala: A New Model for International Criminal Justice Mechanisms," *Journal of International Criminal Justice* 8, no. 1 (2010): 53–74.

10. "Agreement between the United Nations and the State of Guatemala on the establishment of an International Commission Against Impunity in Guatemala ('CICIG')," conclusion date: December 12, 2006, *United Nations Treaty Series*, registration no. 44373, https://treaties.un.org/Pages/showDetails.aspx?objid=0800000 28006222c&clang=_en.

11. Washington Office on Latin America, *The CICIG: An Innovative Instrument.*

12. Under Article 116 of the Guatemalan Penal Code, a "querellante adhesivo" or private prosecutor takes part in the charges and the investigation process as a joint plaintiff.

13. Washington Office on Latin America, "Fact Sheet."

14. Ibid.

15. Ibid.

16. *Informe Final de Cierre: El Legado de Justicia en Guatemala #JuntosLosHicimos* (Comisión Internacional Contra la Impunidad en Guatemala, 2019), p. 52.

17. Washington Office on Latin America, *The CICIG.*

18. Beltrán, "Will the Rebellion for the Rule of Law Prevail."

19. Adriana Beltrán, "A New Era of Accountability in Guatemala?" *Washington Office on Latin America*, November 3, 2015, https://www.wola.org/analysis/a-new -era-of-accountability-in-guatemala/.

20. Cora Currier and Danielle Mackey, "The Rise of the Net Center: How an Army of Trolls Protects Guatemala's Corrupt Elite," *The Intercept,* April 7, 2018, https://theintercept.com/2018/04/07/guatemala-anti-corruption-trolls-smear-campaign/.

21. Ibid.

22. *Guatemala: Un Estado Capturado* (Comisión Internacional Contra la Impunidad en Guatemala, 2019), and Sandra Cuffe, "Guatemala's anti-corruption CICIG body to shut down: What to know," *Al Jazeera*, September 1, 2019, https:// www.aljazeera.com/news/2019/08/guatemala-anti-corruption-cicig-body-shut-1908 30225625800.html.

23. *Guatemala: Un Estado Capturado* (Comisión, 2019).

24. Beltrán, "Will the Rebellion for the Rule of Law Prevail."

25. Ibid.

26. Comisión Internacional contra la Impunidad en Guatemala, *Financiamiento de la Política en Guatemala* (Comisión Internacional contra la Impunidad en Guatemala, 2015).

27. Election Guide: Democracy Assistance & Election News, http://www.elec tionguide.org/elections/id/3153/.

28. Asociación de Investigación y Estudios Sociales, Comisión Internacional contra la Impunidad en Guatemala, and Instituto Internacional para la Democracia y la Asistencia Electoral, *Sistema Político-Electoral* (Comisión Internacional Contra la Impunidad en Guatemala, 2019), https://www.cicig.org/wp-content/uploads/2019/08 /SistemaPoliticoElectoral_layout_F.pdf.

29. Freedom House, *Freedom in the World 2017 Report: Guatemala* (Freedom House, 2017). https://freedomhouse.org/country/guatemala/freedom-world/2017, and Kevin Pallister, "Guatemala: The Fight for Accountability and the Rule of Law," *Revista de Ciencia Politica* 37, no. 2 (2017): 471-491.

30. Comisión Internacional contra la Impunidad en Guatemala, *Financiamiento de la Política*.

31. Ibid.

32. Ibid.

33. "International IDEA discusses 'Private financing of politics in Guatemala and its effects on democracy'," *International IDEA*, November 21, 2017, https://www .idea.int/news-media/news/international-idea-discusses-private-financing-politics-gu atemala-and-its-effects.

34. Asociación de Investigación y Estudios Sociales, Comisión Internacional contra la Impunidad en Guatemala, and Instituto Internacional para la Democracia y la Asistencia Electoral, *Sistema Político-Electoral*.

35. Comisión Internacional contra la Impunidad, *Caso: Cooptación del Estado de Guatemala*, Junio 2, 2016, https://www.cicig.org/casos/caso-cooptacion-del-estad o-de-guatemala.

36. Michael Lohmuller, "Guatemala's Government Corruption Scandals Explained," *InSight Crime*, June 21, 2016, https://www.insightcrime.org/news/analys is/guatemala-s-government-corruption-scandals-explained/.

37. Felipe Puerta and Steven Dudley, "Guatemala Politics and the Patriot Party's Theory of 'Eternal Return,'" *Insight Crime*, August 16, 2018.

38. Luis Fernando Alonso, "Interpol Issues Warrant for Prominent Guatemala Businesswoman," *InSight Crime*, September 9, 2016, https://www.insightcrime.org/n ews/brief/interpol-issues-warrant-for-guatemala-businesswomen/.

39. Puerta and Dudley, "Guatemala Politics and the Patriot Party's Theory."

40. Ibid.

41. Ibid.

42. Ibid.

43. Five government ministers and the head of the Social Security Institute from the Pérez Molina administration gave more than $4.7 million over 3 years to buy the president birthday gifts. Former attorney general Aldana said the money was used to buy Pérez Molina a powerboat in 2012, a luxury beach house in 2013, and a $3.5 million helicopter in 2014.

44. The "Construction and Corruption" case accuses Sinibaldi of receiving $10 million dollars in bribes from national construction companies which he funneled through shell companies. In exchange, he awarded these companies' preferential treatment in contracts during his time as minister of housing, infrastructure, and communications.

45. US Department of State, "Public Designation, Due to Involvement in Significant Corruption, of former Guatemalan Minister Alejandro Sinibaldi," *U.S. Embassy in Guatemala*, December 3, 2019, https://gt.usembassy.gov/public-designat ion-due-to-involvement-in-significant-corruption-of-former-guatemalan-minister-a lejandro-sinibaldi/.

46. An investigation into the 2015 presidential elections found that the UNE party used private companies to collect and manage contributions parallel to the official campaign finance information and collection. The funds funneled through the private companies went unreported and were the results of kickbacks in the form of returned tax credits that became merged with the UNE's campaign funds.

47. An investigation into the 2015 presidential elections found that the *Líder* party had received at least USD2 million in unreported campaign donations that the party failed to justify upon notification. The investigation also revealed that third party entities had paid for political advertisements without reporting to the TSE.

48. Harald Waxenecker, *Redes ilícitas y crisis política: La Realidad Del Congreso Guatemalteco* (Guatemala: Comisión Internacional contra la Impunidad en Guatemala, Fundación Myrna Mack, Nómada, 2019), https://myrnamack.org.gt/images/redes_ilicitas/Documento_RedesIlicitasVF-1.pdf.

49. Ivan Briscoe and Marlies Stappers, *Breaking the wave: critical steps in the fight against crime in Guatemala* (Impunity Watch and Clingendael Institute, 2012), p. 7; and Inter-American Commission on Human Rights, *Situation of Human Rights in Guatemala: Diversity, Equality and Exclusion* (Inter-American Commission on Human Rights, 2015), p. 15.

50. *Guatemala's Justice System: Evaluating Capacity Building and Judicial Independence* (Washington Office on Latin America and The Myrna Mack Foundation, 2019), p. 6

51. *Guatemala's Justice System: Evaluating Capacity Building*, pp. 6

52. Mirte Postema, *Running Out the Clock: How Guatemala's Courts Could Doom the Fight Against Impunity* (New York: Human Rights Watch, 2017), pp. 13–14.

53. Ibid.

54. *La Lucha contra la Impunidad en Guatemala: Evaluando el Nivel de Cooperación con la Comisión Internacional contra la Impunidad en Guatemala* (Washington Office on Latin America and The Myrna Mack Foundation, forthcoming).

55. Postema, *Running Out the Clock,* p. 3.

56. Ibid.

57. Comisión Internacional contra la Impunidad en Guatemala, *Guatemala: Un Estado Capturado* (Comisión Internacional contra la Impunidad, 2019), https://www.cicig.org/wp-content/uploads/2019/08/Informe_Captura_Estado_2019.pdf

58. International Legal Assistance Consortium, *ILAC Rule of Law Assessment Report: Guatemala* (International Legal Assistance Consortium, 2018), http://www.ilacnet.org/wp-content/uploads/2018/05/Guatemala-Rule-of-Law-Assessment.pdf.

59. Ibid.

60. Ibid.

61. Jaime Chavez Alor and Lauren McIntosh, *Judicial Nominations in Guatemala: Pockets of Resistance in a Closing Space* (Stockholm: International Legal Assistance Consortium, 2019), https://newilac.wpengine.com/wp-content/uploads/2019/11/ILAC-Policy-Brief-Guatemala2-2.pdf.

62. Adriana Beltrán, "Will the Rebellion for the Rule of Law Prevail," pp. 36–60.

63. Ibid.

64. Chavez Alor and McIntosh, *Judicial Nominations in Guatemala.*

65. Ibid.

66. Beltrán, "Will the Rebellion for the Rule of Law Prevail," pp. 36–60.

67. For more information see: *Guatemala's Justice System: Evaluating Capacity Building*.

68. For more information see: Steven Dudley, "The Tennis Shoe King Who Became Guatemala's Gentleman Lobbyist," *InSight Crime*, September 15, 2014, https://www.insightcrime.org/investigations/guatemala-lopez-villatoro-corruption -lobbyist/.

69. Kelly Grant, "Arrest of Guatemala's 'Tennis Shoe King' Could Impact Prosecutor Selection Process," *InSight Crime,* February 27, 2018, https://www.ins ightcrime.org/news/analysis/arrest-of-guatemalas-tennis-shoe-king-could-impact-p rosecutor-selection-process/.

70. Ibid.

71. Ibid.

72. The process was supported by a technical secretariat composed of the CICIG, the attorney general, and the Human Rights Ombudsman, with the support of the office of the UN High Commissioner for Human Rights. At the national level, more than 1,500 people participated in the dialogues, and nearly 250 reform proposals were submitted. From June to August 2016, nearly eighty participants held weekly working group meetings to discuss the proposed reforms in an effort to reach consensus. See: https://www.wola.org/analysis/guatemala-crossroads-reinforce-fight-corruption -reinstate-hidden-powers/.

73. UN Human Rights Council, *Annual Report of the United Nations High Commissioner for Human Rights and Reports of the Office of the High Commissioner and Secretary General* (New York: United Nations General Assembly, 2017), p. 5.

74. Ibid.

75. "¿Está de acuerdo en que la Cicig siga en Guatemala?" ProDatos, Encuesta Libre, data visualization by Sergio Espada, https://gnwebprensalibrerootwest.s3-us -west-2.amazonaws.com/App_Themes/PL/assets_2017/images/redaccion/07PLMT0 5042019%20CICIG/07PLMT05042019%20CICIG/grafico.html.

76. Washington Office on Latin America, "Fact Sheet."

77. Ibid.

78. According to investigators, the FCN party had reported spending a paltry amount of money for the 2015 campaign. The party had failed to provide the monthly and bimonthly financial reports legally required, and those that it had turned in were incomplete. During the 2015 presidential elections, FCN-Nacion had failed to deliver any financing reports to the tribunal the months the first round and second round of elections took place, and in November during the traditional accounting roundup period. The funds for the campaign came from evangelical churches, religious organizations, ex-military officials, and influential members of the private sector. A drug trafficker also allegedly provided funding to the vice president's son for the campaign, although the claim has not been confirmed. For more information see: Héctor Silva Ávalos and Steven Dudley, "President Jimmy Morales' (and Guatemala's) 'Original Sin,'" *InSight Crime*, August 23, 2020, https:/ /www.insightcrime.org/investigations/president-jimmy-morales-guatemalas-origin al-sin/.

79. Sofia Menchu, "Guatemala President's Brother, Son Held on Suspicion of Fraud," *Reuters*, January 18, 2018, https://www.reuters.com/article/us-guate mala-corruption/guatemala-presidents-brother-son-held-on-suspicion-of-fraud-idUS KBN1522NS. In August 2019, Jose Manuel Morales Marroquin and Samuel Morales Cabrera were cleared of charges in a ruling that convicted eleven other people. According to the court, Morales family had misappropriated public funds, but had not committed fraud.

80. Adriana Beltrán, "Is Guatemala's Fight Against Corruption Under Threat? How Its Enemies Are Undermining Progress," *Foreign Affairs*, June 6, 2018, https ://www.foreignaffairs.com/articles/guatemala/2018-06-06/guatemalas-fight-against -corruption-under-threat.

81. *Situación de la Policía Nacional Civil en Guatemala* (Foro de Organizaciones Sociales Especializadas en Temas de Seguridad, 2018) and Mark L. Schneider, "A Moment of Truth for Anti-Corruption and Security in Guatemala," *Center for Strategic International Studies* (CSIS), September 6, 2018.

82. Changes of the police leadership during Minister Enrique Degenhart's tenure include three directors of the national police and three deputy directors, the sub-directors of Criminal Investigations, Operations, Anti-Narcotics Analysis and Information, Police Academy, Support and Logistics, and Personnel, as well as the head of the US-supported wiretapping unit.

83. Hector Silva Avalos, Felipe Puerta, and Kelly Grant, "Ousting of Police Director May Shift Guatemala's Balance of Power," *InSight Crime*, March 2, 2018, https://www.insightcrime.org/news/analysis/guatemala-removes-police-leadership-a mid-anti-corruption-controversy/.

84. Ximena Enriquez, "5 Ways the Guatemalan Government is Trying to Dismantle CICIG," *Americas Quarterly*, September 18, 2018, https://www.americas quarterly.org/content/5-ways-guatemalan-government-trying-dismantle-cicig.

85. Alex Fernando Rojas, "La Cicig terminará su mandato en 2019," *Prensa Libre*, August 31, 2018, https://www.prensalibre.com/guatemala/politica/cicig-te rminara-su-mandato-en-2019/.

86. Sandra Cuffe, "U.S. Gave Military Jeeps To Guatemala To Fight Drug Trafficking. Instead, They Were Used To Intimidate An Anti-corruption Commission," *The Intercept*, https://theintercept.com/2018/11/09/guatemala-crisis-corruption-cicig/ , November 9, 2018.

87. Irving Escobar and Andrea Orozco, "Gobierno da 72 horas a 11 investiga-dores y abogados de Cicig para abandonar el país," *Prensa Libre*, December 18, 2018, https://www.prensalibre.com/guatemala/politica/gobierno-da-72-horas-a-11-investi gadores-y-abogados-de-cicig-para-abandonar-el-pais/.

88. "Luego de más de 24 horas de tensión, y tras fallo de la CC, investigador de Cicig ingresa al país," *Prensa Libre*, January 6, 2019, https://www.prensalibre.com/ guatemala/politica/persiste-tension-en-el-aeropuerto-por-caso-de-investigador-de-la -cicig-yilen-osorio/.

89. "Jimmy Morales termina el acuerdo de Guatemala con la Cicig," *CNN Español*, January 7, 2019, https://cnnespanol.cnn.com/2019/01/07/jimmy-morales-ter mina-el-acuerdo-de-guatemala-con-la-cicig/.

90. Luis Gonzalez, "DIGECAM cancela licencias de portación de armas a personal de CICIG," *República*, January 8, 2019, https://republica.gt/2019/01/08 /digecam-cancela-licencias-de-portacion-de-armas-a-personal-de-cicig/. Following Morales decision to terminate the agreement with the CICIG, the General Directive for the Control of Weapons and Munitions (DIGECAM) revoked the Commission's license that permitted their security personnel to possess and carry weapons. According to Army spokesman Colonel Óscar Pérez, the CICIG was ordered to hand in their weapons registered with the Digecam on January 8, 2019.

91. *Guatemala 2018 Human Rights Report* (US Department of State: 2018), p. 8.

92. Muna Abbas et al., "Invisible Threats: Mitigating The Risk Of Violence From Online Hate Speech Against Human Rights Defenders In Guatemala," *American Bar Association Center for Human Rights* (2019), pp. 15-16.

93. Jody García, "Jimmy, Baldizón and these Business Executives Organized the Lobby Against Todd and the CICIG (Part 1)," *Nómada*, October 20, 2018, https:/ /nomada.gt/pais/entender-la-politica/jimmy-baldizon-and-these-business-executives -organized-the-lobby-against-todd-and-the-cicig-part-1/.

94. Ibid.

95. The first contract was signed by Marvin Mérida, who at the time was serving as Presidential Ambassador for Migration in the United States. According to reports, the contract was for services for the Presidency of Guatemala. When the contract became public, President Morales tried to distance himself from Merida and was dismissed. For more information see: Garcia, "Jimmy, Baldizón and These Business."

96. The second contract was signed by four members of the Guatemalan Congress who were staunch critics of the CICIG, including Jaime Regalado (Reform Movement Party, MR), who has been accused of links to drug trafficking, Fernando Linares Beltranena (National Advancement Party, PAN), lawyer who has representing drug traffickers, Oscar Quintanilla (Citizen Alliance Party, AC), who was implicated in the Transurbano corruption case, and Julio Lainfiesta (Nationalist Change Union Party, UCN), party with ties to drug cartels. For more information see: Garcia, "Jimmy, Baldizón and These Business Executives."

97. Garcia, "Jimmy, Baldizón and These Business Executives."

98. Colum Lynch, "Corrupt Guatemalans' GOP Lifeline," *Foreign Policy*, February 5, 2019, https://foreignpolicy.com/2019/02/05/trump-republican-lawmak ers-weaken-u-n-anti-corruption-commission-guatemala-jimmy-morales-white-house -putin/.

99. Jonathan Blitzer, "The Trump Administration's Self-Defeating Policy Toward the Guatemalan Elections," *The New Yorker*, May 30, 2018, https://www .newyorker.com/news/daily-comment/the-trump-administrations-self-defeating-poli cy-toward-the-guatemalan-elections,

100. Lynch, "Corrupt Guatemalans' GOP."

101. David C. Adams, "Guatemalan Anti-corruption Effort Under Attack, Accused of Colluding with the Kremlin," *Univision*, May 13, 2018, https://www.uni vision.com/univision-news/latin-america/guatemalan-anti-corruption-effort-under-attack-accused-of-colluding-with-the-kremlin.

102. The "migration case" involved a massive fraud ring in which Guatemalan immigration officials charged up to $50,000 for fake passports and other fraudulent documents. At the time, the department was under the direction of Enrique Degenhart, President Morales' second minister of interior. The Public Prosecutor's Office began the investigation in 2010. The whistleblower who had tipped off prosecutors was tortured and killed three months after sounding the alarm. In 2018, a judge convicted thirty-nine people, including lawyers, human traffickers and immigration officials. Among those convicted was the Bitkov family.

103. Beltrán, "Is Guatemala's Fight Against Corruption Under Threat?"

104. House Foreign Affairs Committee Republicans, "Hearing: Advancing U.S. Interests in the Western Hemisphere (EventID=108530)," Filmed [July 2018]. YouTube video, 4:03:13. Posted [July 2018]. https://www.youtube.com/watch?v =NOwqHqzf7pQ&t=5839s

105. Elizabeth Gonzalez, "Guatemala Update: Torres and Giammattei Head to a Runoff," *Americas Quarterly*, June 17, 2019, https://www.as-coa.org/articles/gua temala-update-torres-and-giammattei-head-runoff.

106. Sonny Figueroa, "El surgimiento del Pacto de Corruptos," *Diario La Hora,* December 28, 2017, https://lahora.gt/surgimiento-del-pacto-corruptos/.

107. Figueroa. "El surgimiento del Pacto."

108. Tulio Juárez, "CC ordena suspensión de la comisión anti–CICIG del Congreso," *El Periódico*, October 7, 2019, https://elperiodico.com.gt/nacion/2019/10 /07/cc-ordena-suspension-de-la-comision-anti-cicig-del-congreso/.

109. Sonia D. Pérez, "Guatemala: acusados de corrupción se quejan ante el Congreso," *AP News*, December 13, 2019, https://apnews.com/bb75a48a516a41d5 8f35c5617a764483.

110. Alex Fernando Rojas, "Estado acciona penalmente contra tres magistrados de la CC," *Prensa Libre*, December 26, 2018, https://www.prensalibre.com/guatemala/ justicia/pgn-denuncia-a-tres-magistrados-de-cc-por-tres-delitos/.

111. Willian Cumes, "Organizaciones internacionales de Derechos Humanos piden respetar independencia de la Corte de Constitucionalidad," *Prensa Libre,* August 2, 2019, https://www.prensalibre.com/guatemala/justicia/organizaciones-int ernacionales-de-derechos-humanos-piden-respetar-independencia-de-la-corte-de-con stitucionalidad/.

112. Washington Office on Latin America, "Fact Sheet."

113. The vehicles had been donated by the US Department of Defense to combat drug trafficking and organized crime in border regions.

114. Mike Pompeo, "Our Relationship with Guatemala Is Important. We Greatly Appreciate Guatemala's Efforts in Counternarcotics and Security," September 1, 2018, 7:57 am, https://twitter.com/SecPompeo/status/1035904498580041730.

115. Lynch, "Corrupt Guatemalans' GOP."

116. Ibid.

117. Adriana Beltrán, "Guatemala Is No Safe Third Country: Why the Asylum Deal Is a Mistake," *Foreign Affairs*, September 25, 2019, https://www.foreignaffairs .com/articles/guatemala/2019-09-25/guatemala-no-safe-third-country.

118. Washington on Latin America, "Fact Sheet."

119. The reforms included stronger oversight of parties' campaign contributions, regulation of paid publicity, the strengthening of the sanctioning powers of the electoral tribunal, among other provisions.

120. Blitzer,"The Trump Administration's Self-Defeating Policy Toward the Guatemalan Elections."

121. Adriana Beltrán and Adeline Hite, "Corruption in the Guatemalan Political System and the 2019 Elections," *Washington Office on Latin America,* June 12, 2019, https://www.wola.org/analysis/corruption-in-the-guatemalan-political-system -and-the-2019-elections/.

122. Maureen Taft-Morales, *Guatemala: Corruption, Uncertainty Mar August 2019 Elections* (Congressional Research Service, 2019), pp. 1–2.

123. Beltrán and Hite, "Corruption in the Guatemalan Political System."

124. Ibid.

125. U.S. Department of Justice, "Guatemalan Presidential Candidate Charged With Conspiring To Import Cocaine Into The United States And Related Firearms Offense," *U.S. Attorney's Office Southern District of New York,* April 17, 2019, https ://www.justice.gov/usao-sdny/pr/guatemalan-presidential-candidate-charged-conspi ring-import-cocaine-united-states-and.

126. Ibid.

127. Beltrán and Hite, "Corruption in the Guatemalan Political System."

128. Jody García, "Giammattei es el ganador y Guatemala se las verá con un Jimmy 2.0 o un autoritarismo más radical," *Nómada,* August 12, 2020, https://no mada.gt/pais/elecciones-2019/giammattei-es-el-ganador-y-guatemala-se-las-vera-co n-un-jimmy-2-0-o-un-autoritarismo-mas-radical/.

129. The law is aimed to increase control over non-governmental organizations by giving the government the ability to unregister an NGO without having to go through a legal procedure or provide a mechanism for defense, and allows for more control over internationally provided funds. President Giammattei signed it into law on February 27.

130. In a closed door session and amidst a "State of Calamity" ordered by the government due to the COVID-19, Congress elected the next five magistrates of the Official Electoral Tribunal (TSE) despite legal actions regarding the process pending before the Constitutional Court.

131. Kenneth Monzon, "Juez del caso "Agua Mágica" denuncia que fue insultado por un hombre y fotografiado por policías," *Prensa Libre,* September 14, 2018, https ://www.prensalibre.com/guatemala/justicia/juez-pablo-xitumul-denuncia-que-es-per seguido-fue-insultado-por-un-hombre-y-fotografiado-por-policias/; Sonia D. Perez, "Face of Guatemala's Anti-corruption Fight Faces Threats," *ABC News,* November 25, 2019, https://abcnews.go.com/International/wireStory/face-guatemalas-anti-co rruption-fight-faces-threats-67284186.

132. Francisco Mauricio Martínez, "La elección de magistrados se ha politizado porque es presionada por grupos de interés," *Prensa Libre,* February 19, 2020, https ://www.prensalibre.com/guatemala/justicia/la-eleccion-de-magistrados-se-ha-polit izado-porque-es-presionada-por-grupos-de-interes/.

Chapter 4

Corruption in Colombia

Fernando Cepeda Ulloa

Colombia has been undergoing dramatic transformations for decades. Until the 1970s, Colombia was considered an honest country with small cases of petty corruption.[1] However, the panorama drastically worsened over time. Larceny, for instance, occurred in official financial institutions (1980–1992) such as the Central Mortgage Bank or "Banco Central Hipotecario," the State Bank or "Banco del Estado," and the Agrarian Bank or "Caja Agraria." The privatization of Colpuertos (1991) (the main Port Authority) led to the creation (1992) of a special fund (Foncolpuertos) for the payment of pensions. The historical records were falsified to inflate the value of many individual pensions. It was a multibillion-dollar corruption scandal. Many lawyers and former workers have been sentenced. In addition, the illicit drugs[2] phenomenon corrupted many public and private institutions and became an important source of financing for illegal armed groups.[3]

The aforementioned factors fomented the emergence of criminal networks, particularly political mafia organizations that, through the use of violence, have been able to infiltrate elements of the Colombian state within its various municipalities and states, producing perverse effects at the national, municipal, and regional level. This explanation, however, contrasts with the opinion offered by Professor Robert Dix in his classic book, which features a debate with Malcolm Deas of Oxford University. He states:

> For many years, Colombia has been a country with strong political competition, a poor government and a formidable severe criticism of it. This pattern did not allow exaggerated "serruchos"—popular Spanish expression to refer to briberies. The small proportion of rich Colombians made visible any economic ascent.

Politicians controlled themselves not because of virtue but due to political hate
or jealousy. Presidents and politicians did not become rich during or after being
in power nor bureaucrats.[4]

He continues:

In the last three decades, this panorama has changed (. . .) . New temptations
and opportunities have appeared in the environment (. . .) . I think this is a more
corrupt country than before.[5]

Colombia has experienced high economic growth and a rising middle
class, dramatically altering expectations. A newly developed ambition to get
rich easily and quickly has also arisen as a result. Colombia has been affected
by the booms of an illegal economy in which contraband, illegal transaction
of emeralds, money laundering, and other criminal activities create conditions
which stimulate corrupt behaviors and practices.

CRISIS OF THE TRADITIONAL VALUE SYSTEM

Colombia has been characterized by its austerity and the high value its
citizens give to honesty, but this panorama has transformed these identifying qualities radically. It has been argued that the diminished influence of
the Roman Catholic Church in the school system has eroded the traditional
values in Colombian society. In addition, the mass media in Colombia has
made certain criminals who obtained their wealth through various illegal
activities into celebrities, which has contributed to the model of corruption
in Colombia. Some of these celebrity criminals have become cultural icons,
while noncriminal Colombians remain unnoticed. In sum, the glorification
of the ostentatious criminal lifestyle contributes to the culture of crime and
corruption.

THE DIVISION AND WEAKENING
OF POLITICAL PARTIES

Colombia has had a two-party system for over two centuries. Despite this
factionalism, one could argue that this strong system defends a value system
against corruption. The necessary alliance between the two political parties
(liberal and conservative) to end intraparty violence led to a Constitutional
system of shared power that existed for sixteen years (1958–1974). This
agreement was later extended until 1991 (with one interruption from 1986

to 1990 when the government-opposition model was introduced). Intraparty violent conflict successfully ended in the national, state, and municipal (executive, legislative, and judiciary) levels.[6]

This scheme, however, was easily corruptible, as demonstrated by various scandals in the 1970s. The Constitution of 1991 that replaced the 1886 Constitution fostered a multiparty system that had over sixty political parties and created political chaos. However, recent electoral reforms which occurred in 2003 have reduced the number of parties to ten. Four parties have a significant representation: The Party of Social Unity, the Liberal Party, and the Conservative Party, and the leftist party, Alternative Democratic Pole (Polo Democrático Alternativo). Party fragmentation has caused Colombia to experience what Italians refer to as "personal parties," which are prone to corrupt political exchanges due to campaign finance regulations. Furthermore, the various organized criminal networks have been able to penetrate the state apparatus. The profits from illegal drugs and other illicit activities have eroded institutions and fomented corruption within Colombia.

To some extent, political parties were substituted by "personal parties" that quickly became electoral small businesses. These parties raise funds for their political campaigns, and afterward, reward donors with jobs, contracts, and favors. In some cases, political parties even began buying votes outright. These corrupt activities contributed to the deterioration of the electoral and political decision-making process within democratic Colombia. The corruption scandal in the capital city, known as "the contracting carrousel of Bogotá" ("*carrusel de la contratación en Bogotá*"), began with dubious agreements during the electoral campaign that translated into profitable contracts. Journalists have been investigating the case for more than two years. Civil servants, contractors, and even the mayor of Bogotá are being prosecuted; some of them have been incarcerated.

Nonetheless, we have the appearance of a city with an organized and vigilant civil society, a robust network of mass media and numerous enterprises interested in obtaining contracts with the city government. If a larceny of such dimensions occurred in a city like Bogotá, it is easy to imagine what can happen in other cities or even in small and remote municipalities in Colombia that are rich in resources.

Prior to the corruption scandal, Bogotá had been governed by honest mayors and praised as a model of progress and effective management. However, it is surprising that such things happen when the mayor and the civil servants involved belonged to the left-wing party Polo Democrático Alternativo. The absence of strong, organized, and centralized parties with efficient mechanisms of internal ethical control has contributed to corruption. The various forms of corruption in capital cities as well as lesser municipalities resemble the behavior of organized criminals.

INEFFICACY OF THE JUDICIAL POWER

Colombia has experienced the paradox of having a state governed by the rule of law (high courts, tribunals, proliferation of law schools of varying degrees of quality, an exaggerated attachment to "legal fetishism,") with simultaneous long periods of violence and, situations of impunity and illegality. Madeleine Albright, as US Secretary of State, wrote an article titled "Colombia's struggles How we can help?"[7] Secretary Albright described Colombia's judicial system in the following terms: "*and Colombia's judicial system is plagued by corruption, inadequate resources and a backlog of 3.5 million cases. Success will not come quickly but progress is possible if the Government has international support.*" Despite its harsh tone, Albright's statement was not debated in Colombia. Other criticisms of corruption were made by the Colombian president Alfonso López Michelsen (1974–1978). Professor Gutiérrez Anzola, a reputed professor of criminal law, wrote in 1962 in his book "Violence and Justice" that Colombia had 15 million inhabitants. He contends that the number of judges did not correspond to the number of cases resulting from such a population. This ended in an accumulation of cases that the judicial system was unable to solve.[8] Based on a report of the criminal procurator of the special District of Bogotá, Professor Gutiérrez quoted the following conclusion: "The Special District of Bogotá was under the tyranny of impunity. . . . Only a small number of processes ended in a resolution or sentence of condemnation (3.89 percent). The rest, approximately 90.67 percent of the complaints exceeded the statute of limitations."[9] Gutiérrez Anzola states: "The judge that is able to affirm that his office is capable of dealing with 3,000 records is incompetent and cannot be considered serious."[10] The report quoted by Gutiérrez, issued by the Ministry of Justice and titled "Five years of apparent criminality," asserts: "We are in the brink of a catastrophic national collapse. (. . .) It is a crazy race that leads to a total demoralization. In Antioquia, in 1959, there was a crime occurrence of 58.4 per cent more than in 1955; in Cundinamarca, 57.1 per cent; in Norte de Santander, 49.3 per cent; in Caldas, 45.8 per cent."[11] The same report identified two critical problems that, for our analysis, are useful to remember:

1. The refusal of society and the ruling class to deal with the problem. As stated by the Ministry of Justice, "a society that is responsible for the emergence of crimes, as the Colombian one, has a ruling class that is deaf to the claims of the judicial system and that does not demand more resources for combatting crime."[12]
2. The absence of a criminal policy or examples of an erroneous criminal policy.[13]

Professor Gutiérrez adds: "For many years, an absurd criminal policy has been established in the country via laws and decrees. There is a general ignorance of the problem."[14] This diagnosis does not differ from the opinion of justice secretaries, high civil servants, and professors. It is alarming the lack of statistics that makes the construction of a public policy for justice administration even more difficult. A report written by two researchers of the Center for the Study of Economic Development of Los Andes University openly differs from the statistics that have been published for decades.[15] The authors of this study do not have any reserve in concluding: "Until today, we cannot measure criminal impunity because there is not an official record of the real entries or crimes that reach the criminal system. It is because of that, figures like the one of 99 per cent impunity is only a dangerous myth. We do not know, with certainty, the true figures of crimes, complaints or entries to the criminal system."[16] The researchers argue, "One of the most important questions that we can ask ourselves after the analysis is if the mediocrity and lack of criminal statistics is the result of a general disorder (incompetence-inefficiency) or if a judicial sector has been decidedly obstructing data recollection." The absence of a reliable system of judicial statistics, historical and current, compounds the problem.[17]

The inefficacy of this judicial system invites corruption. In addition, the 99 percent impunity rate only exaggerates the problems of the Colombian judicial system and helps foster corruption. However, we must also recognize the significant efforts some members of Congress, governors, mayors, judges of the Supreme Court of Justice, the attorney general, and the municipal judges have overcome this situation with courage and diligence.

THE IMPACT OF THE ILLICIT DRUG TRADE

In his August 2, 2000, visit, President Bill Clinton stated that the illicit drugs trade phenomenon had exacerbated all the problems of the country, which obviously includes issues of corruption. The combination of the aforementioned factor continues to foster corruption within the state apparatus and, in essence, the illegal armed groups can only be compared to organized crime. Guerrillas, self-defense forces (often referred to as paramilitary groups), and now criminal groups such as the criminal bands (BACRIM) gathered strength and presence in different regions and municipalities of the country.[18] Therefore, these organizations could determine, in some cases, the electoral results through various means of coercion. They developed the capability to appoint members of these groups to key government positions in various agencies, such as the departments of health, education, and infrastructure.

In this vein, these groups were able to capture large amounts of public resources.

The aforementioned organized criminal groups evolved into criminal networks that had links with various national institutions like the Colombian Congress. This was evident during the demobilization of the "paramilitaries" and the confessions of some of the chiefs of these organizations as well as the information found in their computers.[19]

UNCHECKED DECENTRALIZATION

The 1991 Constitution established an ambitious decentralization scheme both in political terms as well as in administrative and budgetary ones. Mayors since 1988 and Governors since 1991 started to assume office via universal suffrage. In addition, more than 50 percent of the total budget is sent to departments and municipalities. Furthermore, the royalties paid by the gas and mining industry (carbon, gold, nickel, and coltan) were directly paid to some municipalities and departments.

In a context of judicial inefficacy, illegal armed groups (guerrilla and "paramilitaries"), personal political parties, wasted taxes and royalties at the national and municipal level, this situation encouraged the government to submit to Congress a proposal to modify the distribution of royalties. The Legislative Act 5 of 2011 constituted a Unique System of Royalties and modified articles 360 and 261 of the Colombian Constitution. This reform recentralizes the management of royalties to avoid corruption and mismanagement.

The political discourse of "recentralization" appeared again in 2013. The Legislative Act 5 of 2011, however, was the only way to temporally control the resources and combat corruption. Decentralization has been viewed as an anticorruption tool; however, the sociopolitical and judicial context in Colombia and the absence of efficient checks have made it a somewhat perverse strategy.

In the regions, municipalities, and cities, instances of corruption have evolved as a result of organized crime or criminal networks.[20] More than 100 congressmen have been investigated by the Supreme Court,[21] or the General Prosecutor's Office. Fifty members of Congress (senators and representatives) have been convicted, demonstrating the power of organized criminal groups and various actors to penetrate the Colombian system, eroding the institutional capacity and integrity of various state apparatuses. The International Criminal Court produced a long list of the proceedings against congressmen.[22] There has been an association to commit crime between some congressmen and criminal organizations like the "paramilitaries." Judicial cases proved a relation with the illegal armed group FARC-EP (Fuerzas Armadas Revolucionarias de Colombia—FARC) and the National Liberation Army (Ejército de Liberación Nacional—ELN) have not been successful.

Luis Jorge Garay and Eduardo Salcedo-Albarán, well-known researchers in Colombia, investigated the social, political, and economic influence of criminal networks in Colombia. They conclude:

> Social Network Analysis (SNA) and Social Network Analysis for Institutional Diagnosis (SNAID) allow us to understand and demonstrate the institutional impacts of the symbiosis between (i) political agents and public officers, (ii) unlawful armed groups and (iii) other criminal networks like those focused on drug trafficking. Furthermore, SNA and SNAID allow us to see how that symbiosis undermines processes of democracy consolidation and peace building. Both processes are affected when formal democratic institutions and even national administrations are at risk of being manipulated by the action of lawful and/ or unlawful agents carrying out processes of Co-opted State Reconfiguration CStR.[23]

This analysis demonstrates that corruption has evolved. Garay illustrates such arguments using three cases and affirms, "There are serious situations in which political leaders, candidates and civil servants have taken advantage of the coercive capacity of criminal groups to perpetuate their political and electoral power."[24] When referring to illegal armed groups, he discusses the municipality of Soledad in Atlántico, a state in the Caribbean coast: "The interaction of some civil servants of the municipal executive branch with 'paramilitaries' or members of the AUC (Autodefensas Unidas de Colombia) was essential to manipulate administrative and contractual processes and favour the perverse interests of criminals."[25] Garay argues that Soledad, Atlántico, is characterized by "serious faults in the provision of health and education services and important mistakes during contracting processes, among others."[26]

The authors examine the state of Arauca and the influence of the guerrilla armed group ELN and prove that there is a criminal network that started operating with the support and participation of civil society organizations in the 1980s. The guerrilla group could "decide over the administrative procedures, especially the contractual ones."[27] "In this sense, important resources of the national budget aimed to improve education, sanitation and infrastructure ended up in hands of contractors that were allied to the ELN and did not meet the requisites and qualifications for handling complex contracts."[28]

FINANCING POLITICS

Several factors have increased the costs of political campaigns in Colombia:

- The decay of political parties
- The emergence of "personal" parties
- With the 1991 Constitution, the enactment of a national electoral constituency meaning that senators need to campaign in various states or departments
- An increase in the cost of media and new modern electoral technology

State campaign financing is not enough to be elected.[29] The sheer cost of running for office leads to the temptation of making pacts with armed illegal groups, drug traffickers, organized criminal networks, investors, contractors, and various other criminal activities.

THE WEAKNESS OF THE OPPOSITION

Historically, Colombia has experienced party hegemonies and coalition governments. From 1958 on, the only exception has been the 1986–1990 government of President Virgilio Barco. Two-party coalitions were constitutionally ordered from 1958 to 1974. Since then, "adequate and fair participation" was constitutionally ordered. In 1986, the Conservative Party decided not to participate in the Cabinet as it believed that the number of secretaries (three out of thirteen) granted by President Barco was insufficient. From 1991 onward, government coalitions have not been constitutionally enacted but have been necessary to obtain democratic governability.[30] The weakness of the opposition, which today does not represent more than 10 percent of the total votes in Congress, facilitates corruption at the national level. State Assemblies and Municipal Councils lack attentive and watchful servants.

GOVERNMENT WEAKNESS AND TOOLS
TO COMBAT CORRUPTION

Traditionally, Colombia has had weak governments. Even the dictatorship spanning from 1953 to 1957 was called a *dictablanda* or "weak dictatorship." President Álvaro Uribe (2002–2010) fortified the armed forces as well as the state apparatus. However, the efficiency of public institutions leaves a lot to be desired, and weak governments facilitate corruption.

Yet Colombia has valuable experience in fighting some aspects of corruption and can offer its experience to other countries. Its efforts have been significant, but not enough, to deal with the enormous challenges it faces daily such as the power of the various criminal networks. Recently, the attorney general announced a reorientation of the Colombian General Prosecutor's Office strategy to combat organized crime. Colombia has created several useful tools to fight corruption:

1. In 1991, Colombia ruled out parliamentary immunity. A special privilege administered by the Supreme Court of Justice appeared in its place. It is an exemplary measure as the Court has been quite efficient in prosecuting and condemning congressmen.
2. The Colombian Constitution introduced the figure of "*pérdida de investidura*" (political death). It is a measure aimed to sanction elected congressmen, representatives, councilmen, and councilors that violate the Conflict of Interest Statute or other legal norms. More than 50 congressmen and more than 150 elected councilmen and deputies have been sanctioned by the State Council (*Consejo de Estado*).[31]
3. Under the Decree 1895 of 1989, illicit enrichment was criminalized. High public servants and congressmen were called to Court in the famous "8.000 process" that investigated the events surrounding the illegal funding of the 1994 presidential campaign.
4. The general comptroller (article 168 of the Constitution) and the general procurator of the Nation (article 278 of the Constitution) have the power to dismiss public servants via a simplified procedure. The procurator has used this tool more times than the comptroller and has affected members of the National Congress, ministers, governors, and mayors.
5. President Juan Manuel Santos introduced a similar strategy to the one he used when he acted as secretary of defense under the Uribe administration. He identified high-level objectives that are monitored by elite groups (Comptroller, Procurator, Attorney General, National Intelligence service, etc.). Thanks to this strategy, the government was able to identify three critical cases: (1) Corruption within the National Tax Agency (fictitious exportations); (2) An investigation of one of the most prestigious health providers of the country "Saludcoop" for fictitious payments, double payments, and inflated invoices; (3) The existence of "phantom" students and schools. In all three cases, the government could act rapidly and dismantle criminal networks. The capture and initial prosecution of the chiefs and implied servants were shown almost immediately on TV.

Colombia has been successful in applying conventional methods to combat "petty corruption." The efficacy of international treaties and conventions against corruption and the recommendations of multilateral organisms have been precarious. The same can be said of the Anti-Corruption Statues or the Office of the Anti-Corruption Czar. Colombia adhered to the OECD Convention on Combatting Bribery that is very well monitored and has had results in many countries. A March 2013 survey showed that 62 percent of investors and CEO's in Colombia consider that without the payment of bribes no contract or transaction is made. The average bribe payments is of 14.8 percent of the contract value.[32] At the same time, scandals in the private sector complicate the corruption picture. INTERBOLSA, the main actor in the Colombian Stock Exchange, is under investigation both by the pertinent agency and the Prosecutor's Office.[33]

CURRENT DEVELOPMENTS

Corruption in Colombia has evolved since this chapter was originally written. As of November 2017, it is clear that the phenomenon has acquired extraordinary dimensions, to the point that it is practically considered a national emergency and may become the central theme of the ongoing electoral process. The elections were held for the Congress, Departmental Assemblies, Municipal Councils on March 11, 2018, and for the president of the Republic in May 2018.

It is obvious that governmental strategies for combating corruption, such as the one established by the document of the Council of the National Economic and Social Policy on December 9, 2013, have failed. Moreover, the metamorphosis of corruption has led to the proliferation of organizations in the fashion of the drug cartels. They include criminal organizations, such as cartels for municipal contracts, cartels for school meal plans, cartels for health sector programs (to assist nonexistent patients, to relabel expired drugs, to overcharge for medical services, or to treat nonexistent cases of hemophilia). There are also cartels within the education system, and cartels that issue construction licenses without meeting quality requirements, cartels that issue driver's licenses, cartels that issue tender contracts at any level of government (municipal, departmental, national). The most critical and alarming of these has been *el cartel de la toga*, or the gown cartel, integrated by magistrate judges of the Supreme Court of Justice, lawyers, congressmen, and other public servants who manipulate judicial decisions at the highest level. This situation is unprecedented for Colombia and it has resulted in several proposals designed to address these issues.

The issue of corruption, organized crime, and criminal networks has been taking over both the public and the private sectors. They have triggered all alarms and are responsible for a great deal of the distrustfulness and suspiciousness among Colombians toward their institutions and authorities. Public opinion surveys show dramatic figures in this respect. It is worth describing briefly the modus operandi of the gown cartel. Although there had been rumors about its existence, they did not lead to any decisive action. It became clear how it was distorting the functioning of justice at the highest level only after the US Drug Enforcement Administration (DEA) in Miami, in collaboration with the Office of the Attorney General of Colombia, intercepted some recordings of this criminal arrangement. The DEA found a conversation between the ex-national director of Anti-Corruption, Luis Gustavo Moreno, and the ex-governor of the Department of Córdoba, Alejandro Lyons, who was under DEA protection. This conversation revealed that the criminal organization was rooted in the same department of Córdoba, in the National Congress, in the Attorney General Office and in the Supreme Court of Justice. Arguably, the Court and the Office of the Attorney General's were the source of an extortion mechanism against the congressmen accused of links with criminal organizations (*autodefensas*, wrongly named paramilitaries). Magistrate judges, assistant attorneys, and lawyers, among others demanded bribes in exchange for favorable rulings in these cases. The extortion amounts went as high as 10 million pesos (approximately US$3 million) and were lowered down to 2 million pesos after the negotiations. The governor's office has also been involved, as the congressmen used public funds—over which they exerted control through the governor—to pay their extortion fees.

The whole scheme is outrageous. However, even more scandalous is the fact that the congressmen, possibly the most influential ones, victims of this humiliating and insolent blackmail, had no courage to inform the President of the Republic, the Minister of Justice or the Attorney General, to whom they had regular access. If it was not for the DEA recordings in Miami, made public in the mid-2017, we would have never learned about such a serious situation. We had been reading for months the different versions about how this cartel operated. On November 8, for example, the former anticorruption chief, who had been under arrest for several months, described to the commission of investigation and prosecution of the House of Representatives the real workings of this criminal network at the highest levels of the judicial and political systems.

There are more stories in this respect. On November 9, 2017, *El Tiempo* published an "explosive testimony" by a well-known ex-senator from an influential family at the Atlantic Coast, Piedad Zuccardi in which she revealed the details of the extortion scheme that included the use of lawyers recommended by the judges themselves, and the use of false witnesses.[34] One is left wondering, for how long has this cartel operated? How many judicial decisions have been affected? How many innocent high-level officials have been convicted for not accepting these procedures?

The process has started. At least a former president of the Supreme Court has been in prison for over a month. In addition, at least three other judges are under investigation. The former anticorruption director Luis Gustavo Moreno has been under arrest for several months as well. What is even more astonishing is that apparently the same cartel promoted him to the level of an anticorruption chief. Previously, he was a private lawyer.

There is evidence about similar situations in regional tribunals. This may well be the case for courts and attorney general offices. Thus, it is safe to say that the reputation of the justice system in Colombia today is in deep crisis. As San Agustin, the bishop of Hipona, forcefully argues in his famous book *The City of God*, "and without justice, the kingdoms are nothing but big robberies."

The case of the Brazilian multinational Odebrecht, made public in December 2016, revealed criminal activities of the company, which had been operating as a transnational criminal enterprise. The New York judge Robert L. Capers, who shed light on the systemic bribe payments, also mentioned Colombia.[35] He argued that the Odebrecht holding had paid over US$11 million in bribes in Colombia to ensure the contracts for public works that brought more than US$50 million in revenues to the company. The judge provided concrete evidence of a US$6.5 million bribe to a public official who could influence the decisions. Soon after, Colombia's attorney general arrested the official who turned out to be a vice-minister of the Ministry of Transport and Public Works. He quickly accepted the charges and decided to collaborate with the investigation. Today, the public prosecutor assures that these bribes reached over US$30 million. This case compromised the National Infrastructure Agency (Agencia Nacional de Infraestructura—ANI) considered a model institution for distribution of resources for public works both nationally and internationally. Therefore, it became evident that criminal networks had been operating at the three levels of public administration: national, departmental, and municipal. The same senators who were involved in the "gown cartel" scandal are embroiled in the corruption network concerned with infrastructure contracts financed by the national budget or international loans.

Furthermore, allocation of tenders at the departmental and municipal levels has been investigated both by the Colombian Society of Engineers and by the Colombian Infrastructure Chamber. According to the data about the distortion and manipulation of the system, the decrease in the number of bids is alarming. It usually does not exceed three. Besides, there are known mechanisms all over the world that allocate tenders for public works through friendships and favors which makes the whole process just a simulation.

The former president César Gaviria denounced the existence in Colombia of the "politician-contractor" several times. He referred to politicians at different levels of the administration who receive and carry out contracts, often in a precarious manner, with payouts to the corresponding administrations generated from the same exorbitant profits. Without a doubt, it is a mechanism for personal enrichment and, occasionally, an inappropriate way of financing their political activities. The Odebrecht case demonstrated the connection between financing of political campaigns and state contracts for public works. For this reason, the US justice system demanded that Odebrecht provide information about financing political campaigns or politicians.

Unfortunately, there is no clear understanding of this wicked association that has been globalized nowadays. I must admit that I have insisted for decades that at least the presidential campaign be financed completely with public funds. It is of the utmost importance to place presidential candidates above any suspicion of being part of pacts of reciprocity, "do ut des," "quid pro quo," or an exchange of favors that seriously contaminates the policy making process and allocation of contracts. It is a distorted democracy, which is an issue that has long been at the center of discussion in the United States and in the Supreme Court of Justice of Colombia. It was the central theme of the 2016 presidential campaign and is still an unresolved matter both in Colombia and outside.

Unfortunately, the Electoral Observation Mission that was expected to develop an electoral reform in accordance with the Colombian Peace Accords (signed in Havana and Bogotá's Teatro Colón) did not take a decisive stance in this respect and only expressed its support for a greater public financing. With this move, it left open a potential opportunity for the FARC to finance their proselytizing activity with hidden multimillionaire resources. The report by Douglas Farah presented to the US congressional subcommittee, in which he ensured that the FARC had laundered over US$2 million vía Venezuela, Nicaragua, and ad-hoc companies, fuels the worst suspicions in this matter.[36]

We are left wondering how a country with such a respectable tradition as Colombia could have witnessed such a dramatic ethical deterioration of its justice system. Besides the factors mentioned in the chapter, at least two additional ones have been crucial in this disgraceful situation:

1. The judicialization of politics has led to the politicization of justice. The participation of the Supreme Court, the Constitutional Court, and the Council of State in the process of the election of the Attorney General, the Comptroller General of the Republic, and the Prosecutor General resulted in an excessive ambition on the part of these court members to participate in the distribution of positions and contracts within these institutions, that administer bulks of budgets and payrolls. At the same time, the 1991 Constitution granted the authority to the Supreme Court

of Justice to try senators and representatives in court. This created a
dependency that led to the judicialization of politics and to the further
politicization of justice in its worst form.

2. The Comptroller General of the Republic recognizes that the important
democratic advances of the 1991 Constitution, such as the popular election of governors (32), the election of mayors since 1988 (in more than
1,000 municipalities), and the election of senators by a national constituency (quasi mini presidential), generated the need to obtain inexistent
resources for politicians or political parties. This, in turn, led to criminal
behaviors that ranged from criminal organizations (drug cartels, self-
defense groups, and paramilitaries) to the control and manipulation of
public funds at the departmental, municipal, and sometimes, national
levels to ensure the financing of political campaigns. Moreover, it led
to pacts with contractors in advance to obtain resources in exchange for
contracts.

The issue of investiture loss that allows the Council of State to declare
the political death of a congressman has generated a similar situation. This
explains the reason for which this institution, so efficient in its first years
(after 1991), has become less relevant.

For this reason, many experts agree on suggesting two key reforms as
effective tools to combat these new forms of organized crime or criminal
networks. First, to make financing of all campaigns public (it is evident that
the systems of control do not work properly). And second, to prohibit preferential voting, or the use of open electoral rosters that make each candidate
compete against other roster members for the highest number of votes. This
leads almost certainly to the previously described criminal behavior.

Undoubtedly, the effect of drug cartels and other types of criminal organizations have been extremely pernicious and have enormously debilitated
Colombian democracy. Fortunately, the strength of the democratic, civil,
electoral, and legal tradition in Colombia, as well as the courage and honesty of many, have allowed for institutions to endure the permeating threats.
Today, the same Supreme Court judges put their former colleagues on trial,
bringing back the dignity and majesty these institutions deserve.

CONCLUSION

Colombia should be admired as its judges prefer death to bribes. We can say
the same about most of the citizens that have maintained honesty and have
rejected different forms of corruption. The illicit drugs criminal phenomenon
that has stricken the country since the 1970s was instrumental to promote

corrupt behaviors that ended up in criminal networks. This tendency weakened the state and Colombia's law enforcement institutions.

The state and society have combated corruption heroically. Presidential candidates, congressmen, Supreme Court judges, judges, members of the armed forces, governors, mayors, ministers, members of political or business families, and witnesses have been brutally killed or have suffered the effects of extortion and kidnapping. There is a portion of the population, nevertheless, that betrayed trust and honesty.

Colombia's weak democracy could stand against the terrible menace of illegal drugs, corruption, and organized crime. The task, however, is incomplete as today; there are criminal and organized criminal networks that are more dangerous and powerful than the illegal groups of the past. The Supreme Court of Justice, the State Council, the Constitutional Court, the Prosecutor's Office, the procurator, and the comptroller have made extraordinary achievements and their work is recognized as courageous and valuable. Of course, there have been notable exceptions. We should analyze the behavior of honest citizens. Despite many complex and difficult situations like the ones Colombia has suffered, honesty is more present than corruption, a fact that we cannot forget.

NOTES

1. Thanks to Nicolás Ávila for translating this work from Spanish to English. Thanks to Yulia Vorobyeva for her translation assistance. This chapter is from Fernando Cepeda Ulloa, "Corruption in Colombia," in *The Criminalization of States: The Relationship between States and Organized Crime*, eds. Jonathan D. Rosen, Bruce Bagley, and Jorge Chabat (Lanham, MD: Lexington Books, 2019): pp. 255–279.

2. For more on drug trafficking and violence in Colombia, see Jennifer S. Holmes, Sheila Amin Gutiéreez de Piñeres, and Kevin M. Curtin, *Guns, Drugs & Development in Colombia* (Austin, TX: University of Texas Press, 2008).

3. María Alejandra Velez, *FARC-ELN evolución y expansión territroial. Documente 2000-2008* (Bogotá: CECE, Universidad de los Andes, 2000); Pulido Villamarín and Luis Alberto, *El cartel de las FARC* (Bogotá: Ediciones El Faraón, 1996).

4. Malcolm Deas, "Siete especulaciones sobre la corrupción en Colombia." *Política colombiana* 3, no. 3 (1993). Quoted in Fernando Cepeda Ulloa, Narcotráfico, financiación política y corrupción (Bogotá: CO Ecoe Ediciones, 2011), prologue.

5. Ibid.

6. For more on the formation of modern Colombia, see David Bushnell, *The Making of Modern Colombia: A Nation in Spite of Itself* (Berkeley and Los Angeles: University of California Press, 1993); the more complete work on political parties is Felipe Botero, comp., *Partidos y elecciones en Colombia* (Bogotá: Ediciones Uniandes, 2010).

7. (The New York Times, August 10, 1999).

8. J. E. Gutiérrez Anzola, *Violencia y Justicia* (Bogotá: Tercer Mundo, 1962), 12.

9. The data is based on the report written by the government official for criminal issues in Bogotá, Hugo Humberto Rodríguez in 1961.

10. Ibid., p. 105.

11. Ibid., p. 117.

12. Ibid.

13. Ibid., p. 111, 117, and 119.

14. Ibid., p. 121.

15. Elvira María Restrepo y Mariana Martínez Cuéllar, *Impunidad penal: mitos y realidades* (Bogotá: CEDE Document 2004).

16. Ibid, p. 34.

17. Ibid., pp. 34–36.

18. For more on the BACRIM, see Bruce Bagley, *Drug Trafficking and Organized Crime in the Americas: Major Trends in the 21st Century* (Washington, DC: Woodrow Wilson International Center for Scholars, 2012), pp. 7–9. See also Bilal Y. Saab and Alexandra W. Taylor, Criminality and Armed Groups: A comparative study of FARC and Paramilitary Groups in Colombia. *Studies in conflict and Terrorism* 32 (2009): 455–475. See also Mónica Serrano and María Celia Toro, "From Drug Trafficking to Transnational Organized Crime in Latin America," in *Transnational Organized Crime and International Security*, eds. Mats Berdal and Mónica Serrano (Boulder: Lynne Rienner Publishers, 2002). Mauricio Romero, "Changing identities and Contested Settings: Regional Elites and Paramilitaries in Colombia," *International Journal of Politics, Culture and Society* 14, no. 1, (2000): pp. 51–69.

19. L. J. Garay and E. Salcedo, *Redes ilícitas y reconfiguración del Estado: el caso Colombia.* (Bogotá: Fundación Vortex, 2012).

20. Ibid.

21. Corte Suprema de Justicia, Procesos contra aforados constitucionales (parapolítica). Compilación de Autos y Sentencias (Dic. 2007-Sept. 2010).

22. International Criminal Court. Situation in Colombia: Interim Report, Nov. 2012.

23. Institutional impact of criminal networks in Colombia and Mexico, Luis Jorge Garay-Salamanca y Eduardo Salcedo-Albarán, Published online: 25 November 2011. # Springer Science+Business Media B.V. 2011.

24. Garay and Salcedo, *Redes ilícitas y reconfiguración del Estado: el caso Colombia*, pp. 14–15.

25. Ibid., p. 15.

26. Ibid.

27. Ibid.

28. Ibid., p. 7.

29. Fernadno Cepeda Ulloa, *Narcotráfico, financiación política y corrupción* (Bogotá: ECOE, 2011).

30. Fernando Cepeda Ulloa, *La mesa de Unidad Nacional* (Bogotá: ECOE, 2011).

31. Fernando Cepeda Ulloa, *Pérdida de investidura 1991-2011: una herramienta eficaz contra la corrupción de los congresistas, diputados y concejales* (Bogotá: ECOE, 2011).

32. Survey prepared by International Transparency and the Universidad Externado de Colombia, issued March 12, 2013.

33. Alberto Donadio, *El cartel de Interbolsa: Crónica de una estafa financiera* (Colombia: Editorial Sílaba, 2013).

34. Unidad Investigativa, "El explosivo testimonio de Zuccardi contra el 'cartel de la toga,'" *El Tiempo*, 9 de noviembre de 2017.

35. For more, see: "Odebrecht and Braskem Plead Guilty and Agree to Pay at Least \$3.5 Billion in Global Penalties to Resolve Largest Foreign Bribery Case in History," The United States Department of Justice, December 21, 2016.

36. For more, see: Douglas Farah, "Terrorist Groups in Latin America: The Changing Landscape," Testimony Before the House Foreign Affairs Subcommittee on Terrorism, Nonproliferation and Trade, February 4, 2014.

Chapter 5

Corruption in Peru in the Twenty-First Century

A Tsunami of Scandals, A Tsunami of Prosecutions

Cynthia McClintock

As of 2019, all four past Peruvian presidents since the country's return to democracy in 2001 had been prosecuted for corruption. Alejandro Toledo (2001–2006) was in jail in the United States upon Peru's extradition request; Alan García (2006–2011) committed suicide rather than submit to pretrial detention; both Ollanta Humala (2011–2016) and Pedro Pablo Kuczynski (2016–2018) faced trial. In addition, Keiko Fujimori, the runner-up in Peru's 2011 and 2016 elections and the leader of Peru's strongest party, was in pretrial detention.

The prosecution of the entire set of Peru's top 2001–2016 leaders raises numerous questions. First, is corruption in Peru worse than in other Latin American countries? Although corruption, by its hidden nature, is very difficult to measure, the answer is almost certainly: no. Peru's five leaders were charged with wrongdoing related to Brazil's giant construction company, Odebrecht; Odebrecht has reported the payment of $29 million in bribes in Peru, but also $10 million in Mexico, $33 million in Ecuador, $59 million in Panama, $92 million in the Dominican Republic, and $98 million in Venezuela.[1] In expert assessments of the rule of law among Latin American nations, Peru ranks approximately average.[2] In surveys by Latinobarometer between 2005 and 2015, the percentage of Peruvians who had direct knowledge of a corrupt act over the previous year was considerably below the average (although in surveys by the Americas Barometer for a similar time frame, the percentage of Peruvians who reported that they had been solicited for a bribe by a public official over the last year was higher than average).[3]

A second question raised by the prosecution of Peru's 2001–2016 leaders is: In the twenty-first century, did corruption among Peru's top politicians worsen? The next section of this chapter addresses this question; again, although corruption is very difficult to measure, the answer is almost certainly no. Egregious corruption among political elites in Peru has been long-standing since Peru's conquest and colonization. However, as the subsequent section addresses, abetted by the drug trade and organized crime, the opportunities and rewards for corruption are greater in the twenty-first century, and broader swathes of authorities are caught up in corrupt circles than in the past.

This chapter argues that the prosecutions of Peru's 2001–2016 leaders shows that, as democracy took hold after 2000 and hemispheric anticorruption initiatives intensified, Peru's investigative journalists, prosecutors, and judges were more willing and able to combat corruption. Amid the visible evidence on Peru's media, Peruvians' tolerance of corruption dissipated, helping the current president, Martín Vizcarra, to stake his presidency on the anticorruption effort and initiate significant reform efforts. Since 2016, the prosecution of corruption has gone further in Peru than in any other Latin American country except Brazil.[4]

Still, to date, Peru's anticorruption forces have won only a battle: politicians are on clearer notice than ever before that they are not before the law. However, until corruption is in fact dramatically reduced in Peru, the war has not been won. Further, the war could be lost due to concerns that, amid the tsunami of prosecutions, Peru's judiciary has overreached, insufficiently respecting due process. The war could also be lost due to Peruvians' mounting cynicism and dissatisfaction with democracy, possibly leading to its erosion or even breakdown.

Prior to addressing these questions, it must be asked: What is "corruption"? The traditional definition is "the abuse of public power for private gain," but this definition is imperfect; a recent alternative is "the privatization of public policy."[5] The primary concern about the traditional definition is that it omits the role of corporations, criminals, and other private actors in tolerating and instigating corruption; it omits the possibility of the "corporate capture of the state."[6] A second concern is that the traditional definition does not distinguish between petty corruption and grand-scale corruption; arguably, in some contexts petty corruption is more like a tip for service and does not affect public policy or hurt other people.

CORRUPTION IN PERU PRIOR TO
THE TWENTY-FIRST CENTURY

Like most Latin American countries, Peru has a long history of corruption, initiated during the Spanish conquest and colonization. By the estimate of

Alfonso Quiroz, the scholar who has most rigorously studied the problem, the cost of corruption by Peruvian governments since independence was never below 24 percent of public expenditure or 1 percent of GDP.[7] Overall, authoritarian governments were considerably more corrupt than democratic governments, but democratic governments were far from immune.[8] With rare exceptions, impunity was the rule. Most frequently, political leaders took illegal commissions from financial contracts by the state, in particular contracts for public works (such as those by Odebrecht) and military purchases. Also frequently, huge public investments would be made for private purposes; for example, investment in an irrigation project, with the newly fertile land allocated to relatives or cronies.

When in 1532 Francisco Pizarro's forces conquered the Incan empire, they were attracted by Peru's abundant gold, silver, and mercury. Peru became a source of tremendous treasure for Spain. Yet the colonial administration was replete with abuse. At Peru's mines, colonial authorities, merchants, and mine administrators colluded in illegal trade, fraudulent accounting, and the circumvention of technical requirements. The Spanish Crown's district authorities, judges, priests, and landowners disregarded the rules for tribute from Peru's indigenous peoples and collected as much as they could—by force if necessary—and regularly falsely reported revenues

In Quiroz's estimate, the first decade of independence in 1824 was the most corrupt in Peru's history, with the cost of corruption at 139 percent of public expenditures and 6.1 percent of GDP.[9] Rival military caudillos (strongmen on horseback) struggled to gain executive power; they confiscated property and mobilized supporters through promises of future rewards from public office. The caudillo presidents immediately contracted major foreign loans under onerous terms for military expenses and other unproductive endeavors—and almost immediately defaulted. Public credit collapsed.

Another exceptionally corrupt period was provoked by a boom in guano (dung deposited on Peru's shores by sea birds, which in 1840 was discovered to be an excellent fertilizer). Peru's state owned the rights to the guano; to gain the licenses to collect and export the guano, merchants bribed state authorities. The revenues from guano were large—but mismanaged. Ultimately, in the late 1860s to the early 1870s, Peru's guano was depleted and world prices for commodities dropped; a severe financial crisis erupted.

The eleven-year authoritarian government of Augusto Leguía (1919–1930), called the *Oncenio*, is also deemed exceptionally corrupt. Building close ties to the United States, Leguía's regime gained huge loans from the US banks for public works (especially roads) and major investments from the US companies in oil and mining. But the benefits for most Peruvians were scant. By one estimate, at most 30 percent of loan funds were spent on actual public works while 70 percent were diverted by corruption.[10] From 1916 to 1934 only 16 percent of the value of the total sales of the US-owned International

Petroleum Company stayed in Peru in the form of wages, taxes, or other payments.[11]

Amid the Great Depression, the Leguía regime was overthrown in 1930. Unusually, Leguía was arrested on charges of misappropriation of funds and confined until his death in 1932. Under the terms of a special court established by the new government, 664 formal accusations against former officials were made, 75 of the former officials were tried, but only approximately 10 convicted and punished.[12]

In Quiroz's estimate, since Leguía's *Oncenio*, Peru's most corrupt government was the government of Alberto Fujimori, costing Peru more than $2 billion; Fujimori himself stole about $400 million and his partner, Vladimiro Montesinos, $450 million.[13] Elected in 1990, Fujimori carried out a "self-coup" (*autogolpe*) in 1992 and subsequently was widely deemed authoritarian. Among their paths to enrichment were illegal commissions from privatization deals, arms purchases, and import agreements with China as well as the misappropriation of foreign charity funds.[14]

The catalyst of the regime's demise in 2000 was a videotape showing Montesinos bribing a congressman. As evidence of wrongdoing mounted, first Montesinos and then Fujimori fled Peru; Fujimori found safe haven in Japan. Ultimately, however, with a return to democracy, impunity did not reign. Montesinos and Fujimori were tried in Peru, convicted, and imprisoned (where, as of the writing of this chapter, they remain); more than 1,400 individuals were investigated, 187 arrested, and 58 convicted.[15]

Corruption extended way beyond the top tiers of government. Bureaucrats routinely demanded personal payments for their work. "Tramitadores" [people whose job is to make "arreglos"—deals with bureaucrats] were numerous. By one estimate, in the 1980s–1990s, 75 percent of Peru's bureaucrats were guilty of taking payments for their work—usually, small payments, but sometimes large.[16]

CORRUPTION AT THE APEX OF POWER IN THE TWENTY-FIRST CENTURY: THE VAST TENTACLES OF ODEBRECHT

Peru's last four former presidents—Toledo, García, Humala, and Kuczynski—as well as Fujimori were prosecuted for taking bribes for government contracts from Odebrecht and for illegally taking campaign funds from the company. The scandal erupted in mid-2016, when Odebrecht acknowledged, in a plea bargain with the US government, that from approximately 2005–2014 it paid $737 million in bribes across ten Latin American countries, including the $29 million in Peru.[17]

Odebrecht initiated projects in Peru in the late 1970s. During the government of Alberto Fujimori (1990–2000, widely deemed authoritarian after 1992), Odebrecht gained twenty-eight government contracts for public works, spanning roads, irrigation canals, and water treatment plants, and became the country's top construction firm.[18] Odebrecht's head, Marcelo Odebrecht, knew Peru's top leaders personally and, based in Lima since 1997, the company's representative, Jorge Barata, mingled easily with Peru's top business elites.

The most egregious actions by Odebrecht were massive bribes for government contracts for exorbitant projects. Particularly reprehensible were its bribes for contracts for the Interoceanic Highway (also called the Trans-Amazon Highway), which crosses the Amazon and the Andes to connect Brazil and Peru. When construction began in 2005, the project was to cost about $1 billion; but charges ballooned and, when construction was completed in 2010, the cost was more than $4 billion.[19] Per kilometer, the cost was $3.4 million, deemed "incredible" in contrast to the average cost of $900,000 per kilometer in Peru.[20] It was the "most expensive highway ever constructed."[21] Further, the road was very damaging to the fragile environment of the Amazon; not only was forest razed but, with the new road, illegal logging increased.

It was for the contract for the Interoceanic Highway that Odebrecht reported payments of $20 million for Toledo. And, it was for consulting related to the highway that Odebrecht reported payments of $750,000 to one of Kuczynski's firms, Westfield, and more than $4 million to another, First Capital.[22] Although these contracts were not strictly illegal, Kuczynski had served as economic minister and prime minister during the Toledo government, and at one point had opposed the construction of the highway.[23] As president in 2016, Kuczynski denied any dealings with Odebrecht; then, when evidence of payments emerged, he claimed that the arrangements were exclusively between Odebrecht and his business partner, Gerardo Sepúlveda. But amid twists and turns in Kuczynski's accounts, his claim was not credible to most Peruvians. It was in this context that Kuczynski barely survived an impeachment vote in December 2017; however, after the release in March 2018 of a videotape that showed Kuczynski's allies trying to bribe a legislator for his vote against impeachment, he had no chance to survive, and he resigned.

A second major Odebrecht project was the Lima Metro (Line 1), built during the government of Alan García. In contrast to the Interoceanic Highway, the cost of the metro was not exorbitant and, serving more than 300,000 passengers per day, it is environmentally favorable.[24] However, in April 2019, Odebrecht reported $14 million in bribes to high-ranking figures, in particular officials at the Ministry of Transportation and Communication, for the contract.[25]

In addition to bribes for construction projects, Odebrecht made campaign contributions to all major 2006 and 2011 presidential candidates. These contributions were not reported as required by law and, accordingly, were prosecuted as crimes of money laundering. For the 2011 election, Odebrecht donated $3 million to the winner, Humala; $1.2 million to the runner-up, Keiko Fujimori; $700,000 to Toledo; and $300,000 to Kuczynski.[26] It was for these crimes that Ollanta Humala, his wife Nadine, and Keiko were charged. In addition, in 2013, Odebrecht provided $3 million to the then mayor of Lima, Susana Villarán, for the defeat of a recall effort against her; she was also prosecuted.

GLOBAL TRADE AND THE BROADENING SWATHE OF CORRUPTION IN THE TWENTY-FIRST CENTURY

Although it is very unlikely that corruption among Peru's top leaders was greater in 2000–2016 than in the twentieth century, it is likely that the swathe of corruption was broader, ensnaring a larger number of Peruvians. Beginning in the 1980s, the illicit global drug trade escalated; in the twenty-first century, new hemispheric environmental norms emerged, catalyzing illicit practices in mining and logging.

Despite decades of the "war on drugs," including regular offensives by Peru's security forces against coca cultivators and traffickers, global demand for cocaine has continued, and supply from the Andean nations has too. Since the 1980s, Peru and Colombia have vied as the world's largest cultivators of coca; the area under cultivation in Peru between 2010 and 2017 was between 40,000 and 60,000 hectares.[27] In the 2010s, the area of greatest cultivation was in the Valley of the Apurímac, Ene, and Mantaro Rivers (VRAEM), on the remote eastern slopes of the Andean mountains. In the VRAEM, drug producers and traffickers allied with about several hundred remnant fighters from the Shining Path (*Sendero Luminoso*) insurgency, which ignited war in Peru from 1980 to 1992.

The drug trade is immense. By one estimate, the value of Peru's coca-based exports was $22 billion in 2008—Peru's leading export and approximately 70 percent of the value of all legal exports.[28] In another estimate, the number of Peruvians involved in some way in the drug trade was about $2 million, or seven percent of the population.[29] In 2012, just one of many money launderers active in one remote coca-producing area of Peru was laundering more than $100 million.[30] Perhaps fifteen drug kingpins, controlling Peru's major exit points for drugs (several ports on the Pacific coast, especially Callao, bordering Lima, and airstrips near Bolivia and Brazil), amassed wealth to the tune of "tens of millions."[31]

With these revenues, drug traffickers bribed security forces for the safe transit of drugs, bribed judges for favorable rulings, and bribed politicians for both goals. Corruption was severe. Peru's security forces were so compromised that cocaine was at times transported from the VRAEM to Callao in military helicopters.[32] In the metaphor of a retired general, "[Assigning Peru's military to counternarcotics in the VRAEM is tantamount to assigning] four street dogs to guard a plate of beefsteak."[33] One notorious scandal during García's 2006–2011 term was dubbed the *narcoindultos*: the commutation of the sentences of more than 3,000 convicted drug traffickers by a high-level commission, almost always in exchange for bribes. At least 20 of the 130 legislators elected to Peru's congress in 2016 were reported to be complicit in the drug trade.[34]

Corruption at the regional and local level was also severe. Although historically Peru's government was centralized in Lima, twenty-five "regions"—very similar to states in the United States—were established in 2002. Of the twenty-five regional governors elected in 2006, eight years later eleven had either been jailed for corruption or had fled, often on drug-related charges.[35] The ties at these levels between the party of Keiko Fujimori and drug traffickers were particularly strong.[36]

Similarly, in the twenty-first century, in Peru's exceptionally remote Amazonian rain forest, mining (in particular for gold) and logging (in particular for mahogany, a very valuable wood) have expanded. In 2007, under the terms of Peru's free trade agreement with the United States, Peru committed to the protection of its rain forest, and requirements for the verification of the legal origin of gold and timber exports were introduced. However, "tens of thousands of people" worked in illegal mining and logging in the Amazonian rain forest.[37] As in the case of the drug trade, security forces were repeatedly dispatched to the area; but, after they departed, the miners and loggers returned, bribing local officials to approve false documents and, if arrested, bribing the judges for their release.[38]

Corruption was also problematic in legal mining enterprises. During the twenty-first century, global demand for minerals skyrocketed. By the 2010s, approximately 20 percent of Peru's land was contracted to mining concessions, affecting more than half of Peru's indigenous communities, and minerals comprised roughly 40 percent of Peru's legal exports.[39] Indigenous communities perceived damage to their land, their water, and their culture, and conflict escalated. Various national programs were introduced to assuage communities' concerns, including the canon (the allocation of certain percentages of a mining company's taxes to near-by districts) and requirements for environmental impact reports and prior consultation with communities. Yet amid the pro-market orientation of Peru's national government, the weakness of Peru's political parties, and enduring poverty and inequality, local leaders were often co-opted by the mining companies and sometimes misappropriated canon funds.[40] And, accordingly, conflict continued.

THE 2016–2019 BATTLE AGAINST CORRUPTION

Peru's 2016–2019 battle against corruption was fierce. The forces of the status quo were strong. They included Peru's oldest party, the American Popular Revolutionary Alliance (Alianza Popular Revolucionaria Americana—APRA), led by Alan García, and its largest party, Popular Force (Fuerza Popular, also called the Fujimorista party), led by Keiko Fujimori, the daughter of Alberto. Primarily due to aggressive efforts by García during his second term, APRA dominated Peru's judiciary.[41] And, although Popular Force had won only 36 percent of the 2016 legislative vote, the party gained 56 percent of the legislative seats, primarily due to the effects of the D'Hondt proportional representation formula.[42] Keiko Fujimori was angry at her second presidential loss and in no mood for compromise with the opposition. Further, APRA and Popular Force were allied.

Yet opponents mounted a successful assault. Amid democratic government, Peru's investigative journalists and judges were able to work effectively to provide evidence of corruption. As Peruvians became more aware of the enormity of corruption, their anger increased and became a key resource in the battle. By all appearances, they had the new president, Vizcarra, on their side.

The Political, Judicial, and Economic Context

In the twenty-first century, Peru has changed considerably. First, as of 2019, democracy had survived almost twenty years—longer than ever before in Peru. Historically, as democracies are consolidated, they become better at fighting corruption.[43] By definition, with democracy come free media, as corruption is investigated and reported, popular demands for its combat increase, and it is more and more in the interest of political leaders to fight it.

In this context, new anticorruption institutions were established. Peru's government introduced new laws and procedures for its auditing agency; for the transparency of public information and public procurement; for the prevention of money laundering; for political parties and campaign finance, including asset disclosure requirements.[44] The government also encouraged anticorruption NGOs, in particular Transparency International.

In addition, in Peru's most recent constitution in 1993, the judiciary became more independent of the executive than in the past. Peru's judges and prosecutors were appointed by the seven members of the National Magistrates Council (Consejo Nacional de Magistratura—CNM); these seven members were elected in secret vote by a spectrum of legal and judicial institutions as well as by university presidents, with no role for the executive or the legislature.[45] By contrast, in the earlier 1979 constitution, Peru's judges were appointed by the president, "upon the proposal of the CNM" and Supreme Court judges were ratified by the Senate.[46] (Overall, trends in the degree of judicial power and independence provided by Peru's constitution are not anomalous for the region.[47])

Peru was also active in hemispheric anticorruption initiatives. Like its neighbors, Peru ratified conventions against corruption established by the Organization of American States and the United Nations.[48] Amid hemispheric exchanges of information about best practices, Peru gained new procedures. Of particular significance were new tools for the review of electronic information and the adoption of plea-bargaining.[49] As of 2013, as in the United States, Brazil, and elsewhere, prosecutors in Peru could offer reduced sentences to suspects who admitted guilt in exchange for testimony and evidence about their crimes. Plea bargains are not uncontroversial; by definition, they reduce criminals' sentences and, by reducing sentences in return for information, they may tempt suspects to make false statements against others. However, it was through a plea bargain with the US, Brazilian, and Swiss prosecutors that Odebrecht first admitted to its payment of egregious bribes around the world.

Another major change in Peru has been its robust economic growth—in the twenty-first century, among the most robust in the region. With economic growth came better education and a larger middle class.[50] Today, as elsewhere in Latin America, majorities in Peru use cell phones and are aware of global norms, including norms about corruption. They know that corruption constrains economic growth and reduces public goods.

Accordingly, tolerance of corruption plummeted. The traditional statement, "He [the political leader] steals, but he gets things done," is now rarely heard. In the 2018 Latinobarometer survey, 30 percent of Peruvians agreed with the statement, "It is okay to pay the price of corruption if the country's problems are resolved"—well below the Latin American average of 40 percent and third lowest in Latin America.[51] In addition, Peruvians were much more likely to consider corruption a serious problem; in the 2018 Latinobarometer survey, 19 percent of Peruvians deemed corruption "the country's most important problem"—the second highest percentage in the region and an increase from four percent in 2004–2006 and nine percent in 2011–2015.[52]

Key Protagonists: Investigative Journalists

In recent years, Peru's civil society and media have been fundamental to the country's anticorruption effort.[53] Investigative journalists worked hard to uncover corruption and the media widely disseminated the evidence of wrongdoing.

Particularly important was the work of Gustavo Gorriti, a veteran award-winning investigative journalist who directs IDL-Reporteros (Instituto de Defensa Legal Reporteros (Legal Defense Institute Reporters).[54] In October 2018, in an annual survey among influential Peruvians, Gorriti was ranked the eighteenth most powerful person in Peru—a higher rank than any other Peruvian outside of political or business leaders with the exception of the Cardinal of the Catholic Church.[55] Intrepid throughout his life, in earlier decades Gorriti revealed hidden facts about Peru's insurgents, its drug traffickers, and the authoritarian Fujimori regime. During the Fujimori regime, Gorriti weathered repression; amid the 1992 *autogolpe*, he was briefly arrested and worked in exile in Panama until the regime's demise.

Throughout 2016–2019, Gorriti's team worked relentlessly and fearlessly. Collaborating with official investigations, the team secured emails and documents from Odebrecht, audiotapes of corruption among Peru's judges, and text messages among Popular Force leaders. Even amid democracy, Gorriti worried about repression. In July 2018, a top prosecutor, Víctor Raúl Rodríguez Monteza, demanded—without success—that IDL-Reporteros reveal its sources and surrender all its recordings or face charges. After García's suicide, IDL-Reporteros faced protests in front of its office by APRA militants. The IDL-Reporteros office is well guarded.

Also very importantly, Peru's media broadly disseminated IDL-Reporteros' work. Peru's major news outlets, including its daily newspapers and its top-rated Sunday evening broadcast television programs *Panorama* and *Cuarto Poder*, regularly devoted lengthy segments to IDL-Reporteros' documents, audiotapes, and text messages. And social media took up the gauntlet as well.

The Revolution in Peru's Judiciary

The revolution was sparked in July 2018 by audiotapes released by IDL-Reporteros, which was investigating illicit ties between drug rings and judges. The audiotapes revealed the corruption of dozens of senior judges. In one audiotape, the president of the Callao Superior Court, Walter Ríos, was heard offering to sell a judicial appointment for $10,000. Further audiotapes indicated that various members of the National Magistrates Council (CNM) were guilty of accepting rewards in exchange for appointments.

Most significantly, audiotapes implicated a Supreme Court Justice and president of the Second Transitory Criminal Court, César Hinostroza. Previously, Hinostroza had dismissed money-laundering charges against Keiko Fujimori. In one audiotape, he asked an intermediary whether the perpetrator of the rape of a young girl wanted to be acquitted or have his sentence reduced. In another audiotape, he was heard arranging a meeting between a businessman and "Señora K." "Señora K" was almost universally assumed to be Keiko Fujimori.

Upon these revelations, popular outrage was ferocious. The pressure on legislators—even Popular Force legislators—was intense. In October, Congress unanimously approved a motion accusing him of participation in organized crime. Hinostroza fled to Spain, but he was quickly arrested by Interpol; Peru is requesting his extradition.

About a month before this crisis, a new attorney general, Pedro Chávarry, had been named by the Board of Higher Prosecutors (Junta de Fiscales Supremos), which included many prosecutors sympathetic to APRA and Popular Force. As Chávarry took office, he was heard in an audiotape speaking with Hinostroza, and calls for his resignation began. Evidence of contacts between Chávarry and corruption suspects mounted.

On October 10, the judge who headed Peru's anticorruption investigation, Richard Concepción, who had previously ordered the pretrial detention of the Humalas, ordered the pretrial detention of Keiko Fujimori for ten days. The charge was faking campaign fund-raising events to disguise Odebrecht's 2011 illicit donations. Evidence included a memo from Marcelo Odebrecht that stated "increase Keiko by 500 and make a visit," which had appeared frequently in Peru's media for many months, as well as copies of forged documents and bank transfers. However, in the event, Keiko served only seven days. Appellate judges ordered Fujimori's release on the grounds of insufficient evidence; she filed a motion for Concepción's recusal from the case.

Then, on October 31, Concepción again ordered Keiko's pretrial detention—this time, for three years. In the interim, Concepción's team persuaded a key Fujimorista legislator, Rolando Reátegui, to accept a plea bargain and become a witness for the state in the case against Keiko.[56] With the assistance of Reátegui and work by IDL-Reporteros, text messages and other communications between Keiko and Fujimorista legislators were obtained; they showed an uncompromising Keiko, coordinating criticism of the lead prosecutor for her case, José Domingo Pérez. The unflattering messages were widely disseminated on Peru's media. In this new context, Concepción charged that Keiko headed a "de facto criminal organization" within Popular Force and that, if Keiko were free, she would obstruct the investigation into the party's finances. This time, Concepción's position prevailed.

Popular opinion had turned strongly against Keiko. In late 2018, she was deemed "the most corrupt person in the country" by a plurality of Peruvians—29 percent (versus only 4 per cent in late 2017).[57] Approximately two-thirds of Peruvians believed that her pretrial detention was "justified."[58]

Suddenly, on New Year's Eve, Chávarry announced that he was dismissing lead prosecutor Domingo Pérez as well as another top prosecutor. Immediately, Peruvians rose up in anger. On January 2, massive demonstrations were held across four cities.

The Vizcarra administration called for Chávarry's departure. Chávarry refused, arguing that the prosecutors opposing him were "Vizcarra lackeys." Yet a few days later, a leaked videotape showed a break-in by Chávarry and members of his staff of an office sealed for the protection of evidence. Domingo Pérez and the second prosecutor were reinstated—and, Chávarry resigned. Chávarry was succeeded by former Supreme Court prosecutor Zoraida Avalos, who enjoyed support from Domingo Pérez and Gorriti. However, among critics, there were concerns that, during the Humala government, she had endorsed Humala's wife's cousin in his bid for the attorney general position.

The cooperation among key anticorruption actors that led to the revolution in Peru's judiciary and the pretrial detention of Keiko Fujimori is aptly described by ConsultAndes:

> While the Prosecution received information about the details of Fuerza Popular's 2011 campaign financing [largely from members of Fujimori's inner circle who agreed to testify due to plea bargains], the media obtained copies of messages exchanged between party leaders in a WhatsApp chat group . . . [used for] instructions from Keiko Fujimori and her closest advisers. The messages . . .—splashed on the front pages of most dailies—have proven deadly for Fuerza Popular.[59]

Vizcarra's Reform Initiatives

During 2018, as the evidence of politicians' guilt and the concomitant public outcry mounted, Vizcarra gained the capacity for bold anticorruption initiatives. In July, he proposed a referendum on four reforms: stricter regulation of political parties and campaign finance; prohibition of the reelection of legislators; a new system for the appointment of judges and prosecutors; and the establishment of a second legislative chamber. Subsequently, upon changes to Vizcarra's proposal for the second legislative chamber by the congress, Vizcarra withdrew his endorsement of this reform. But the three other proposals were overwhelmingly approved in the referendum on December 9.

For the anticorruption effort, the reform of the system for the appointment of judges is particularly important. As noted earlier, previously appointment was by the CNM, and its seven members were elected in secret votes by a spectrum of institutions—but the process was not open to the public. Although the goal was to reduce the influence of politicians and the process was not entirely anomalous in Latin America, the result was to increase the trafficking of appointments.[60] Amid the scandal described earlier, the CNM was suspended and then abolished; in the Vizcarra government's reform, the CNM is replaced by a National Justice Panel (Junta Nacional de Justicia—JNJ). This panel is to be selected on the basis of a public contest, including tests of legal knowledge, organized by a committee including the head of the Supreme Court and the attorney general.

In April 2019, the Vizcarra government put additional reform proposals before the congress. These proposals included a critical anticorruption measure: the removal of decisions for the lifting of legislative immunity from prosecution in anticorruption cases from congress to the Supreme Court. A few days after congress rejected this reform, Vizcarra increased the pressure against it; in his annual address to the nation on July 28, he called for early elections, in April 2020 rather than April 2021, for both congress and the executive.

Vizcarra's proposals were strongly supported by Peruvians, but, of course, strongly opposed by the legislators (many of whom were tainted by corruption and, in any case, according to the referendum provision, were barred from reelection). As of the writing of this chapter, the prospects for these proposals are uncertain.

OUTCOMES OF THE 2016–2019 BATTLE
AGAINST CORRUPTION

Amid the victory in the 2016–2019 battle by the forces for change, prosecutions were launched not only against Keiko but also Humala, Toledo, García, and Kuczynski—and a swathe of other authorities. As of mid-2019, approximately 250 investigations due to complicity with Odebrecht had been launched in Peru.[61] The tsunami of prosecutions gave notice to Peruvian authorities that corruption would not be tolerated.

Yet, significant concerns existed. For example, were some procedures, especially pretrial detention, abusive? On the one hand, in Peru and elsewhere, pretrial detention is necessary to prevent suspects' flights and interference with the investigation. The rate of pretrial detention is not significantly higher in Peru than in other Latin American countries (or indeed the United States, where release is usually granted only upon the payment of bail).[62] On the other hand, in Peru, a suspect can be sentenced for up to three years of pretrial detention, even without an indictment—much longer than in the United States although not longer than in some other Latin American countries.

Further, were Peru's judicial rulings rigorous and consistent? Or, did political bias endure? Were judges sometimes swept up in Peruvians' "lock-the-rascals-up" outrage? APRA and Popular Force politicians, as well as Alejandro Toledo and Ollanta Humala, have loudly charged that Peru's aggressive prosecutors were politically motivated and, in some cases, if the prosecutors were to entirely refute the politicians' charges, greater evidence about their cases was necessary.[63]

For these prosecutions, evidence of guilt was a sine qua non and, accordingly, information from Odebrecht was also. In the final months of 2018, as the forces for change were winning the anticorruption battle, Peru's prosecutors and Odebrecht representatives worked toward a cooperation accord. In December, Peru agreed not to prosecute Odebrecht officials and to allow Odebrecht to continue its operations in Peru; in exchange, Odebrecht was to share the pertinent documents about its bribes for at least six contracts and provide testimony from Barata and other complicit employees. In addition, Odebrecht would pay almost $200 million in compensation to Peru.

The first former president to be prosecuted was Alejandro Toledo. In 2016, Toledo was indicted in Peru on charges of laundering Odebrecht bribes through the purchase of property in Lima by Ecoteva Consulting, a company owned by Toledo's friend and business partner, Josef Maiman. In February 2017, after police raided Toledo's Lima home, Toledo fled to the United States. Since that time, Peru sought his extradition from the United States. But, apparently, evidence was insufficient, and Toledo's defense team argued that he could not receive a fair trial in Peru. However, in early 2019, Peru's prosecutors made a plea bargain with Maiman, and Maiman stated that he had taken Odebrecht's bribes for Toledo. Peruvian authorities reasserted the extradition request. In July 2019, authorities arrested Toledo in California and denied bail on the grounds that he was a flight risk.

The second former president to be prosecuted was Ollanta Humala. In July 2017, he and his wife, Nadine (who had headed his party and controlled much of his campaign finance) were sentenced to eighteen months of pretrial detention. Charged with taking illegal campaign contributions from Odebrecht, they were imprisoned on the grounds that they were flight risks and could use their party's funds to obstruct the investigation against them. Then, in April 2018, in a four against three vote, Peru's Constitutional Tribunal ruled that the pretrial detention violated the Humalas' presumption of innocence; the Humalas were released subject to periodic monitoring and other restrictions. The arguments and evidence that enabled the Humalas to await trial out of prison at about the same time that imprisonment was pursued for Keiko Fujimori are not clear. In any case, prosecutors have asked for a sentence of twenty years for Ollanta Humala and twenty-six for Nadine—long sentences for crimes of illegal campaign finance.

On April 17, 2019, the police arrived at García's house to arrest him and take him to pretrial detention; he went upstairs and committed suicide. Just a few days previously, Gorriti had released details about more than $1 million in bribes from Odebrecht to García's presidential secretary, Luis Nava, through an account in Andorra.[64] At the same time, Peru's prosecutors were pressing a former vice president of Peru's state oil company, Miguel Atala, as well as Odebrecht's Barata for evidence in the García case; and, they were succeeding. García was a two-time former president and a towering figure in Peruvian politics for more than thirty years; his suicide shocked the country and increased concern that the norms of pretrial detention in Peru violated suspects' rights.

At the same time as García's suicide, pretrial detention for up to three years was ordered for Kuczynski, who was eighty years old and in the hospital. A few days later, after García's suicide, the order was relaxed; the former president was placed under house arrest.

CONCLUSION

For centuries, the toll of corruption on Peru's society, polity, and economy has been immense. In the war against corruption, battles were won during 2016–2019. Amid almost two decades of democracy, Peru's investigative journalists and judicial authorities fought corruption much more vigorously than in the past. As information about corruption became more available, Peruvians took to the streets to say "Enough."

Yet caution is necessary; the war to dramatically reduce corruption in Peru is far from over. Even with the best of judicial intentions, it is likely that some rulings were inconsistent or excessive; if wrongdoing were to emerge, the outcome of the next battle for dominance of the judiciary could be quite different.

Further, as the depth and breadth of corruption were revealed, Peruvians—like citizens in other nations around the globe—tended to infer that corruption was worsening and could not be controlled amid democratic processes. Accordingly, citizens' satisfaction with democracy eroded—and the specter of its demise emerged. In Latinobarometer surveys, support for democracy as a system of government was only 43 percent among Peruvians in 2018, the lowest percentage in Peru since the survey began in 1995 with the exception of 2005 (and below the Latin American 2018 average of 48 per cent).[65]

Furthermore, in the 2018 survey, only 11 percent of Peruvians were satisfied with how the country's democracy was working—the second lowest in Latin America (after Brazil).[66]

Against significant odds, Peru won the 2016–2019 battle against corruption. To win the war, Peru will need the continued commitment of resolute investigative journalists, prosecutors, judges, and citizens.

NOTES

1. Marta Rodríguez Martínez, "What Is the Odebrecht Corruption Scandal in Latin America, and Who Is Implicated?" *Euronews*, April 18, 2019.

2. For example, during 2005–2014, Peru ranked exactly at the Latin American average in Transparency International's Corruption Perception Index; it ranked slightly below average in the World Bank's "control of corruption" indicator, as reported in Kevin Casas-Zamora and Miguel Carter, *Beyond the Scandals: The Changing Context of Corruption in Latin America* (Washington, DC: Inter-American Dialogue, 2017), p. 14. But, Peru ranked slightly above average for "rule of law," including an independent judiciary and administrative capacity, as of 2012, in Leonardo Morlino, *The Quality of Democracies in Latin America* (Stockholm: International Institute for Democracy and Electoral Assistance, 2016), p. 64.

3. Casas-Zamora and Carter, *Beyond the Scandals: The Changing Context of Corruption in Latin America*, p. 12.

4. Michael Reid Bello, "The Ultimate Political Act," *The Economist*, April 27, 2019.

5. Casas-Zamora and Carter, *Beyond the Scandals: The Changing Context of Corruption in Latin America*, pp. 8–9.

6. Francisco Durand, "The Odebrecht Tsunami," *NACLA Report on the Americas* 51, no. 2 (Summer 2019): pp. 146–152.

7. Alfonso W. Quiroz, *Corrupt Circles: A History of Unbound Graft in Peru* (Baltimore, MD: Johns Hopkins University Press, 2008), pp. 448–450.

8. Ibid., pp. 448–450.

9. Ibid., p. 448.

10. Peter Flindell Klarén, *Peru: Society and Nationhood in the Andes* (New York: Oxford University Press, 2000), p. 266.

11. Michael Reid, *Forgotten Continent* (New Haven, CT: Yale University Press, 2008), p. 39.

12. Quiroz, *Corrupt Circles: A History of Unbound Graft in Peru*, p. 239.

13. Ibid., pp. 381, 440, 447, and 448–450.

14. Ibid., p. 381.

15. "Corruption in Peru: Cleaner-than-thou," *The Economist*, October 9, 2004, p. 34.

16. Gustavo Reyna Arauco, "Cultura Política y Gobernabilidad en un Espacio Local," in *Cultura Política en el Perú: Tradición Autoritaria y Democratización*

Anómica, eds. Gonzalo Portocarrero, Juan Carlos Ubilluz, and Victor Vich (Lima: La Red para el Desarrollo de las Ciencias Sociales en el Perú, 2010), p. 199.

17. Durand, "The Odebrecht Tsunami," p. 148.

18. Francisco Durand, *Odebrecht: La empresa que capturaba gobiernos* (Lima: Pontificia Universidad Católica del Perú y Oxfam, 2018), pp. 106–111.

19. "Gasto por Interoceaníca pasó de US $1.000 mills. A US 4.5 mlls," https://el comercio.pe/politica/actualidad/gasto-inteoceanica-paso-us-1-000-mls-us-4-500-mlls -401937

20. "I km de viá Interoceaníca costó hasta US $3.4 millones," February 15, 2017, www.diariosinfronteras.pe/2017/02/15/1-km-de-via-interoceanica-costo-hasta-us-3-4 millones

21. Durand, *Odebrecht: La empresa que capturaba gobiernos*, p. 223.

22. Mitra Taj and Teresa Cespeda, "Odebrecht paid firms linked to Peru's Kuczynski $4.8 million: document," December 13, 2017, https://www.reuters.com/a rticle/us-peru-odebrecht-kuczynski-id USKBN1E8088

23. Durand, *Odebrecht: La empresa que capturaba gobiernos*, p. 190.

24. Valle Avilés Pinedo, "El Caso de Negocio para la Infraestructura Sostenible: Linea 1 del Metro de Lima," October 28, 2015, https:iadb.org.bidinvest/es/el-caso -de-negocio-para-la-infraestructura-sostenible-linea-1-de-metro-de-lima/, accessed August 15, 2019.

25. Daniel Alarcón, "Letter from Lima: Executive Decision: What led Peru's Former President to take His Own Llife?" *The New Yorker*, July 8 and 15, 2019, p. 33.

26. Durand, "The Odebrecht Tsunami," p. 151.

27. UNODC (United Nations Office on Drugs and Crime), *Perú: Monitoreo de cultivos de coca 2015* (Lima, Peru: UNODC, 2016) and ConsultAndes, S.A., *"Peru Key Indicators 18-927,"* December 23–December 30, 2018, p. 6.

28. "Drug Trafficking Grows in Peru, Newspaper Says," *Latin America Herald Tribune*, no date, www.laht.com/article.asp?Articleid=340845&categoryid_14095, accessed September 23, 2019 and Richard Webb and Graciela Fernández Baca, *Perú en Números 2010* (Lima: Cuánto, 2010), p. 881.

29. Simeon Tegel, "Peru's Booming Cocaine Business Is Turning It into Latin America's Newest Narco State," February 9, 2016, simeontegel.com/2016/02/p erus-booming-cocaine-business-is-turning-it-into-latin-americas-newest-narco-state/, accessed September 22, 2019.

30. Frank Bajak and Carla Salazar, "Peru Rebel Brothers Lead Retooled Shining Path," *Associated Press*, May 29, 2012.

31. Tegel, "Peru's Booming Cocaine Business Is Turning It into Latin America's Newest Narco State."

32. Enrique Chávez, "El VRAEM es una bomba de tiempo," [interview with Rubén Vargas], *Caretas,* June 23, 2016, pp. 33–35.

33. Frank Bajak, "The Peruvian Military Is Letting Planes Filled with Cocaine Fly Right under their Noses," *Business Insider*, October 14, 2015.

34. "Peru's Drug Fight," *ConsultAndes Sector Report*, July 2016, p. 7.

35. John Crabtree and Francisco Durand, *Peru: Elite Power and Political Capture* (London: Zed Books, 2017), p. 145.

36. Alberto Vergara, speaking on the panel "Fujimorismo Twenty Years After the Fall of Alberto," at the Latin American Studies Association meeting, Boston, MA, May 25, 2019.

37. "Can Peru's Military End Illegal Mining in the Amazon?" *Latin America Advisor*, Inter-American Dialogue, March 15, 2019, p. 3 (comment by Rafael Saliés).

38. See, for example, William Neuman and Andrea Zarate, "Corruption in Peru Aids Cutting of Rain Forest," *New York Times*, October 19, 2013, pp. A1 and A8.

39. Fabiana Li, *Unearthing Conflict: Corporate Mining, Activism, and Expertise in Peru* (Durham: Duke University Press, 2015), pp. 16–17 and Anthony Bebbington, Abdul-Gafaru Abdulai, Denise Humphreys Bebbington, Marja Hinfelaar, and Cynthia A. Sanborn, *Governing Extractive Industries: Politics, Histories, Ideas* (Oxford: Oxford University Press, 2018), p. 39.

40. Anthony Bebbington, Abdul-Gafaru Abdulai, Denise Humphreys Bebbington, Marja Hinfelaar, and Cynthia A. Sanborn, *Governing Extractive Industries: Politics, Histories, Ideas,* pp. 65–68.

41. Carlos Basombrío Iglesias, "Corruption in the Andean Region: Is Progress Being Made?" (Washington, DC: Inter-American Dialogue, 2009), p. 5; Cesar R. Nureña and Federico Helfgott, "Rings of Corruption in Peru," *NACLA Report on the Americas* 51, no. 2 (Summer 2019): p. 168 and ConsultAndes, S.A., *"Peru Key Indicators 18-919,"* October 28–November 4, 2018, p. 4.

42. Eduardo Dargent and Paula Muñoz, "Peru: A Close Win for Continuity," *Journal of Democracy* 27, no. 4 (October 2016): p. 151.

43. Casas-Zamora and Carter, *Beyond the Scandals: The Changing Context of Corruption in Latin America,* p. 10.

44. Ibid., pp. 27–32.

45. See Article 155 of Peru's 1993 constitution for details.

46. See Article 245 of Peru's 1979 constitution for details. In the Spanish, the president is to name judges *"a propuesta del"* CNM.

47. Daniel M. Brinks and Abby Blass, *The DNA of Constitutional Justice in Latin America* (New York: Cambridge University Press, 2018), pp. 34–36.

48. Ibid., pp. 26–28.

49. "Corruption Prosecutions in the Americas: A Comparative Perspective," event sponsored by the Inter-American Dialogue and the Inter-American Development Bank, February 5, 2019, Washington DC, which included Brazilian prosecutor Rodrigo Janot, former Peruvian prosecutor José Ugaz, and former Guatemalan attorney general Claudia Paz y Paz.

50. Ludwig Huber and Leonor Lamas, *Deconstruyendo el Rombo: Consideraciones sobre la nueva clase media en el Perú* (Lima: Instituto de Estudios Peruanos, 2017).

51. Corporación Latinobarómetro, *Informe 2018*, https://www.latinobarómetro.org, p. 65, accessed July 18, 2019.

52. Ibid., p. 59 and Casas-Zamora and Carter, *Beyond the Scandals: The Changing Context of Corruption in Latin America*, p. 15.

53. In the "capacity to combat corruption" index developed by *Americas Quarterly*, Peru's "civil society, media, and the private sector" ranked high. See "The Capacity to Combat Corruption Index," *Americas Quarterly* 13, no. 3 (2019): p. 63.

54. Alarcón, "Executive Decision: What Led Peru's Former President to take His Own Life?"

55. "Los 30 Más Poderosos," *Semana Económica*, October 28, 2018, pp. 44–46.

56. "Peru: Fuerza Popular in Meltdown," *Latin America Weekly Report,* October 25, 2018, p. 4.

57. Ibid.

58. Ibid.

59. ConsultAndes, S.A., *"Monthly Political Analysis,"* October 2018, p. 3.

60. For similar problems in Guatemala, see "Guatemala's Judiciary: Buy any Deans Necessary," *The Economist,* July 27, 2019, p. 29.

61. Ben Filler and Fernanda Uriegas, "The Decade's Most Iconic Corruption Cases," *Americas Quarterly* 13, no. 3 (2019), p. 26.

62. Richard M. Aborn and Ashley D. Cannon, "Prisons: In Jail, But Not Sentenced," *Americas Quarterly* 7, no. 1 (2013), pp. 27–31.

63. See, for example, Alejandro Toledo's accusations at https://toledofacts.net.

64. Alarcón, "Executive Decision: What Led Peru's Former President to Take His Own Life?" p. 31.

65. Corporación Latinobarómetro, *Informe 2018*, https://www.latinobarómetro.org, pp. 15–16.

66. Ibid., p. 35.

Chapter 6

"The Police Are Involved in Everything"

Corruption and the Corrupt in Bolivia

Marten Brienen

I was first personally introduced to the concept of bribery living in Bolivia as a young scholar in the mid-1990s. I had, of course, been familiar with the concept, but had never encountered it in real life until I had to arrange an extension of my courtesy visa so that I could remain another six months to finish up my research. The requirements were straightforward, but the process was not. For weeks, I slogged from office to office with ridiculous paperwork and for as many weeks it just appeared that I hit upon brick wall after brick wall. "Come again tomorrow," some official would say, and I would come again the next day and get nothing accomplished. It was ultimately the police officer from whom I needed my *antecedentes* (criminal record) who after weeks of visiting his office in vain pulled me in closer and quietly indicated that all this could be done in a much more efficient manner, so long as I greased the wheels a little. For a Dutchman, it was so far removed from anything approaching my previous reality that it was almost like being asked to enter a spaceship in the middle of the Plaza Murillo. For me personally, it was a tremendous relief: at long last I understood what had been going wrong and that there was a simple way to fix it. I stayed another eight months to finish up my research.

For Bolivians, the fact that any official act must be greased is a simple given. Bolivia has consistently ranked toward the very bottom in the region in terms of rates of corruption, generally competing only with Haiti for the bottom slot. This is true in terms of the common perception of corruption, but notably also with regard to actual victimization. The Latin American Public Opinion Project (LAPOP) in its surveys has consistently found that around 40 percent of Bolivians report having been asked to pay a bribe in the previous year, a number that has stayed remarkably stable over the years since 2004. By comparison, this rate is roughly double the average for the region, which stood at 20.6 percent for 2016/2017.[1]

Indeed, Bolivian newspapers offer a constant barrage of corruption allegations and scandals, reaching virtually every office high and low and ranging from government ministers to local mayors. Just since February of 2020—the past month—this included a vice-minister for education (Yola Nery Mamani Callisaya), the chief of the financial unit of the Ministry of Culture (Jorge M.), the director-general of strategy of the Ministry of Communication, and the head of the state communications enterprise Entel (Elio Montes).[2]

While it is true that corruption is especially pervasive in Bolivian society, and clearly more so than in the rest of the region, some scholars have raised questions with regard to the issue effectively positing that corruption may not be in and of itself all that harmful. There are effectively two schools of thought on the subject of corruption and its effect on national development. On the one hand, there are scholars who would argue that bribery is what makes efficiency possible in highly inefficient bureaucratic structures. In effect, it has been argued that faced with reams of red tape, the small act of bribery allows businesses and individuals to get around all the unreasonable obstacles put in their way and get on with business. This is the "greasing the wheels hypothesis."[3]

The "sanding the wheels" hypothesis, on the other hand, holds that rather than lubricating economic activity, corruption undermines economic development and faith in institutions such that foreign direct investment is discouraged, and already weak political systems are further undermined. Likewise, the hypothesis holds that the incentives for officials will be to preserve undeserved income and thus maintaining structural inefficiencies. Thus, the reams of red tape that bribery can circumvent will never be reduced or removed, since this would rob countless petty officials of illicit earnings.[4]

I will present a view of public corruption in Bolivia from the "sand" perspective, arguing not only that corruption undermines economic growth, but that it also undermines the political system to the point of extreme volatility, thus further hampering prospects for Bolivian society, its economy, and its people.

UNDERSTANDING THE ISSUE

As with any illegal activity, reliable data regarding corruption is rather hard to come by. While we do have good survey data—for example from LAPOP— with regard to victimization rates for ordinary individuals, it would be difficult to construct a survey for politicians where they might indicate that they accept bribes, meaning that our systematic insight into corruption is necessarily one-sided, leaving us to depend on cascades of corruption scandals to give us any sense of how widespread corruption is among officials themselves. This leaves us with a very limited understanding of the corrupt themselves.[5]

One of the major shortcomings of the "greasing" model is that corruption, in the Bolivian case, extends to every layer of every institution.[6] It is thus not just a question of whether or not one can bypass reams of red tape in order to establish a business—which would in principle benefit society—but also a question of whether one can avoid speeding tickets, arrest, whether one can access necessary healthcare, whether one can bribe one's way out of a conviction, and whether one can obtain "bonus points" for a better grade in school.[7] There is ample evidence to suggest that one's ability to access healthcare depends on one's ability to bribe the individuals involved in providing that care.[8]

In a society in which there is already tremendous inequality—although Bolivia's GINI coefficient has steadily been improving, dropping from 61.6 in 2000 to an all-time low of 42.2 in 2018[9]—this pervasive corruption necessarily means that for those whose socioeconomic status is low, access to public goods and resources is restricted by the inability to pay bribes. For the poor, this obstructs access to healthcare as much as to education, while for those who are further up the social ladder it means the ability to engage in illicit behavior unpunished: policemen are easily bribed, and if necessary, judges can be bribed, too. This creates injustice for the poor and impunity for the rich.

Moreover, these are merely the relatively benign instances where one can obtain an unearned benefit with graft. Unfortunately, corruption in Bolivia is not limited to these types of "greasing the wheel." It is also known for much more malign schemes operated by corrupt officials that are, by any measure, obviously harmful to the country. One quite well-publicized example was the case of Jacob Ostreicher, who fell victim to a conspiratorial scheme involving fifteen officials, including the judge who ordered him incarcerated, several prosecutors, and government officials tied to the justice system. The US investor was held on accusations of money laundering for eighteen months without charges, while prosecutors and officials sold off 13,000 tons of rice, along with agricultural equipment, and other valuables belonging to the businessman and extorted him for large amounts of money in return for his freedom.[10]

While the Ostreicher case is an extreme example, it does shed light on the fact that widespread and unchecked corruption very directly harms the institutions themselves, by providing perverse incentives and in the absence of any real systematic efforts to crack down on this social problem. Moreover,

Bolivia is also an integral part of the region's cocaine economy, as the third largest supplier of cocaine and its precursors, which in turn creates an environment in which transnational organized crime flourishes and in which corrupt officials stand to make very large amounts of money. Indeed, without the active collaboration of officials at every level, the relatively peaceful drug economy would be impossible.[11]

Bolivian informants in the drug trade readily back up the assertion that corruption is the means through which the system functions:

> "The narcos [*sic*] work at the highest level, always with the police, to cover their operations. Usually there's a Bolivian middleman who acts as the bridge between the Colombians and the police. [. . .] Police corruption is the key to underworld activities here in Bolivia. The police are involved in everything. I personally know of a case where police were contracted to kidnap someone who had some outstanding debts. They charged $6000. [. . .] But it is not just the police who are corrupt. If by some miracle you actually get arrested and charged, you can buy most judges off for $20,000."[12]

Another informant indicated that

> "[s]ometimes one of us is detained, say for fighting, for being drunk or whatever, or in some cases for selling small quantities of drugs; we are talking about 300 to 500 grams that you can sell in Yapacani. If the police find that, then you are detained and taken to the police station. That is when our boss calls the colonel, and the colonel makes sure we are freed. [. . .] If, however, he is detained by the FELCN [the anti-narcotics police] in another part, it usually takes two days to arrange for his release. [. . .] Yes, there is one above them all, and he usually only comes once, maybe twice, a year to the zone. [. . .] [He] has a political position, he is some kind of minister. We have only seen him from a distance, but we know what he looks like from the television."[13]

Authorities arrested General René Sanabria Oropeza, the former head of the Special Antinarcotics Force (Fuerza Especial de Lucha contra el Narcotráfico—FELCN), in 2015 in Panama for the production of large quantities of cocaine destined for the US market.[14] In that same year, a total of twenty prosecutors and twelve police officials were under investigation for corruption.[15]

It is simply not the case that we are looking at a simple means to circumvent red tape but at something significantly more nefarious and destructive. The incentive structure and the general impunity creates an environment that promotes corrupt actions of a much more aggressive nature, where those in positions of power actively exploit those who lack it, while officials and transnational criminal organizations become deeply intertwined in an illicit economy that by far dominates its licit cousin. In the case of Bolivia, this corruption manifests in such a way that the most likely manner in which any Bolivian will encounter it in daily life is in contact with the police: 28.6 percent of Bolivians report having been asked for a bribe by a police officer in the past year, again taking the number one slot region-wide.[16]

UNDERMINING FAITH IN INSTITUTIONS

The pervasive nature of corruption in Bolivia has several notable effects. As I noted earlier, the close cooperation between transnational criminal organizations and Bolivian officials means that parts of the state apparatus along with local authorities have effectively been subverted and co-opted by criminal elements. As Theo Roncken put it in 1997, "They use a strategy of peaceful coexistence with the state, which has successfully guaranteed their lucrative businesses, generally without resorting to violence. As a result, antidrug interdiction policies are usually directed towards the least powerful sectors of the coca-cocaine circuit: coca producers, processors, and small-scale transporters of the chemicals used in refining."[17] The fact that the guilty can walk away from their crimes without repercussion has created an atmosphere of impunity, at least for those with means. Unsurprisingly, this affects how Bolivians view their chances of obtaining justice when they have been wronged: 68.1 percent do not believe that the criminal justice system will punish the guilty, while a further 28.4 percent do not believe that the police would respond within three hours or at all if a crime is reported.[18]

It is this environment in which ordinary Bolivians cannot count on institutions for their overall security or indeed to actively punish those who engage in criminal behavior that we have seen the phenomenon of "street justice" rise to the forefront. Unable to rely on police for protection or on the criminal justice system to deliver justice, marginalized communities around Bolivia have come to rely on what they would describe as "communal justice," in which accused delinquents are frequently lynched in protracted and public displays of ultraviolence, often ending with a public burning, burial alive, of battering to death.[19] The practice almost exclusively targets outsiders who are viewed with suspicion, and involves no process to determine guilt or innocence, leading to tragedy upon tragedy for the unfortunate individual in the wrong place at the wrong time. It should be noted that almost without exception, these public murders themselves go without investigation and without punishment. Impunity brings about yet more impunity.

It is not just the justice system and law enforcement that are impacted by high levels of corruption, however. Two thirds of Bolivians believe that more than 50 percent of politicians are corrupt, indicating a very low level of trust in government as a whole.[20] Likewise, no more than 16.3 percent of Bolivians trust political parties, leading to a level of alienation visible in the percentage of people who identify with a political party themselves, at no more than 16.9 percent—near the very bottom for the entire region.[21]

The result is a precarious political system that lacks broad support among Bolivians. The volatile nature of the system is perhaps best illustrated by the sudden and unexpected ouster of President Juan Evo Morales in November of 2019.[22] Morales had been the longest serving and notably most popular president in Bolivian history. His ouster came as a result of accusations of electoral fraud, but it is important to point out that no one at all doubted that he had come out as the winner. Yet despite his popularity, a lack of support from police and military meant that he could not hang on to power. Bolivian politics are so volatile that no one sector of society can ever hold on to power without broad support. In an environment where there is very little trust in the institutions, the parties, and the system as a whole, it is exceedingly difficult to maintain the coalitions that are necessary to maintain stable government. So much so that even a popular president, having won an election, cannot do it.[23]

A CRUSHING WEIGHT

There are several overwhelming forces that bear down upon Bolivian society. In the first place, there is the perpetual weakness of the state, which has historically meant that it cannot overcome widespread discontent. Bolivians have long had the ability to paralyze the nation through marches, strikes, and protests, and this was both how Mr. Morales gained power initially in 2003–2006 and how he lost it again in 2019, forced to leave the country in a hurry much like Gonzalo Sánchez de Lozada and a host of others before him. In Bolivia, stable government requires at least the tacit ascent of broad swaths of society—from *cocaleros* to *mineros* and from police to military. This makes it exceedingly difficult to make hard choices and undertake serious reforms other than the ones that have historically proven quite popular—nationalization of foreign interests chief among them—even if never quite successful at improving the lives of ordinary Bolivians. The truth is that despite the very popular narrative of a small elite wielding absolute power over an indigenous majority for most of the country's history, this has never quite been true: the elites may have firmly held on to the trappings and symbols of power, but never power itself. They always needed broad support, without which they could not retain their positions.[24]

The structure of the Bolivian state reflects a number of historical peculiarities as well as the underlying political volatility. The state was designed as an institution that was intended to function like its rich counterparts in Europe and North America, providing all of the basic modernizing services that these did and continue to do. Thus, the Bolivian state has been tasked with national healthcare, national defense, education for all citizens, regulating business, housing, labor, and so on. However, it must attempt to do so with only a fraction of the resources that its European and North American counterparts possess. Rather than trimming down the responsibilities of the state to something more manageable, the Bolivian solution has been continuing to insist that the state provide these services without adequate funding. This has meant that each and every office has responsibilities it effectively cannot meet, tasking officials with impossible jobs in return for salaries that cannot sustain life.[25]

Moreover, Bolivia's very long history of patronage and clientelism has meant that people in positions of power use the offices controlled by the state as rewards for their clients in order to guarantee their loyalty and cohesion. This gives rise to the tradition of *empleomanía*; when a new party takes over the reins of power, each and every official in every government office, down to the shoe-shine boy, is replaced with those whose loyalty lies with the new administration.[26] The prize is not the generally abysmal salary that comes with these positions, but rather the potential for graft, which can be many times as lucrative.[27] Indeed, some positions are especially coveted for their profitability, such as any in the customs office.

The result is a rather strange beast, a sprawling bureaucracy that has all the trappings of a modern state, but virtually none of its abilities. Outside of import and export tariffs on raw materials, the Bolivian tax office is not very good at raising taxes, leaving the state perpetually strapped for cash.[28] To make up for this very long-standing problem, tradition has always dictated that the state should attempt to supplement its revenues by raising more indirect taxes, generally in the form of stamps and fees for any official acts—such as filing a police report. Each new bureaucratic step presents a new manner of extracting revenues for the state.[29] This, of course, is how one builds a bureaucracy so inefficient that it appears to exist to impede economic development and diversification, one that ranks near the bottom of the pile on the Ease of Doing Business Index.[30]

The results are predictable: government offices are staffed by individuals who obtain positions due to connections and favors, not competence. The purpose of these offices is to extract money, while the officials in them extract yet more to supplement insufficient salaries. This has led to a tradition of byzantine bureaucracy that serves as an obstacle to business at large that most choose to circumvent it altogether by entering the enormous informal sector, which comprises some 77 percent of the Bolivian workforce and 68 percent of its GDP, making it the largest informal sector in the region.[31]

This, of course, negates any of the progressive measures to ensure workers' happiness in recent years: minimum wage increases mean nothing for those in the informal sector, nor do regulations with regard to safety, nor any other aspect of working conditions. In effect, the majority of individuals affected by government regulations regarding labor and labor conditions are those who work for the government themselves. It also deprives the state of tax revenues that it would be able to capture, were it possible for anyone who does not have an army of lawyers and deep pockets to navigate their way to a business license in a formalized manner.

In effect, when we look at the Bolivian economy, we observe a state of unregulated lawlessness in the informal sector, due in no small measure to the incompetence and ineffectiveness of the state, which has not the means to bring the informal sector to heel. It is an environment that unfortunately extends to illegal logging and illegal mining, both activities that produce tremendous environmental damage and further rob the state of desperately needed revenues.[32]

We are thus left with a state infrastructure that appears mostly to mimic a state infrastructure, while performing very few of its functions. It is difficult to make an argument about the efficiency or social purpose of an office that regulates labor conditions through a variety of licensing and inspection requirements, each of which comes with its own set of stamps and fees, when 77 percent of the market is informal and thus entirely beyond the reach of these offices. It does not exist to facilitate the smooth functioning of society, but rather to extract resources for the state and create opportunities for graft.

Much the same argument can be presented with regard to the other functions of the state. The Bolivian police force appears wholly incapable of solving crime, but is very good at demanding bribes from citizens, who consequently do not count on it for their security. It is effectively an institution that is made to look like a police force, but without any of the normal attributes of one save the external features, such as uniforms. It is a cargo cult's vision of a police force.

The next great weight upon the back of Bolivian society is the biggest prize of them all: the trade in illicit substances, namely cocaine and its precursors, mainly to neighboring countries such as Brazil and Argentina, both of which have become major consumers of *pasta base* and powder cocaine.[33] This trade, due to its illicit nature, is necessarily an informal one and yet it generates tremendous profits—or rather, precisely because of its illicit nature. I have argued elsewhere that it is to some extent the corruptibility of Bolivian officials—at any level—that explains how Bolivia has this far avoided the death spiral that grips other countries as deeply involved in the trade in cocaine.[34] Unlike Colombia or Mexico, Bolivia remains relatively peaceful and secure. In large part, I attribute this to the social cohesion of the communities responsible for the cultivation of *Erythroxylum coca*, but the fact transnational criminal organizations have the easy option of bribing officials into looking away has meant that there has been little need for violence, somewhat mimicking the situation such as it was in Mexico prior to 2007.[35]

The tradeoff is that so long as police officers and judges make their money in the trade in illicit substances, they need not concern themselves particularly much with the needs of the Bolivian public. Just like anyone else, they answer to those who pay them. What this means in the simplest of terms is that bureaucrats, policemen, judges, and other officials effectively do not exist to serve the needs of the Bolivian people, but offer a much more personalized service to those who have the means.

CONCLUSION

The result is that anything ranging from healthcare outcomes and student learning to how one might be treated in the justice system depends on financial clout. Those who have money are simply unlikely ever to be arrested for speeding or to have difficulty obtaining necessary medical care, while those who lack such resources can be barred even from attaining good grades and advancing in life. This sort of preselection guarantees that grades are a measure of money more than performance, just as arrest records are more indicative of money than of lawful behavior.

As such, corruption puts up significant barriers to economic development while simultaneously undermining faith in democracy and its institutions to such an extent that it produces exceptional political volatility, which has manifested itself time and time again. Bolivians simply do not believe that the institutions of the state exist to serve them, and they have no faith at all in political parties and politicians, with the exception of a handful of *caudillos políticos* who inspire personal loyalty, such as Mr. Morales.

Although I am very clearly on the side that views corruption more as sand than as grease, it is important conceptually to understand that the phenomenon exists because it solves a problem. In countries such as the Netherlands and Finland, there is little need for petty corrupt acts because it is perfectly simple and straightforward to obtain a business license or to engage in other economic traffic. The system itself is set up to encourage such behavior as being in the best interest of society as a whole. Likewise, there is little incentive for a police officer to accept a bribe in return for overlooking an infraction because the benefit, relative to the officer's salary, is not great enough to risk losing the position altogether. These circumstances have conspired to create an environment in which most officers would look upon any attempt to bribe them as a direct insult and an infraction to be acted upon in its own right.

The daily reality for Bolivians is starkly different. The country groans under a bureaucratic system that makes simple transactions painfully difficult and expensive. Obtaining a business license is not straightforward, but rather an arduous march through office after office for month after month, ultimately producing an environment that seems specifically designed to discourage economic formalized traffic and activity. Seemingly simple bureaucratic transactions require endless stamps and paperwork to create a byzantine structure that would have made Franz Kafka despair. The historical reason for the emergence of this death-knell is the eternal underfunding of the state. One must regard every stamp, license, and official document as a series of indirect taxes through which the Bolivian state attempts to fund itself in the absence of any ability to raise revenues through more conventional means. The result, of course, has been a structure so impossible to navigate that it serves any individual to figure out how to circumvent it altogether. For many, this simply means operating completely in the informal sector, where no office visits are required, no minimum wages apply, and no stamps are needed.

In this sense, corruption does indeed offer a solution to an otherwise intractable problem: the structures of the Bolivian state are designed to extract money from anyone hoping to engage in economic traffic to such an extent that it directly hinders the ability to do so. The corruption of Bolivian officials creates a pathway to proceed and thus enables the existence of a formal sector. This, of course, does raise the price of formal participation and thus discourages those who lack the means to engage in this form of circumvention and are therefore left with no choice but to eschew formality altogether.

This leaves ordinary Bolivians entirely out in the cold. Most of them view the state with a mixture of disdain and mistrust, the latter of which appears justified. They are, in effect, correct to assume that the institutions are not there to serve them or to facilitate their economic activity. The state exists primarily to extract resources from society to sustain itself and offers very little in return. Its offices are a means by which politicians can reward their friends and allies with salaried jobs and opportunities for graft. It supports institutions that in many ways look like the institutions we might find in Finland or Canada, but that are fundamentally different in nature.

In that environment of institutions that, even though they look awfully much like real institutions, do not perform any of their usual functions, it is little wonder that communities would take it upon themselves to appropriate those functions. For marginalized communities in Bolivia, which cannot afford to pay for private security, security comes in the form of extrajudicial lynchings of accused delinquents. For most of society, it means that the state and officialdom are something to avoid, leaving society largely unregulated with at times dire consequences for both citizens and environment.

NOTES

1. Mollie Cohen, Noam Lupu, and Elizabeth Zechmeister, eds., *Political Culture of Democracy in the Americas, 2016/17* (LAPOP, 2017): p. 56.

2. Ángel Guarachi, "Gobierno de Áñez es afectado por al menos cuatro casos de corrupción." *La Razón*, February 20, 2020. Section: Nacional.

3. Graham Brooks, *Preventing Corruption: Investigation, Enforcement and Governance* (New York, NY: Palgrave Macmillan, 2013); Paul J. Beck and Michael W. Maher, "A Comparison of Bribery and Bidding in Thin Market." *Economics Letters* 20/1 (January 1986).

4. Paolo Mauro, "Corruption and Growth." *Quarterly Journal of Economics* 110 (1995): pp. 681–712. Pierre-Guillaume Méon and Khalid Sekkat, "Does Corruption Grease or Sand the Wheels of Growth?" *Public Choice* 122 (2005): pp. 69–97.

5. David Murphy, "Public Sector Corruption in Bolivia." *The Journal of Government and Financial Management* 53/3 (2004): pp. 44–52.

6. Sofia Wickberg, *Overview of Corruption and anti-Corruption in Bolivia* (Transparency International, 2012).

7. Aurolyn Luykx, *The Citizen Factory: Schooling and Cultural Production in Bolivia* (Albany, NY: SUNY Press 2006): pp. 241–244.

8. Roberta Gatti, George Gray-Molina, and Jeni Klugman, "Determinants of Corruption in Local Health Care Provision: Evidence from 108 Municipalities in Bolivia." In *Proceeds from the XIV Conference of the Società Italiana di Economia Pubblica* (Pavia, 2002): pp. 1068–1086.

9. World Bank. https://data.worldbank.org/indicator/SI.POV.GINI?locations=BO, retrieved February 29, 2020.

10. Ernesto Calizaya, "Caso Ostreicher devela red de corrupción en 2 ministerios." *La Razón*, November 28, 2012. Section Seguridad Nacional. Carlos Corz, "Desbaratan red de corrupción y extorsión en la que operaban dos asesores del Ministerio de Gobierno." *La Razón*, November 27, 2012. Section: Nacional.

11. Marten W. Brienen, "Coca, Organized Crime, and (Non-)Violence in Bolivia." In In Jonathan D. Rosen, Bruce Bagley, and Jorge Chabat (eds.), *The Criminalization of States: The Relationship Between States and Organized Crime* (Lanham, MD: Lexington Books, May 2019): pp. 299–322.

12. Jeremy McDermott, "Voices from Bolivia's Underworld." *InSight Crime*, October 13, 2014. https://www.insightcrime.org/investigations/voices-from-the-bolivia-underworld/, retrieved May 12, 2019.

13. As quoted in McDermott, "Voices from the Bolivian Underworld."

14. Drug Enforcement Administration, "Four Bolivian National, Including Retired Police General, Charged with Drug Trafficking," Press Release dated February 28, 2011. https://www.dea.gov/press-releases/2011/02/28/four-boli

vian-nationals-including-retired-police-general-charged-drug, retrieved December 01, 2019.

15. Kyra Gurney, "Bolivia Steps Up Fight Against Corruption." *Insight Crime*, January 12, 2015.

16. Cohen, Lupu, and Zechmeister, *Political Culture*, p. 87.

17. As quoted in: Theo Roncken, "Bolivia: Impunity and the Control of Corruption in the Fight Against Drugs." https://www.tni.org/en/article/stub-276?content_languag e=en, retrieved November 25, 2019.

18. Cohen, Lupu, and Zechmeister, *Political Culture*, pp. 83–91.

19. Marten W. Brienen, "Spectacular (In)Justice: Impunity and Communal Violence in Bolivia." In Hanna S. Kassab and Jonathan D. Rosen (eds.), *Violence in the Americas* (Lanham, MD: Lexington Books, 2018), pp. 33–46.

20. Cohen, Lupu, and Zechmeister, *Political Culture*, p. 60.

21. Cohen, Lupu, and Zechmeister, *Political Culture*, p. 24.

22. Keith Johnson, "Why Is Evo Morales Suddenly No Longer President of Bolivia?" *Foreign Policy*, November 11, 2019. https://foreignpolicy.com/2019/11/11 /evo-morales-resigns-president-bolivia/ retrieved February 23, 2020.

23. Marten Brienen, "The Ungovernable State: Bolivia in the Age of Morales." In Jonathan D. Rosen and Hanna S. Kassab (eds.), *Fragile States in the Americans* (Lanham MD: Lexington Books, 2018), pp. 185–204.

24. For a detailed analysis, see Marten W. Brienen, "The Ungovernable State: Bolivia in the Age of Morales." In Jonathan D. Rosen and Hanna S. Kassab (eds.), *Fragile States in the Americas* (Lanham, MD: Lexington Books, 2019), pp. 185–204.

25. Murphy, "Public Sector Corruption."

26. Willem Assies, "Bolivia: A Gasified Democracy." *European Review of Latin American and Caribbean Studies* 76 (2004): pp. 25–43.

27. Murphy, "Public Sector Corruption."

28. Richard Bird, "Tax Reform in Latin America: A Review of some Recent Experiences." *Latin American Research Review* 27/1 (1992): pp. 7–36.

29. Carmenza Gallo has written on Bolivia's history with indirect taxes: Carmenza Gallo, *Taxes and State Power: Political Instability in Bolivia 1900-1950* (Philadelphia PA: Temple University Press, 1991): pp. 105–112.

30. Top be outdone only by Venezuela. Doing Business (World Bank), *Doing Business 2020* (New York: World Bank, 2019).

31. World Bank, "Increasing Formality and Productivity of Bolivian Firms." In *World Bank Country Study* (New York: World Bank, 2009).

32. Victor Hugo Gutiérrez Vélez and Kenneth MacDicken, "Quantifying the Direct Social and Governmental Costs of Illegal Logging in the Bolivian, Brazilian, and Peruvian Amazon." *Forest Policy and Economics* 10/4 (2008): pp. 248–256. Sébastien Boillat et al., "Protected Areas and Indigenous Peoples in Bolivia and Peru: Dilemmas, Conflicts, and Ways Out." In Hans Hurni and Urs Wiesmann (eds.), *Global Change and Sustainable Development: A Synthesis of Regional Experiences from Research Partnerships. Perspectives / NCCR North-South: Vol. 5* (Bern, Schweiz: Geographica Bernensia).

33. Renata Rigacci Abdalla, Clarence S. Madruga, Marcelo Ribeiro, et al., "Prevalence of Cocaine Use in Brazil: Data from the II Brazilian National Alcohol and Drugs Survey (BNADS)." *Addictive Behaviors* 39, no. 1 (2014): pp. 297–301. United Nations Office on Drugs and Crime (UNODC), *World Drug Report 2013* (Vienna: United Nations, 2013): p. 42.

34. Brienen, "Coca, Organized Crime, and (Non-)Violence in Bolivia."

35. Rosen and Kassab, "Introduction: Fragile States in the Americas." In Jonathan D. Rosen and Hanna S. Kassab (eds.), *Fragile States in the Americans* (Lanham, MD: Lexington Books, 2018), pp. xi–xx. A. D. Morton, "The War on Drugs in Mexico: A Failed State?" *Third World Quarterly* 33/9 (2012): pp. 1631–1645.

Chapter 7

Organized Crime and the State in Brazil

Michael Jerome Wolff

The nature of organized crime and its relationship to the state in Brazil is probably too complex to be understood within any single explanatory framework.[1] Territorially, Brazil is larger than the continental United States, and many of the social, economic, and political factors that normally shape the dynamics of organized crime vary significantly from one region to another. Moreover, Brazil's "strong" federalism has meant that subnational governing institutions, which are largely autonomous of their federal counterparts and whose behavior varies in accordance with local political cultures, have dealt with corruption and organized crime (disrupting, shaping, or fostering it) in very different ways. That said, developments over the last few decades point to an eventual convergence in most Brazilian states around a common model of political-criminal relations that, as I will argue in the chapter, reflects a deepening symbiosis between state institutions and organized crime.

Understanding these developments is a particularly urgent matter in Brazil today. The related problem of criminal violence has had a marked political salience since the 1980s, but homicides have more than tripled since then, exceeding 61,000 (or approximately 10 percent of the global total) in 2017 alone.[2] The majority of this lethal violence afflicts poor urban communities that are controlled to varying degrees by drug trafficking gangs or racketeering organizations, and whose populations consequently exist outside of the legal purview of the state. Variously dubbed "parallel polities,"[3] "authoritarian enclaves,"[4] or "private sovereignties,"[5] this relegation of millions of people to de facto governance of non-state armed groups—the street-level branches of organized crime—have led to the criticism that Brazilian democracy is one without citizenship.[6] In its place, there has emerged a system of fragmented sovereignty in which political democracy and citizenship pertains mostly to the wealthy, while much of the country's poor are beholden to what Diane Davis has called "new imagined communities" and "alternative networks of commitment" that undermine the legitimacy of the national state.[7]

Organized crime thus clearly poses a serious threat to state sovereignty in Brazil. However, it would be misguided to view organized crime as a parallel power (as in the context of insurgency), or to interpret its expansion across national territory as merely a predatory siege on the state itself, for at all stages of its evolution, state agents and institutions have both shaped its development and have benefited (directly or indirectly) from is presence. Directly, local police forces extort money from drug gangs while allowing them free reign over sprawling slum communities,[8] and elected officials funnel public money to mafia organizations in exchange for guaranteeing an electoral constituency.[9] Indirectly, governments reduce spending on prison management by allowing criminal gangs to govern inmate populations,[10] and police and politicians can claim credit for reducing homicides when such reductions are in fact the consequence of criminal organizations monopolizing territorial control and imposing social order for their own benefit.[11] Moreover, the development and expansion of organized crime is often an unintended consequence of state policy, as when mass incarceration becomes a de facto recruiting mechanism for prison gangs, or when the transfer of prison gang leaders to out-of-state prisons facilitates the spread of criminal organizational repertoires and trade networks.[12]

If organized crime does not constitute a parallel power, how then can we best understand its relationship with the state? Peter Lupsha's *stage-evolutionary* model of organized crime presents a compelling starting point.[13] According to the model, criminal organizations are supposed to initiate either confrontational or corrupting interactions with state agents and institutions as they seek to expand their wealth and protect their business from legal prosecution. To the extent they are successful, their relationship to the state evolves in stages from *predation* (i.e., confrontation) to *parasitism* (i.e., corruption) and eventually to *symbiosis*. In this last stage, political-criminal relations are interdependent, mutually beneficial, and relatively stable, and consequently present the greatest challenge to democratic governance and the rule of law.

In Brazil, the political-criminal nexus might best be described as symbiotic, as organized crime and the state often operate in conjunction with one another for mutual benefit, whether directly or indirectly. However, the relationship is in no way a stable one, and its terms are given to constant renegotiation, the primary mechanisms of which are confrontation and corruption.[14] This helps to explain why we tend to see high overall levels of violence punctuated by occasional and dramatic reductions in homicides on one end, and periods of heightened, sometimes highly coordinated violence directed at the state itself on the other. Theoretically, this implies that the nexus of political-criminal relations is constantly swinging back and forth between predation and symbiosis as criminal organizations and the state jockey for a more favorable position in an ever-shifting balance of power.

This chapter examines the relationship between politics and organized crime through an analysis of Brazil's preeminent criminal organizations and their evolution over several decades. As in most other Latin American countries, it was the astronomical rise in cocaine consumption in North America and Europe during the 1980s and 1990s that initially fueled the growth of organized crime in Brazil by channeling narcotics shipments through Brazil's major export hubs.[15] In addition, it was the democratizing and liberalizing reforms of the same period that created gaping institutional holes through which political-criminal alliances have been able to penetrate the state and expand both vertically and horizontally.[16] Ultimately, however, organized crime in Brazil has manifested in unique ways, varying substantially at the subnational level and only recently beginning to converge around a common model nationwide. My analysis begins in the next section with a cursory overview of Brazil's most visible drug trafficking gangs. I then discuss another mode of organized criminality that has emerged from within the state's own criminal justice institutions, the notorious police-run racketeering mafias and death squads popularly referred to as *milícias*. However, as I make clear in the final section, it is the development and expansion of prison gangs over the last two decades that is most responsible for the convergence across Brazil around a common model of political-criminal relations, one that is increasingly symbiotic in nature, and which has only deepened the fragmentation of Brazilian society.

"COCAINE POLITIES"

Brazil's archetypical organized crime group is the *Comando Vermelho* (CV), a drug trafficking organization that emerged in the early 1980s in Rio de Janeiro and came close to monopolizing the city's cocaine retail market by the end of the decade. Although the CV fragmented in the early 1990s, giving rise to rival factions such as the *Terceiro Comando* (TC) and the *Amigos dos Amigos* (ADA), each group reproduced the same basic organizational structure, modes of behavior, and political significance. Their organizational base lies in the state's prison system, from where the leadership of each faction loosely directs the actions and behavior of their affiliate drug-selling gangs outside of prison, which maintain territorial monopolies and impose social order in the city's sprawling favela communities.[17] For decades, this particular modality of organized crime was unique to Rio de Janeiro. As I discuss in the latter part of this chapter, however, it has in the last twenty years or so begun to spread and reproduce itself across Brazil due in no small part to national trends in mass incarceration.

According to the CV's story of origin, the organization was born out of the cohabitation of political prisoners and common criminals at the Cândido Mendes prison complex on Ilha Grande, an island off the coast of Rio de Janeiro, during the final years of Brazil's military government. Its initial purpose was to promote inmate solidarity and improve prison conditions, as well as to facilitate escape from the prison itself, but in order to finance this mission its members engaged in criminal enterprise on the outside. At first, they focused on bank robberies like their urban guerrilla counterparts did in the 1960s, but by the mid-1980s, local cocaine consumption had boomed in Rio de Janeiro, and the well-organized CV was uniquely poised to take advantage of it. They soon went to war, eliminating or co-opting most of Rio's independent, favela-based cocaine dealers, and by the end of the decade, they controlled around 70 percent of the city's drug trade.[18]

Parts of this narrative are certainly exaggerated and romanticized, but it serves to illustrate that the state has been integral to the development of the CV since its inception. First, its formation as a prison gang (whether or not this had anything to do with political prisoners) reflected the state's willingness to deal with rapidly growing incarceration rates amid deepening economic crisis by handing the greater share of prison administration and inmate governance responsibilities to prisoner collectives, often called "Solidarity Commissions."[19] These collectives, which were typically defended by the political Left as pro-democratic forces that were necessary in order to ensure that basic human rights were respected in Brazil's notorious prisons, were simultaneously demonized by the political Right and much of the news media, which exaggerated both their power and their criminal orientation.[20] For the CV, such polarization ultimately meant both more autonomy and notoriety, and consequently, a greater ability to project its power both inside and outside of prison walls.[21]

The state was also integral to the CV's development as a political authority in the favelas of Rio de Janeiro, creating what Elizabeth Leeds has called "Cocaine Polities," where nearly a fourth of the city's inhabitants now live without recourse to basic rights of citizenship.[22] Here, the CV not only succeeded in monopolizing the drug trade, but also engaged in basic governing functions like dispute resolution, welfare provision, and the regulation of social order. While poverty and inadequate state presence are partly to blame for this, the state's role in fostering the growth of organized crime was also more direct. In the realm of electoral politics, public officials had long nurtured clientelistic relationships with informal authority figures in Rio's favelas in exchange for votes, and when it became clear that the heavily armed drug gangs could be similarly useful, they quickly forged new political-criminal alliances with gang leaders. Seeing the opportunity in this, the CV began systematically driving out existing community leaders and replacing them with civilian cronies that could act as legitimate conduits between them and political elites. From this, a sort of "two-tiered" clientelism developed, still very much in practice today, in which patronage filters down from political elites through local drug gangs before finally being distributed among favela residents.[23]

The police, too, directly fostered and reinforced the development of the CV and its rival factions in Rio de Janeiro. Corruption is largely to blame. The favela-based cocaine trade provided lucrative opportunities for the police to extort drug gangs, which were often allowed free reign to fight for territorial control (and then do as they pleased once control was monopolized) as long as they kept up with their payments. Police interference in gang governance was thus only sporadic and invariably temporary, generating high death tolls but doing little to disrupt the growth of territorially embedded organized crime. Moreover, police violence itself served to reinforce gang authority in Rio's favelas. Often indiscriminate in its application, it helped to drive non-criminal residents into a de facto alliance with drug traffickers.[24]

Both the scale of police violence and the scope of gang governance increased significantly during the 1990s and 2000s. By this time, the CV had split and several prison-based criminal factions now competed for control of Rio's favelas. Their pitched battles were not only highly visible to the out-side public, but often directly obstructed the daily life and security of Rio's wealthier inhabitants, who in turn demanded tougher police action against gangs. In response, right-wing politicians made good on their promises to increase police military capacity and carry out *mano dura*-style crackdowns on crime. By the late 1990s, Rio's police forces had been fully equipped with high-power automatic rifles, machine guns, armored trucks, and helicopter gunships, and on occasion were even assisted directly by national army units as they made regular incursions into gang-controlled favela communities. Police lethality began to skyrocket, eventually reaching a peak of 1,330 *autos de resistencia*[25] (individuals killed during police operations) in 2007 alone.

The crackdowns and increasing levels of police violence may have kept Rio's drug gangs fragmented, but they also helped deepen the cultural and institutional divide between the city's formal neighborhoods (o *asfalto*) and its favelas (o *morro*).[26] Favelas became vilified as enemy territory, and their resident populations were assumed to be complicit and even loyal to criminal gangs. State presence deteriorated still further as a result. Service providers (both public and private) such as educators, medical professionals, social workers, trash collectors, and repair technicians either ceased to come to work in favelas or came only occasionally, and judicial agents refused to enter favelas at all. In the widening vacuum of power that emerged, guaranteeing social order and providing basic services in Rio's favela communities became a competitive strategy of organized crime. The so-called *Lei do Tráfico*, the unwritten legal code of drug gangs that govern social life in Rio's favelas, expanded and was much easier to enforce where state institutions were absent or severely compromised.

This dynamic began to change after 2008. Shifts in political power at the national level and the accumulative impact of nearly a decade of rapid economic growth produced the surge in political capital needed for Rio de Janeiro's government to invest in major police reform. The rise of Leftwing president Luiz Ignacio "Lula" da Silva (2002–2010) and his Workers Party (PT) meant that the focus of such reforms would reflect concerns about human rights and citizenship, and increased government revenues meant that, at least in the short term, there would be plenty of money to throw at new projects. In 2007, for example, Lula's administration inaugurated a new federal ministry in 2007 call PRONASCI,[27] the specific purpose of which was to orient state governments toward implementing more citizen-oriented police reforms.[28]

In line with this new thinking, Rio de Janeiro's governor Sergio Cabral inaugurated his first the Pacifying Police Unit (Unidade de Policia Pacificadora—UPP), a community-oriented policing initiative intended to reassert state authority in Rio's gang-controlled favelas, in December of 2008 in Morro da Santa Marta. Several more UPPs were inaugurated over the following months, and initial impact assessments boasted positive and dramatic results: homicides had decreased by as much as 75 percent in UPP communities, armed confrontations almost ceased altogether, and survey data indicated significant improvements in resident's sense of security.[29] Cabral's UPP program then surged forward on a wave of more good news. In 2009, it was announced that Rio de Janeiro would host both the 2014 World Cup Games and the 2016 Summer Olympics. Eyeing a unique investment opportunity, Brazil's richest venture capitalist, Eike Batista, spearheaded the development of a public-private partnership to help fund the expansion of the UPPs. Thirty-eight units, employing nearly 10,000 new officers occupying nearly a fourth of Rio's favelas, were operative by 2014.[30]

Although the UPPs seemed to represent a fundamental change in state-society relations and a potential end to the territorial embeddedness of organized crime in Rio de Janeiro, the program ran into serious problems as Brazil's national economy fell into crisis after 2013. By 2015, private investment vanished, Rio's state government was near insolvency, and three consecutive years of negative economic growth at the national level eliminated the federal government as an effective contributor to state-level public security programs. For the police, this meant hiring and salary freezes, and consequently a significant loss of manpower and basic resources available to the UPPs. And as policing capabilities declined, the relative capabilities of drug gangs increased. Many favela communities that had been celebrated as UPP success stories only a few years earlier once again erupted in violence as rival gangs intensified their territorial wars. The consequent increase in violent crime sparked a renewed conservative reaction in public opinion, and *mano dura*-style crackdowns soon returned as the dominant policing strategy. Police killings, having reduced by around 70 percent during the heyday of Cabral's UPPs, again skyrocketed, and in February 2018, claiming that "organized crime has taken control of our cities," Brazil's president Michel Temer deployed federal army troops to assume public security responsibilities on the streets of Rio de Janeiro.[31]

The frequency and high-profile nature of confrontational violence between Rio's drug gangs and the police have led many to describe organized crime there as a kind of parallel power or insurgency, which according to Lupsha's stage-evolutionary model, would imply that it moves somewhere between the predatory and parasitic stages. A closer examination of the economic and political linkages between the organized crime and the state, however, reveals a more mutually beneficial, indeed symbiotic, relationship. A drug trade that is territorially rooted in favelas characterized by their poverty and informality not only make for an easily taxable source of wealth for corrupt state agents, but also creates opportunities for politicians to take advantage of criminal authority structures to garner block votes during election times, and there is no shortage of evidence to suggest that these relationships are systemic.

Yet how can we explain confrontational violence? Part of it is performative. According to anthropologist Erika Larkins, it is a spectacle that is commodified and consumed in the capitalist market, and which gives meaning to local social institutions and cultural codes.[32] It also has a more directly functional purpose in regulating the political-criminal nexus. The relationship between organized crime and the state may be symbiotic generally speaking, but both sides of that coin are composed of a multitude of competing actors and interests whose relative capabilities are in constant flux. Shifts in the balance of power between criminal and state actors are therefore commonplace, provoking at every step efforts of one actor or another to renegotiate the terms of their relationship. Here, confrontational violence acts as the primary bargaining chip of renegotiation.

MILÍCIAS AND POLICE DEATH SQUADS

In 2006, Brazilian media began reporting on a supposedly new kind of criminal organization rapidly emerging in Rio de Janeiro called *milícias*, loosely defined as protection racketeering groups composed largely of state agents (including police, firemen, and prison guards) that control territory and impose a strict form of social control for political and economic gain.[33] Although it is not uncommon for off-duty police officers and other state agents in Brazil to exercise some degree of informal authority in the communities they live, and extortionist police death squads existed in most Brazilian cities, the sudden proliferation of so-called *milícias* throughout most of Rio de Janeiro's West Side favelas in the first decade of the twenty-first century represented something much more organized, criminal, and threatening to both human life and democratic governance than anything seen before. By 2008, when state and federal offices opened investigations, an estimated ninety favelas and several hundred thousand residents were under the direct control of these groups, which in turn had leveraged their territorial monopolies to accrue vast amounts of wealth and penetrate the higher echelons of the state via electoral fraud.[34]

The emergence of *milícias* was closely tied to the rise of Rio's notorious drug gangs. During the 1980s and 1990s when the CV and its rivals were taking control of favela after favela, bringing drugs and heightened violence with them, an almost folkloric countermovement developed in the West Side favela of Rio das Pedras. A group of local residents there, including off-duty police officers, organized themselves to kill or expel all of the drug dealers in their community and completely ban the sale and use of drugs from then on. Their organization, which became known as the *Liga da Justiça* (Justice League), soon took over the local Residents Association and began asking residents and local business owners for financial contributions to maintain their antidrug regime. By the late 1990s, they had fully monopolized political power within the favela, and through the offices of the Residents Association established a governing organization with an array of social services and regulatory enforcement capabilities.[35]

Although the Justice League had clearly evolved into a protection racketeering organization by then, it was popularly embraced in Rio de Janeiro as a heroic counterforce to the spreading plague of drug violence. Riding this wave of popularity, and relying on coercion to mobilize voters in Rio das Pedras, the Justice League's leader, Nadinho, ran for office in the 1998 state legislature elections and won. He then won a seat on Rio de Janeiro's city council in 2000, for which he was reelected in 2004.[36] From there, he was able to funnel public resources and secure government contracts for the Residents Association in Rio das Pedras, enriching himself and consolidating his political power further. In the years following his 2004 election, the Justice League and other rival *milícias* invaded dozens of other favelas on Rio's West and North zones, expelling embedded drug gangs and imposing their own authoritarian social order while extorting local populations. This constituted what Ignacio Cano has called a "political project," in which public officials actively fostered and perhaps even directed the invasion of favelas by *milícias* for the purpose of political power and financial gain.[37]

In the case of *milícias*, organized crime made evident headway toward overtly capturing state power. A 2008 parliamentary investigation indicted eighteen elected officials in Rio's city council and state legislature for criminal conspiracy and involvement in *milícia* activity, while Rio's former mayor, Cesar Maia, had for a time openly endorsed the electoral campaigns of known *milícia* leaders.[38] A coordinated effort by state and federal investigatory institutions revealed shortly afterward that hundreds of active and retired police and military officers had been involved. The threat of state capture became evermore apparent with the 2011 assassination of Judge Patricia Acioli, which was part of the larger campaign to intimidate law enforcement and judicial agents responsible for investigating *milícia* activity.[39] The state crackdown after 2008, however, was largely successful in breaking up the most egregious forms of political-criminal conspiracy exposed by the *milícia* phenomenon, and within a few years media reports about the matter had dwindled. Police-run mafias and death still impose social order and run protection rackets in many of Rio's favelas today, but they are far less visible and less politically powerful than before.

Although largely driven underground, the model of organized crime that Rio's *milícias* developed has significant growth potential throughout Brazil. In fact, similar police-run mafias proliferated in many cities in Brazil's northeast region in the mid to late 2000s, likely inspired by or even directly connected to organized crime groups in Rio de Janeiro. Although none of them achieved the notoriety of their counterparts in Rio, and federal-state collaboration in criminal investigations dismantled a great many of them early on, the continuing spread of drug violence and widespread perceptions of state ineptitude has helped maintain the popularity of organized vigilantism, and with it, opportunities for coercion-wielding actors to seek wealth and power in the name of social solidarity and moral virtue in the future.

MASS INCARCERATION AND THE EMERGING POLITICAL-CRIMINAL ORDER IN BRAZIL

The territorially embedded drug gangs described in the first section of this chapter had long been exceptional to Rio de Janeiro, arguably Brazil's most enigmatic city. Over the last two decades, however, a similar model of organized crime has begun to emerge in cities across the country, bringing with it even greater levels of violence than those seen decades earlier as the CV and its rivals first battled for control of Rio's favela-based drug trade. The chief vector of this contagion, I argue here, has been mass incarceration, which has fomented the nationwide rise of prison gangs whose ability to exercise power inside and outside of prison walls has made them both a formidable threat to state sovereignty and a useful, often lucrative ally in an ever deepening political-criminal partnership with state authorities.

Following a general trend throughout much of the Western Hemisphere, Brazil's incarceration rates and total prison population have surged almost unceasingly since the 1980s. The national inmate population, approximately 800,000 in 2018, has quadrupled in the last 20 years alone. Meanwhile, state spending on prison construction and management has not kept up, resulting in severe inmate overpopulation on one hand, and on the other, a greater tendency of state authorities to delegate basic prison administration and governance responsibilities to self-selecting inmate collectives. As several scholars have argued, these collectives are often critical to the welfare and dignity of Brazil's prison populations, as they serve to both provide social order among prisoners and help to articulate prisoner needs to state authorities.[40] But as inmate numbers skyrocketed, a complex mix of pressures and opportunities has pushed a growing number of these collectives into overt criminality.

The first Brazilian states to be impacted by mass incarceration were Rio de Janeiro and São Paulo in the 1980s and 1990s. As mentioned earlier, this fueled the rise of the CV and its splinter gangs over the next two decades. But it was in São Paulo where a doubling of the prison population between 1992 and 2002 would contribute to the formation of what is today Brazil's preeminent criminal organization, the *Primeiro Comando da Capital* (PCC), which since its inception in 1993 has wrestled control of some 90 percent of all prisons, jails, and other detention centers across São Paulo state, and has established significant influence in numerous other prisons across the country.[41]

Throughout most of the 1990s, the government of São Paulo officially denied the existence of the PCC in an attempt to undermine its influence. After finally admitting its existence in 2001, the government sought to weaken it by other means, transferring key leaders to other prisons, imposing a harsher disciplinary regime on current inmates, and even fomenting the creation of rival gangs.[42] In response, the PCC organized its first "mega-rebellion," mobilizing an estimated 28,000 inmates in 80 prisons and detention centers simultaneously. The highly coordinated rebellion proved to an unknowing public as well as the state that the PCC was a force to be reckoned with, and helped the criminal faction consolidate its power within the state prison system.[43]

From that point on, the continuing flood of new prisoners that resulted from the state's recent imposition of *mano dura* public security policies would serve only to strengthen the PCC. The fact that the PCC now had the capacity to punish or reward prisoners almost anywhere in the penitentiary system meant that prisons themselves became mass recruitment centers for organized crime. And as their control of prisons deepened, the PCC's ability to project its power outside of prison increased.[44] By 2003, this projection of power reached a majority of São Paulo's low-income, peripheral neighborhoods and favelas. The monopoly of territorial control it soon achieved helped enrich the PCC, but it also had an astounding impact on public security: Total homicides in São Paulo fell by 45 percent, and in some areas by as much as 90 percent, between 2000 and 2005.[45]

Almost overnight, then, the consolidation of a prison-based organized crime syndicate caused São Paulo's removal from the list of Brazil's most violent states. This came as a pleasant surprise to police authorities and government officials, who jumped at the opportunity to take credit for the sharp decline in homicides. And such credits had become much more politically salient in the first decade of the twentieth century, for the ascendency of President "Lula" and the PT after 2002 ushered in a new era of national political discourse that prioritized issues of social equality, citizenship, and human rights. The right to life—or the right not to be killed—was heralded as a particularly important matter to address, and from this point on criteria for measuring the performance of government administrations and their public security policies would be based largely on homicide reduction.[46] In the streets of São Paulo as well as in its prisons, a political-criminal symbiosis thus gradually evolved out of convenience, a mutually beneficial arrangement in which state authorities would grant the PCC relatively free reign to do as it pleased in its occupied territories, and in turn the PCC would use its organizational and coercive capacity to impose social order and keep levels of lethal violence at a minimum.

Symbiosis does not imply stasis, however, and the power equilibrium it needs to maintain itself is in constant flux. In São Paulo, while tacit arrangements between the PCC and state authorities allowed the criminal group to expand and consolidate its power, the state continued its attempts to punish and fragment it, imposing ever harsher disciplinary measures on inmates and threatening to transfer the PCC's leaders to maximum security facilities. At the same time, São Paulo's prison population continued to grow at astounding rates, increasing by another 45 percent between 2003 and 2006 alone. On May 12, 2006, the PCC responded to the accumulating pressures by launching its most audacious mega-rebellion yet. Tens of thousands of inmates put 84 prisons on lockdown, and in an impressive show of force, PCC "*soldados*" launched hundreds of coordinated attacks on state institutions, police stations, and public transport buses throughout São Paulo, killing dozens of state security officials in the process.[47]

In the wake of the 2006 mega-rebellion, state forces cracked down on the PCC in even greater force, killing hundreds of supposed PCC-members in retaliation. Despite this, the rebellion was successful insofar that it served to consolidate the PCC's monopoly power in the state's penitentiary system almost completely, and more importantly, to secure its reputation as Brazil's preeminent criminal organization. In the years that followed, this meant that PCC affiliates in prisons across Brazil would have more credibility to wrestle control of inmate collectives, impose internal order, recruit new members, and as a consequence vastly expand their networks of illicit trade and coercive power.

By 2010, moreover, mass incarceration had become a national phenomenon, especially impacting Brazil's North and Northwest regions. The introduction of crack cocaine in these regions during the previous decade had sparked a marked increase in theft and violent crime that caught incompetent public security institutions off guard. While homicides and other violent crimes were rarely solved, tens of thousands of alleged criminals were put behind bars, many of them waiting years just to be sentenced. As before, new prison construction and management did not keep up, and by the mid-2000s, prison management largely fell to inmate collectives. Now, however, the PCC provided them with both a successful organizational template and the keys of access to a rapidly expanding transnational crime network. Soon local prison gangs in Bahia, Pernambuco, Amazonas, and several other Brazilian states began using their control of prison populations to project their power out on the streets, directing the behavior of territorially embedded favela-based drug gangs in ways that mirror the modality of the CV in Rio de Janeiro and the PCC in São Paulo.

While the PCC's monopolization of the criminal underworld has led to a significant decrease in lethal violence in São Paulo, the emergence of similarly organized prison gangs in much of the rest of Brazil has coincided with dramatic increases in violence. This is due to the fact that although the PCC's organizational reach extends to prisons across the country, no other state penitentiary system has been monopolized by a single organization, with the possible exception of Amazonas, where the *Família do Norte* (FDN) prison gang recently launched its own mega-rebellion during which they succeeded in murdering 130 rival gang members.[48] Consequently, rival prison gangs and their affiliate favela-based drug gangs have done much to increase overall levels of violence as they wage constant war for control of lucrative drug markets.

Yet despite this increased violence, symbiotic relationships between the state and organized crime have continued to develop. First, whether or not organized crime is fragmented, the wealth it produces continues to be an easy target for extortion by state authorities. Secondly, even though overall levels of violence have increased, the consolidation of criminal governance has led to significant drops in homicides within some communities, thereby still giving state authorities something positive to take credit for. In Salvador, Bahia, for example, police commanders frequently settle into tacit arrangements with local drug gangs to share authority and avoid confrontation in exchange for maintaining low levels of lethal violence. Reports of homicide reductions then filter up the chain of command and into the higher echelons of state government, reaping significant political rewards in the process.[49]

CONCLUSION

In many ways, the evolving relationship between organized crime and the state in Brazil has been consistent with broader trends across Latin America over the course of the last several decades. The phasing out of authoritarian regimes and their replacement with much more decentralized and democratic ones in the 1980s and 1990s coincided with grave economic crises, rapid demographic shifts, and an explosion in cocaine consumption worldwide, the compounded effect of which helped fuel the rise of organized crime and facilitated its penetration of state institutions. Where the relationship differs, however, has much to do with Brazil's strong federalist structure. Whereas in most other Latin American countries the political-criminal nexus is rooted deep in national political institutions, Brazilian federalism has kept the primary locus of political-criminal relations in state and municipal-level governments, and there is significant variation in the degree to which different subnational governments engage with organized crime.

As I have argued in this chapter, however, political-criminal relations in Brazil are beginning to converge around a common model despite the relative autonomy of subnational governments, and this convergence is largely being driven by national trends in mass incarceration and the resulting spread of prison gangs. Prison gangs like the CV, the PCC, and the FDN today govern the lives of inmates in the majority of Brazil's prisons, which consequently act as mass recruitment centers for organized crime and as operational bases from which prison gangs can direct the behavior and actions of affiliated criminal groups out on the streets. Consequently, the "cocaine polities" once unique to the favelas of Rio de Janeiro and São Paulo have now begun to emerge in large and medium cities across Brazil, bringing with them the same modalities of territorially embedded criminality and the same taunting opportunities for political-criminal partnership.

Although this partnership can best be described as symbiotic—both organized crime groups and state authorities benefit politically and economically from coexistence—it is far from being stable. The relative capabilities of the great many actor groups within and outside of the state, all with their own interests, are in constant flux, and their arrangements of coexistence always up for renegotiation, for which violence is the primary bargaining chip.

The long-term implications of this symbiosis are dire. Although in some places and times it might lead to reductions in lethal violence and the perception of a more stable social order, as occurred in the case of the PCC in São Paulo in the mid-2000s, this best-case scenario comes at the cost of excluding a substantial portion of the population from basic rights of Brazilian citizenship and the relegation of entire communities to criminal governance. Much more likely, high levels of violence will continue to affect many communities as rival criminal factions fight for control over densely populated areas left virtually abandoned by the state. Worse still, to the extent that law enforcement and judicial institutions attempt to crack down on organized crime, their efforts will likely continue to backfire, as prisons themselves have become de facto recruiting grounds and operational bases for organized crime.

NOTES

1. This chapter is from Michael Jerome Wolff, "Organized Crime and the State in Brazil." In *The Criminalization of States: The Relationship between States and Organized Crime*, eds., Jonathan D. Rosen, Bruce Bagley, and Jorge Chabat (Lanham, MD: Lexington Books, 2019): pp. 323–339.

2. Fórum Brasileiro de Segurança Pública, *Atlas da Violência: 2017* (Rio de Janeiro, RJ: FBSP, June 2017).

3. Elizabeth Leeds, "Cocaine and Parallel Polities in the Brazilian Urban Periphery: Constraints on Local-level Democracy," *Latin American Research Review*, 31:3 (1996): pp. 41–83.

4. Desmond Enrique Arias, "Faith in Our Neighbors: Networks and Social Order in Three Brazilian Favelas," *Latin American Politics and Society*, 46:1 (2004): pp. 1–38.

5. Jailson Souza e Silva, "As Unidades Policiais Pacificadoras e os novos desafios para as favelas cariocas," *Seminário Aspectos Humanos da Favela Carioca, Rio de Janeiro*, RJ (2010).

6. Teresa Caldeira and James Holston, "Democracy and Violence in Brazil," *Comparative Studies in Society and History*, 41:4 (1999): pp. 691–729.

7. Dianne Davis, "Undermining the Rule of Law: Democratization and the Dark Side of Police Reform in Mexico," *Latin American Politics and Society*, 48:1 (2010): pp. 55–86.

8. Erica Robb Larkins, *The Spectacular Favela: Violence in Modern Brazil* (Berkeley: University of California Press, 2015).

9. Ignacio Cano and Thais Duarte, *No Sapatinho: A evolução das milícias no rio de Janeiro (2008-2011)* (Rio de Janeiro, RJ: Fundação Heinrich Boll, 2012).

10. João Apolinário, "Sistema prisional e segurança pública: analise sobre a contenção da criminalidade a partir do sistema prisional," *Observatório de Segurança Pública*, UNIFACS, Salvador, BA. (2017).

11. Graham Denyer Willis, "Deadly Symbiosis? The PCC, the State, and the Institutionalization of Violence in Sao Paulo, Brazil." In *Youth Violence in Latin America: Gangs and Juvenile Justice in Perspective*, eds., Gareth A. Jones and Dennis Rodgers (New York: Palgrave Macmillan, 2009): pp. 167–182.

12. Karina Biondi, *Sharing this Walk: An Ethnography of Prison Life and the PCC in Brazil*, translated by John F. Collins (Chapel Hill: University of North Carolina Press, 2016).

13. Peter A. Lupsha, "Transnational Crime versus the Nation-State," *Transnational Organized Crime*, 2:1 (1996): pp. 21–48.

14. John Bailey and Mathew Taylor, "Evade, Corrupt, or Confront? Organized Crime and the State in Brazil and Mexico," *Journal of Politics in Latin America*, 1:2 (2009): pp. 3–29.

15. Frank Mora, "Victims of the balloon effect: Drug trafficking and US policy in Brazil and the Southern Cone of Latin America," *Journal of Social, Political, and Economic Issues*, 21:2 (1996): pp. 115–140.

16. Fiona Macauley, "Federalism and State Criminal Justice Systems." Iin *Corruption and Democracy in Brazil: The Struggle for Accountability*, eds., Timothy Powers and Mathew Taylor (Indiana: University of Notre Dame Press, 2011): pp. 218–249.

17. Michael J. Wolff, "Building Criminal Authority: A Comparative Analysis of Drug Gangs in Rio de Janeiro and Recife," *Latin American Politics and Society*, 57:2 (2015): pp. 21–40.

18. Carlos Amorim, *Comando Vermelho: A historia secreta do crime organizado* (Rio de Janeiro: Record, 1993).

19. Sacha Darke, "Inmate Governance in Brazilian Prisons," *The Howard Journal of Criminal Justice*, 52:3 (2013): pp. 272–284.

20. Marcos César Alvarez, Fernando Salla, and Camila Nunes Dias, "Das Comissões de Solidariedade ao Primeiro Comando da Capital em São Paulo," *Tempo Social*, 25:1 (2013): 61–82.

21. Benjamin Lessing, "Counterproductive Punishment: How Prison Gangs Undermine State Authority," *Rationality and Society*, 29:3 (2017): pp. 257–297.

22. Elizabeth Leeds, "Cocaine and Parallel Polities in the Brazilian Urban Periphery: Constraints on Local-level Democracy."

23. Enrique Desmond Arias, "Drug Trafficking and clientelism in Rio de Janeiro Shantytowns," *Qualitative Sociology*, 29:4 (2007): pp. 427–445.

24. Wolff, "Building Criminal Authority: A Comparative Analysis of Drug Gangs in Rio de Janeiro and Recife."

25. Brazilian authorities refer to deaths of civilians as a result of confrontation with police as *autos de resistencia*, or "Cases of Resistance."

26. Ben Penglase, "The Bastard Child of the Dictatorship: the Comando Vermelho and the birth of 'narco-culture' in Rio de Janeiro," *Luso-Brazilian Review*, 45:1 (2008): pp. 118–145.

27. *Programa Nacional de Segurança Pública com Cidadania.*

28. Vicente Riccio and Wesley G. Skogan, "Gangs, Drugs, and Urban Pacification Squads in Rio de Janeiro," in *Police and Society in Brazil*, eds., Vicente Riccio and Wesley G. Skogan, *Routledge Pub* (New York: Routledge, 2017): pp. 135–150.

29. Ingacio Cano, *"Os Donos do Morro": Uma Avaliação Exploratória do Impacto das Unidades de Polícia Pacificadora (UPPs) no Rio de Janeiro.* Fórum Brasileiro de Segurança Pública, May 2012.

30. Michael J. Wolff, "Policing and the Logics of Violence: A Comparative Analysis of Public Security Reform in Brazil," *Policing and Society*, 27:5 (2015): pp. 560–574.

31. Ernesto Londoño and Shasta Darlington, "Brasil pone al ejército al mando de la seguridad en Río de Janeiro ante ola de violencia," *The New York Times*, February 16, 2018.

32. Erika Robb Larkings, *The Spectacular Favela: Violence in Modern Brazil* (Berkeley: University of California Press, 2015).

33. Ignacio Cano and Carolina Looty, "Seis por meia dúzia? Um estudo exploratório do fenômeno das chamadas milícias no Rio de Janeiro," in *Segurança, Tráfico, e Milícias no rio de Janeiro* (Rio de Janeiro, RJ: Fundação Heinrich Boll, 2008).

34. Cano and Duarte, *No Sapatinho.*

35. Marcelo Baumann Burgos, *A utopia da comunidade: Rio das Pedras, uma favela carioca* (Rio de Janeiro, RJ: Editora PUC-Rio, 2002).

36. Alba Zaluar and Isabel Siqueira Conceição, "Favelas sob o controle das milícias no Rio de Janeiro," *São Paulo em Perspectiva*, 21:2 (July–December 2002): pp. 89–101.

37. Cano and Duarte, *No Sapatinho: A evolução das milícias no rio de Janeiro (2008-2011).*

38. Cano and Duarte, *No Sapatinho: A evolução das milícias no rio de Janeiro (2008-2011).*

39. "Juiza assassinada etava marcada para morrer, diz polícia," *O Globo*, August 12, 2011. http://g1.globo.com/rio-de-janeiro/noticia/2011/08/juiza-assassinada-e stava-em-lista-de-marcados-para-morrer-diz-policia.html, accessed April 2, 2018.

40. Darke, "Inmate Governance in Brazilian Prisons."

41. Biondi, *Sharing this Walk: An Ethnography of Prison Life and the PCC in Brazil.*

42. Alvarez, Salla, and Dias, "Das Comissões de Solidariedade ao Primeiro Comando da Capital em São Paulo,"

43. Biondi, *Sharing this Walk: An Ethnography of Prison Life and the PCC in Brazil.*

44. Lessing, "Counterproductive Punishment: How Prison Gangs Undermine State Authority."

45. Willis, "Deadly Symbiosis? The PCC, the State, and the Institutionalization of Violence in Sao Paulo, Brazil."

46. Wolff, "Policing and the Logics of Violence: A Comparative Analysis of Public Security Reform in Brazil."

47. Bailey and Taylor, "Evade, Corrupt, or Confront? Organized Crime and the State in Brazil and Mexico."

48. Chris Feliciano Arnold, "Brazil Has Become a Gangland," *Foreign Policy*, June 6, 2017. http://foreignpolicy.com/2017/06/06/brazil-has-become-a-gangland -prison-riot/, March 14, 2018.

49. Michael J. Wolff, "Community Policing in the Brazilian Slum," *NORIA* (2018).

Selected Bibliography

Arias, Enrique Desmond. "Drug trafficking and clientelism in Rio de Janeiro Shantytowns," *Qualitative Sociology* 29, no. 4 (2007): pp. 427–445.

Bagley, Bruce M. and Jonathan D. Rosen, eds. *Colombia's Political Economy at the Outset of the Twenty-First Century: From Uribe to Santos and Beyond.* Lanham, MD: Lexington Books, 2015.

Bagley, Bruce M. and Jonathan D. Rosen, eds. *Drug Trafficking, Organized Crime, and Violence in the Americas Today.* Gainesville, FL: University Press of Florida, 2015.

Bailey, John and Mathew Taylor. "Evade, corrupt, or confront? Organized crime and the state in Brazil and Mexico," *Journal of Politics in Latin America* 1, no. 2 (2009): pp. 3–29.

Davis, Diane E. "Undermining the rule of law: Democratization and the dark side of police reform in Mexico," *Latin American Politics and Society* 48, no. 1 (2006): pp. 55–86.

Diamond, Larry. "Consolidating democracy in the Americas," *The Annals of the American Academy of Political and Social Science* 550, no. 1 (1997): pp. 12–41.

Durand, Francisco. "The Odebrecht Tsunami: The Odebrecht scandal highlights the phenomenon of corporate capture of the state in Brazil and Peru. Yet new investigative tools show promise in detecting and responding to multinational graft," *NACLA Report on the Americas* 51, no. 2 (2019): pp. 146–152.

Goodfriend, Hilary. "Prosecuting Presidents in El Salvador: Corruption prosecutions against former presidents in El Salvador did little to punish thieving public officials, but they did help tip the balance of power back toward the Right—revealing the limits and biases of anti-corruption discourse today," *NACLA Report on the Americas* 51, no. 2 (2019): pp. 141–145.

Holmes, Jennifer S. Kevin M. Curtin, and Sheila Amin Gutiérrez de Piñeres. *Guns, Drugs, and Development in Colombia.* Austin, TX: University of Texas Press, 2008.

Lessing, Benjamin. "Counterproductive punishment: How prison gangs undermine state authority," *Rationality and Society* 29, no. 3 (2017): pp. 257–297.

———. *Making Peace in Drug Wars: Crackdowns and Cartels in Latin America.* New York, NY: Cambridge University Press, 2018.

Macauley, Fiona. "Federalism and State Criminal Justice Systems." In *Corruption and Democracy in Brazil: The Struggle for Accountability*, eds. Timothy Powers and Mathew Taylor. Indiana: University of Notre Dame Press, 2011: pp. 218–249.

Marques, Ben. "From the panama papers to Odebrecht: Illicit Financial Flows From Brazil," *Business and Public Administration Studies* 13, no. 1 (2019): pp. 22–31.

Morris, Stephen D. "Corruption, drug trafficking, and violence in Mexico," *The Brown Journal of World Affairs* 18, no. 2 (2012): pp. 29–43.

———. and Joseph L. Klesner. "Corruption and trust: Theoretical considerations and evidence from Mexico," *Comparative Political Studies* 43, no. 10 (2010): pp. 1258–1285.

Quiroz, Alfonso W. *Corrupt Circles: A History of Unbound Graft in Peru.* Baltimore, MD: Johns Hopkins University Press, 2008.

Shelley, Louise. "Corruption and organized crime in Mexico in the post-PRI transition," *Journal of Contemporary Criminal Justice* 17, no. 3 (2001): pp. 213–231.

Index

About the Editors and Contributors

Jonathan D. Rosen is assistant professor of criminal justice at Holy Family University, located in Philadelphia, PA. Dr. Rosen earned his master's in political science from Columbia University and received his PhD from the University of Miami. He has published eighteen books. His recent publications include the following: Jonathan D. Rosen, *The Losing War: Plan Colombia and Beyond* (2014); Roberto Zepeda and Jonathan D. Rosen, eds., *Cooperation and Drug Policies in the Americas: Trends in the Twenty-First Century* (2014); Bruce M. Bagley and Jonathan D. Rosen, eds., *Drug Trafficking, Organized Crime, and Violence in the Americas Today* (2015); Jonathan D. Rosen and Marten W. Brienen, eds., *Prisons in the Americas in the Twenty-First Century: A Human Dumping Ground* (2015); Marten W. Brienen and Jonathan D. Rosen, eds., *New Approaches to Drug Policies*: *A Time for Change* (2015); and Bruce M. Bagley and Jonathan D. Rosen, eds., *Colombia's Political Economy at the Outset of the Twenty-First Century: From Uribe to Santos and Beyond* (2015).

Hanna S. Kassab is teaching assistant professor at East Carolina University. He holds degrees in political science and history from McMaster University, York University, and the University of Miami. His interests include international relations theory, national security, politics of the far-right and nationalism, acts of political suicide, and foreign policy. Dr. Kassab's recent publications include Hanna Samir Kassab, *Weak States in International Relations Theory: The Cases of Armenia, St. Kitts and Nevis, Lebanon, and Cambodia* (2015); Bruce M. Bagley, Jonathan D. Rosen, and Hanna S. Kassab, eds., *Reconceptualizing Security in the Americas in the Twenty-First Century* (2015); Hanna Samir Kassab and Jonathan D. Rosen, *Institutions,* *and Fragile States* (2019); Hanna Samir Kassab and Jonathan D. Rosen, *Illicit Markets, Organized Crime, and Global Security* (2018).

Adriana Beltrán has championed the promotion of a comprehensive, rights-based approach to tackling insecurity, violence, and the growing influence of organized crime in Central America. As head of the Citizen Security Program for the Washington Office on Latin America (WOLA), a US-based research and advocacy organization, she promotes policies that identify and address the root causes of violence and improve the effectiveness and account-ability of police and judicial systems. Beltrán's longtime advocacy for a UN-sponsored commission to investigate and prosecute organized criminal networks linked to the state helped establish the International Commission against Impunity in Guatemala (CICIG) in 2007. She has written and coau-thored various reports and articles on police reform, organized crime, and violence in Latin America, including *Protect and Serve? The Status of Police Reform*, and *Hidden Powers in Post-Conflict Guatemala*, a groundbreaking study documenting the rise and impact of criminal networks since the end of the civil war in that country. Beltrán has testified before Congress and is a frequent commentator in the media—including *The Washington Post, The New York Times*, and leading outlets in Latin America. She holds a master's degree in International Public Policy from the Johns Hopkins School for Advanced International Studies (SAIS).

Marten Brienen is Associate Professor at the School of Global Studies at Oklahoma State University. Dr. Brienen taught in both the African and Latin American Studies Programs at the University of Miami from 2004 to 2013. From 2011 to 2013, he served as the director of the Latin American Studies Program at the University of Miami. While he has worked on a variety of subjects, the fundamental principle that binds them together is his ongoing interest in the struggle between marginalized populations and the interests of states in the process of national construction in Africa and Latin America. From that perspective, he has in recent years focused primarily on energy security, drug trafficking, and complex emergencies. His recent publications include: Marten W. Brienen and Jonathan D. Rosen, eds., *New Approaches to Drug Policies: A Time for Change* (2015); Jonathan D. Rosen and Marten W. Brienen, eds., *Prisons in the Americas in the Twenty-First Century: A Human Dumping Ground* (2015).

Fernando Cepeda Ulloa graduated as Doctor in Derecho y Ciencia Politicas at the National University, in Bogotá, Colombia (1962). He did graduate work at The New School for Social Research, New York (1961–1962). Dr. Cepeda promoted the Political Science Department, the School of Law, the Center for

Regional Interdisciplinary Studies, and the Center for International Studies at the Universidad de los Andes, in Bogotá, where he was secretary general, vice rector, acting rector, and dean of the School of Law. He was Visiting Fellow at Saint Antony's College, Oxford University. He was a member of the Permanent International Court of Arbitration. Dr. Cepeda was minister of the interior (1986), minister of communications (1987–1988), and presidential advisor (1978). He has been the ambassador in the United Kingdom (1988–1990), United Nations (1991), Canada (1992–1994), Organization of American States (1997–1998), and France (2006–2011). He has published several books and academic papers. He was a columnist in the daily newspaper *El Tiempo* for several decades.

Cynthia McClintock is professor of political science and international affairs at George Washington University. She holds the BA degree from Harvard University and the PhD from the Massachusetts Institute of Technology. Dr. McClintock was president of the Latin American Studies Association in 1994–1995. Also, she was a member of the Council of the American Political Science Association in 1998–2000, and served as the chair of its Comparative Democratization Section in 2003–2005. During 2006–2007, Prof. McClintock was a Fellow at the Woodrow Wilson International Center for Scholars. Based on her research at the Center, she published a book on the implications for democracy of runoff versus plurality rules for the election of the president in Latin America.

Bradford R. McGuinn holds a PhD in international studies, with concentration in Middle Eastern studies, from the University of Miami. Dr. McGuinn is a senior lecturer with the Department of Political Science and associate director of the Master of Arts in International Administration program at the University of Miami. His fields of research and teaching include international security, Middle Eastern studies, civil-military relations, and political violence. For many years Dr. McGuinn has lectured to groups in the US military and law enforcement community on questions of violence and insurgency. He has contributed book chapters dealing with security questions in the Middle East, Latin America, and the Caucasus.

Michael Jerome Wolff earned his PhD in political science from the University of New Mexico and joined the faculty at Western Washington University in 2016. His research focuses on organized criminal violence and policing in Latin America, and seeks to understand how state policy and behavior shape the development of different types of criminal groups, as well as how organized crime and violence influence politics. Dr. Wolff currently has ongoing research projects in Mexico and Brazil. Dr. Wolff teaches a range of courses in the subfields of Comparative Politics and International Relations. Special course topics include Civil Wars and Political Violence, Gangs and Organized Crime, Development and Inequality, Politics of Brazil and Mexico, and Comparative Border Studies.

Roberto Zepeda is a researcher at the Centro de Investigaciones sobre América del Norte (CISAN) at the Universidad Nacional Autónoma de México (UNAM). Previously, he was research professor at the Institute of International Studies at the Universidad del Mar in Huatulco, Mexico. Dr. Zepeda holds a PhD in politics from the University of Sheffield as well as a master's in international studies at the University of Sinaloa (UAS), focusing on North America. He has taught politics at UNAM in Mexico City, and in the Department of Politics at the University of Sheffield. His most recent publications include Roberto Zepeda, "Collateral Effects of Migration in the Americas: Security Implications," in *Reconceptualizing Security in the Americas in the Twenty-First Century*, eds. Bruce M. Bagley, Jonathan D. Rosen, and Hanna S. Kassab (2015); Peter Watt and Roberto Zepeda, *Drug War Mexico: Politics, Neoliberalism, and Violence in the New Narcoeconomy* (2012); Roberto Zepeda, "Disminución de la tasa de trabajadores sindicalizados en México durante el periodo neoliberal," *Revista Mexicana de Ciencias Políticas* (2009). He is a member of the National System of Researchers (SNI, level II) in Mexico since 2014. He has published nine book chapters, eighteen articles in academic journals, and five books.

www.ingramcontent.com/pod-product-compliance
Lightning Source LLC
Chambersburg PA
CBHW022320280326
41932CB00010B/1169